Pagan Christianity

OTHER BOOKS BY FRANK VIOLA

Volume 1: Rethinking the Wineskin
The Practice of the New Testament Church

Volume 2: Who is Your Covering?
A Fresh Look at Leadership, Authority, and Accountability

Volume 4: So You Want to Start a House Church?
First-Century Styled Church Planting
(Due 2003)

Volume 5: From Nazareth to Patmos:
The Saga of the New Testament Church
(Due 2004)

**Visit the Present Testimony Ministry Web Site for
Free Downloads and Ordering Information:**

www.ptmin.org

PAGAN CHRISTIANITY

*The Origins of Our
Modern Church Practices*

Frank Viola

PAGAN CHRISTIANITY:
THE ORIGINS OF OUR MODERN CHURCH PRACTICES

*To my forgotten brothers and sisters throughout the ages
who courageously stepped outside the safe-bounds of
institutional Christianity at the risk of life and limb.
You faithfully carried the torch, endured persecution,
forfeited reputation, lost family, suffered torture,
and spilled your blood to preserve the primitive
testimony that Jesus Christ is Head of His
church. And that every believer is
a priest . . . a minister . . . and
a functioning member of
God's house. This book
is dedicated to you.*

CONTENTS

FOREWORD

This book should have been written 300 years ago. If it had, the course of Christian history would be totally different than the path that it has taken.

If every minister in the world read this book today, either they would all leave the ministry tomorrow or live a life of hypocrisy.

Most of our practices of the Christian faith have absolutely nothing to do with the New Testament. Practically everything we do today as Christians came to us as happenstance. Virtually all our major practices came to us within 50 years of the Emperor Constantine (A.D. 324) or within 50 years of the beginning of the Reformation (A.D. 1517).

Mr. Viola has done us a great service by tracing the origin of all we Protestants practice.

My one regret is that this book will be only one out of 100,000 Christian books issued in the year it was printed.

Three hundred years ago—or even two hundred years ago—*Pagan Christianity* would have been one of only a few hundred books . . . and therefore, read by a large portion of Christians. You can help remedy this by telling all your friends about this book.

By the way, you too will face a crisis of conscience after *you* read this book. You will know the heathen and non-biblical origins of all we do today. You cannot ever say again, "We are Bible centered. We do *everything* based on the New Testament." We do virtually nothing that is New Testament, as you will see.

But there is a greater tragedy here. We take the New Testament and twist it, making the New Testament endorse what we do today. This mindset—which is universal—a mindset common to both laymen and clergy . . . *this* mindset has—and is—destroying the Christian faith.

We are left in a situation today where we have absolutely no idea how our faith *should be* practiced.

What is needed? Concerning our present day practice of the faith, we must totally start over from the ground up, laying aside *all* that we practice today.

Secondly, we need to learn the first-century story, and then go after it in our own practices.

May I once again encourage you to not only read this book, but to tell every other Christian you know to also read it.

And then? Follow your conscience. Do this, and we will see a re-emergence of those simple, primitive practices of the first century.

Gene Edwards
Jacksonville, Florida

Experience supplies painful proof that traditions once called into being are first called useful, then they become necessary. At last they are too often made idols, and all must bow down to them or be punished.
-J.C. Ryle

ACKNOWLEDGMENTS

Important ideas are first ridiculed, then attacked, and finally taken for granted.
-Schopenhauer

Not long after I left the religious system, I sought to understand how the Christian church ended up in its present state. For years I tried to get my hands on a documented book that traced the origin of every non-biblical practice we Christians observe every week.[1]

I searched scores of bibliographies and card catalogs. I also contacted a raft of historians and scholars, asking if they knew of such a work. My quest yielded one consistent answer: *No such book has ever been penned.* So in a moment of insanity, I decided to put my own hand to this plow.

I will shamelessly admit that I wish someone else had taken on this overwhelming project. Someone like a childless professor without a day job! It would have saved me an incalculable number of painstaking hours and a great deal of frustration. Nevertheless, now that the work is complete, I am glad I had the privilege of breaking new ground in this all-too neglected area.

Some may wonder why I saw fit to expend so much sweat and blood to document the origin of our modern church practices. It is rather simple. Understanding the genesis of our church traditions can very well change the course of church history. As philosopher Soren Kierkegaard once put it, *"Life is lived forwards, but understood backwards."* Without understanding the mistakes of the past, we are doomed to a flawed future. It is for this reason that I have set out to make the first stab at this Himalayan project.

My hope in publishing this work is as simple as it is somber: That the Lord would use it as a tool to bring His church back to her

---

[1] The only work that I could find which traces the origins of our modern church practices is Gene Edwards' little volume *Beyond Radical* (Jacksonville: Seedsowers, 1999). While this is a fantastic book, it is neither documented nor footnoted.

original roots. On that note, I would like to make the following acknowledgments:

To Gene Edwards for blazing the trail.
Without your pioneering efforts and your personal
encouragement, I could not have widened it.

To Frank Valdez for your keen insight and your
unwavering friendship.

To Neil Carter for your willing tenacity to help me research
everything under the sun. Thanks also for the hours you put in
proofing the manuscript.

To Howard Snyder for that invaluable feedback
which only scholars can give.

To Chris Lee and Adam Parke for making repeated trips to
the library and lugging countless stacks of
dusty books into my study.

To Dave Norrington for periodically mailing me valuable leads
from across the Atlantic.

To Mike Biggerstaff, Dan Merillat, Phil Warmanen, Eric Rapp,
and Scott Manning for your editing help.

To those seminary professors whose names are too numerous
to list for kindly responding to my endless and
persistent inquiries.

Those who cannot remember the past are condemned to repeat it.
    -George Santayana

PREFACE

*And why do you yourselves transgress the commandment
of God for the sake of your tradition?*
-Jesus Christ

When the Lord Jesus walked this earth, His chief opposition came from the two leading religious parties of the day: The Pharisees and the Sadducees.

Those of the Pharisaical party *added* to the sacred Scriptures. They tacked on to the Word of God reams of human law that were passed on to subsequent generations. This body of time-honored customs, often called "the tradition of the elders," came to be esteemed as equal with Holy Writ.[1]

The error of the Sadducees moved in the opposite direction. They *subtracted* whole segments of Scripture—only deeming the Law of Moses worthy to be observed.[2] (The Sadducees denied the existence of spirits, angels, the soul, the after-life, and the resurrection.[3])

The net effect was that when the Lord Jesus entered the drama of human history, His authority was arduously challenged.[4] The reason was simple. He did not fit into the religious mold of either camp. Jesus was viewed with suspicion by both the Pharisee and Sadducee parties. It did not take long for this suspicion to turn to

---

[1] *Nelson's Illustrated Bible Dictionary* (Nashville: Thomas Nelson Publishers, 1986), pp. 830-831. See also Matt. 23:23-24. The Pharisees obeyed the Law of God as it was interpreted and applied by the scribes. Scribes were experts in the Law who lived pious and disciplined lives. They became the official interpreters of God's Word and were endowed with the power of creating tradition (*Nelson's Illustrated Bible Dictionary,* pp. 957-958).

[2] The "Law of Moses" refers to the first five books of the Old Testament, i.e. Genesis to Deuteronomy. It is also called the "Torah" (the Law) and the "Pentateuch," which is a Greek term meaning "five-volumed."

[3] *New Bible Dictionary: 2nd Edition* (Wheaton: Inter-Varsity Fellowship, 1982), p. 1055.

[4] Mark 11:28.

hostility. And both the Pharisees and Sadducees took steps to put the Son of God to death!

We live in a day when history is reliving itself. Modern Christianity has fallen into the errors of both the Pharisees and the Sadducees.

In the tradition of the Sadducees, the great bulk of first-century practices has been *removed* from the Christian landscape. My book, *Rethinking the Wineskin*, unearths some of the forgotten practices that characterized the life of the first-century church.[5]

But modern Christianity is also guilty of the error of the Pharisees. That is, it has *added* a raft of humanly-devised traditions that have suppressed the living, breathing, functional Headship of Jesus Christ in His church.

Even so, the Pharisee and the Sadducee both teach us this oft-ignored lesson: It is just as harmful to dilute the authority of God's Word by addition as it is by subtraction. We break the Scripture equally by burying it under a mountain of human tradition as we do by ignoring its principles.

This book is dedicated to exposing the traditions that have been tacked onto God's way for His church. In so doing, it makes an outrageous proposal: *That the modern institutional church does not have a Biblical nor a historical right to exist!*

This is not a work for scholars. So it is by no means exhaustive. An exhaustive treatment of the origins of our modern church practices would fill volumes. But it would be read by few people. Although this is a single volume, it packs a great deal of history into a small space. In fact, it can rightly be said that what is contained in these pages is the summary of an entire library!

The book does not chase every historical sidelight. Rather, it focuses on tracing the *central* practices that define mainstream Christianity today.[6]

---

[5] Such practices are presently being restored on a small scale by those daring souls who have taken the terrifying step of leaving the safe camp of institutional Christianity.

[6] This book focuses on *Protestant* Christian practices. And its main scope is "low church" Protestantism rather than "high church" denominations like Anglican, Episcopal, and some stripes of Lutheran. The book touches on Catholic and "high church" practices only in passing.

Because the roots of our modern church practices are so important to grasp, I wish that every literate Christian would read this work.[7] Consequently, I have chosen not to employ technical language, but to write in plain English. At the same time, footnotes containing added details and sources have been liberally peppered throughout each chapter. (I want my readers to know that I am not blowing bubbles or building castles out of thin air!)

Reflective Christians who wish to verify my statements and obtain a more indepth understanding of the subjects covered should read the footnotes. Those who care little for such things should ignore them.

Finally, this book can be placed alongside my first book, *Rethinking the Wineskin: The Practice of the New Testament Church*. Both books show two sides of the same coin. *Wineskin* demonstrates beyond dispute that those who have left the fold of institutional Christianity have a *Scriptural* right to exist. The book you hold in your hands turns that coin around and shows that they have a *historical* right to exist as well.

Frank Viola
Brandon, Florida
December 2002

---

[7] As Bacon once said, "It is not St. Augustine's nor St. Ambrose's works that will make so wise a divine as ecclesiastical history thoroughly read and examined."

"*But* the Emperor has nothing at all on!" Said a little child. "Listen to the voice of innocence!" exclaimed the father; and what the child had said was whispered from one to another. "But he has nothing on!" at last cried all the people. The Emperor was vexed, for he knew that the people were right; but he thought, "The procession must go on now!" And the lords of the bed-chamber took greater pains than ever to appear holding up a train, although, in reality, there was no train to hold.

-Hans Christian Anderson

INTRODUCTION

HAVE WE REALLY BEEN DOING IT BY THE BOOK?

The unexamined life is not worth living.
-Socrates

*W*e do everything by the Word of God! The New Testament is our guide for faith and practice! We live . . . and we die . . . by this Book!

These were the words that thundered forth from the mouth of Pastor Farley as he delivered his Sunday morning sermon. Winchester Spudchecker, a member of Pastor Farley's church, had heard them dozens of times before. But this time it was different. Dressed in his blue suit, frozen in the back pew with his wife, Trudy Spudchecker, Winchester stared off at the ceiling as Pastor Farley ranted on about *"doing everything by the sacred Book."*

One hour before Pastor Farley began his sermon, Winchester had a fuming fight with Trudy. This was a common occurrence when Winchester, Trudy, and their three daughters, Felicia, Gertrude, and Zanobia, got ready for church on Sunday morning.

His mind began replaying the event . . .

"Truuuddyy! Why aren't the kids ready!? We're always late! Why can't you ever get them prepared on time!?" . . . were the words that hurled from Winchester's lips.

Trudy's response was typical. *"If you ever thought to help me this wouldn't happen all the time! Why don't you start giving me a hand in this house!?"* The argument went back and forth until Winchester turned on the children: *"Zanobia Spudchecker! . . . Why can't you respect us enough to get ready on time!? . . . Felicia, how many times do I have to tell you to turn off your Play Station before 9 A.M.!?"* Often one or more of the three children would cry as the bantering was brought to a high-fever pitch.

Wearing their Sunday best, the Spudchecker family drove to church at breakneck speed. (Winchester hated to be late and had received three speeding tickets this past year—all liberally given to him on Sunday mornings!)

As they raced to the church building, the silence in the car was deafening. Winchester was steaming. Trudy was sulking. With heads down, the three Spudchecker daughters were trying to prepare their minds for something they hated . . . enduring another boring hour of Sunday School!

As they pulled up to the church parking lot, Winchester and Trudy gracefully exited their car seats, sporting large smiles. They held each other arm-in-arm, greeted their fellow church members, chuckling and putting on the pretense that all is well. Felicia, Gertrude, and Zanobia followed their parents with chins pointed upward.

These were the fresh, yet painful memories that coursed through Winchester's mind that Sunday morning as Pastor Farley continued his sermon. Brooding in condemnation, Winchester began to ask himself some searching questions: *"Why am I dressed up prim and proper looking like a good Christian when I acted like a heathen just an hour ago?"* . . . *"I wonder how many other families have had this same pitiful experience this morning? Yet we're all smelling nice and looking pretty for God."*

Such questions had never before entered Winchester's consciousness.

As he peeked over to see Pastor Farley's wife and children sitting prim and proper on the front pew, Winchester mused to himself: *"I wonder if Pastor Farley screamed at his wife and kids this morning!? Hmmm . . ."*

Winchester's mind continued to race in this direction as he watched Pastor Farley pound the pulpit and raise his Bible with his right hand. The Pastor continued his fire-brand ranting . . . *"We at First Bible New Testament Community Church do everything by this Book! EVERYTHING! This is the Word of God, and we cannot stray from it . . . not even one millimeter!"*

As the bellowing words left Pastor Farley's lips, Winchester suddenly had a thought he had never before had: *"I don't re-*

member reading anywhere in the Bible that Christians are supposed to dress up to go to church. Is that by the Book!?"

This single thought unlocked a torrent of other barbed questions. As scores of frozen pew-sitters filled his horizon, Winchester's mind was flooded with these questions. Questions that no Christian is supposed to ask. Questions like:

"Is sitting in this uncushioned pew, staring at the back of five rows of heads for 45 minutes doing things by the Book? Why do we spend all this money to maintain this building when we're only here twice a week for a few hours? Why is half the congregation barely awake when Pastor Farley preaches? Why do my kids hate Sunday School? Why do we go through this same, predictable, yawn-inspiring ritual every Sunday morning? Why am I going to church when it bores me to tears and does nothing for me spiritually? Why do I wear this uncomfortable necktie every Sunday morning when all it seems to do is cut off blood circulation to my brain!?"

Winchester struggled within himself as the questions continued to pour into his mind. He felt unclean and sacrilegious to think such things. Yet something was happening inside of him that compelled him to doubt his entire church experience. These thoughts had been lying dormant in Winchester's subconscious for years. Today, they surfaced.

Interestingly, the questions that Winchester had that day are questions that virtually never enter the conscious thinking of most Christians. Those creases simply do not appear on our brains. Yet the sober reality is that Winchester's eyes had been opened.

As startling as it may sound, most everything that is done in our modern churches has no basis in the Bible. As pastors roar from their pulpits about being "Biblical" and following the "pure Word of God," their words betray them. Alarmingly, precious little that is observed today in modern Christianity maps to anything found in the first-century church.

Questions We Never Think to Ask

Socrates (470-399 B.C.) is considered by some historians to be the father of philosophy. Born and raised in Athens, his custom was to go about the town relentlessly raising questions and analyzing issues.[1] Socrates boldly questioned the popular views of his day. He thought freely on matters that his fellow Athenians felt were closed for discussion.

Socrates' habit of pelting people with searching questions and roping them into critical dialogues about their accepted customs eventually got him killed. His incessant questioning of tightly-held traditions provoked the leaders of Athens to charge him with "corrupting the youth." As a result, they put Socrates to death. A clear message was sent to his fellow Athenians: All who question the established customs will meet the same fate![2]

Socrates was not the only philosopher to reap severe reprisal for his nonconformity: Aristotle was exiled, Spinoza was excommunicated, and Bruno was burned alive. Not to mention the thousands of Christians who were tortured and martyred by the institutional church because they dared to challenge its teachings.[3]

As Christians, we are taught by our leaders to believe certain ideas and behave certain ways. We have a Bible, yes. But we are conditioned to read it with the lens handed to us by the Christian tradition to which we belong. We are taught to obey our denomination (or movement) and never to challenge what it teaches.

(At this moment, all the rebellious hearts are applauding and are plotting to wield the above paragraphs to wreak havoc in their churches. If that is you, dear rebellious heart, you have missed my point by a considerable distance. I do not stand with you. My advice: Either leave your church quietly, refusing to cause division, or be at peace with it. There is a vast gulf between rebellion and taking a stand for what is true.)

If the truth be told, we Christians never seem to ask why we do what we do. Instead, we blithely carry out our religious traditions, never asking where they came from. Most Christians who claim to uphold the integrity of God's Word have never sought to see if

---

[1] Socrates believed that truth is found by dialoguing extensively about an issue and relentless questioning it. This method is known as *dialectic* or "the Socratic method."

[2] For a concise treatment of Socrates' life and teaching, see Samuel Enoch Stumpf's *Socrates to Sartre* (New York: McGraw-Hill, 1993), pp. 29-45.

[3] Ken Connolly's *The Indestructible Book*, Grand Rapids: Baker Books, 1996 and *Foxe's Book of Martyrs*, Old Tappan: Spire Books, 1968.

what they do every Sunday has any Scriptural backing. How do I know this? Because if they did, it would lead them to some very disturbing conclusions. Conclusions that would compel them by conscience to forever abandon what they are doing.

Strikingly, contemporary church thought and practice have been influenced far more by post-Biblical historical events than by NT (New Testament) imperatives and examples. Yet most Christians are unconscious of this influence. Nor are they aware that it has created a slew of cherished, calcified, humanly-devised traditions[4]—all of which are routinely passed off to us as "Christian."[5]

A Terrifying Invitation

I now invite you to walk with me on an untrodden path. It is a terrifying journey where you will be forced to ask questions that probably have never entered your conscious thoughts. Tough questions. Nagging questions. Even frightening questions. And you will be faced squarely with the disturbing answers. Yet those answers will lead you face-to-face with some of the richest things a Christian can know.

As you read through the following pages, you will be stunned to learn that what we Christians do for Sunday morning church did not come from Jesus Christ, the apostles, or the Scriptures. Nor did it come from Judaism.[6] Shockingly, most of what we do for

---

[4] Edwin Hatch, *The Influence of Greek Ideas and Usages Upon the Christian Church* (Peabody: Hendrickson, 1895), p. 18. Hatch traces the detrimental effects of a church that was influenced by its culture rather than a church that influenced its culture.

[5] It was the Christian philosopher Soren Kierkegaard (1813-1855) who said that modern Christianity is essentially a counterfeit (Soren Kierkegaard, *Attack on Christendom*, ET 1946, pp. 59ff., 117, 150ff., 209ff.).

[6] After the Romans destroyed Jerusalem in A.D. 70, Judaic Christianity waned in numbers and power. Gentile Christianity dominated, and the new faith began to absorb Greco-Roman philosophy and ritual. Judaic Christianity survived for five centuries in the little group of Syriac Christians called *Ebionim*. But their influence was not very widespread. Will Durant, *Caesar to Christ* (New York: Simon & Schuster, 1950), p. 577. According to Shirley J. Case, "Not only was the social environment of the Christian movement largely Gentile well before the end of the first century, but it had severed almost any earlier bonds of social contact with the Jewish Christians of Palestine . . . By the year 100, Christianity is mainly a Gentile religious

"church" was lifted directly out of pagan culture in the post-apostolic period.[7] To be more specific, the great bulk of our church practices were spawned during three time periods: The early post-Constantinian era (324 to 600), the Reformation era (16th century), and the Revivalist era (18th-19th century).

Each chapter will trace an accepted traditional church practice. It will then tell the story of *where* this practice came from. But more importantly, it will explain *how* this practice stifles the functional Headship of Jesus Christ and hampers the functioning of His Body.

If you are unwilling to have your Christianity seriously examined, do not read beyond this page. Give this book to *Goodwill* immediately! Spare yourself the trouble of having your Christian life turned upside down.

However, if you choose to *"take the red pill"* and be shown *"how deep the rabbit hole goes"*[8] . . . If you want to learn the true story of where your Christian practices came from . . . If you are willing to have the curtain pulled back on the modern church and have its traditional presuppositions fiercely challenged . . . then you will find this work to be disturbing, enlightening, and possibly life-changing.

---

movement . . . living together in a common Gentile social environment" (*The Social Origins of Christianity*, New York: Cooper Square Publishers, 1975, pp. 27-28). E. Glenn Hinson writes, "From the late first century on through, Gentiles came to outnumber Jews in the Christian assembly. They imported in subtle ways some of the ideas, attitudes, and customs of Greek and Roman culture" (*Christian History*, Volume XII, No. 1, Issue 37, p. 17).

[7] "Post-apostolic" means after the death of the twelve apostles. Legend tells us that the last surviving apostle, John, died around A.D. 100. According to Paul F. Bradshaw, fourth-century Christianity "absorbed and Christianized pagan religious ideas and practices, seeing itself as the fulfillment to which earlier religions had dimly pointed" (*The Search for the Origins of Christian Worship*, New York: Oxford University Press, 1992, p. 65; *Caesar to Christ*, pp. 575, 599-600, 610-19, 671-672, 650-51).

[8] A quote taken from the very thought provoking hit movie *The Matrix*. In the film, Morpheus gives Mr. Anderson the choice between living in a deceptive dream-world or understanding reality. His words are applicable to the subject at hand: "After this there's no turning back. You take the blue pill, the story ends, you wake up in your bed, and you believe whatever you want to believe. You take the red pill . . . and I show you how deep the rabbit hole goes." I hope that all of God's people would take the red pill!

Put another way, if you are a Christian in the institutional church who takes the NT seriously, what you are about to read will force you to have a crisis of conscience. For you will be confronted by unmovable historical fact.

On the other hand, if you happen to be one of those rare breeds who gathers with other Christians outside the pale of organized Christianity, you will discover afresh that not only is Scripture on your side—but history stands with you as well.

One day, through the primeval wood,
A calf walked home, as good calves should;
But made a trail all bent askew,
A crooked trail as all calves do.

Since then three hundred years have fled,
And, I infer, the calf is dead.
But still he left behind his trail,
And thereby hangs my moral tale.

The trail was taken up next day
By a lone dog that passed that way;
And then a wise bell-wether sheep
Pursued the trail o'er vale and steep,
And drew the flock behind him, too,
As good bell-wethers always do.
And from that day, o'er hill and glade,
Through those old woods a path was made.

And many men wound in and out,
And dodged, and turned, and bent about
And uttered words of righteous wrath
Because 'twas such a crooked path.
But still they followed—do not laugh—
The first migrations of that calf,
And through this winding wood-way stalked,
Because he wobbled when he walked.

This forest path became a lane,
That bent, and turned, and turned again;
This crooked lane became a road,
Where many a poor horse with his load
Toiled on beneath the burning sun,
And traveled some three miles in one.
And thus a century and a half
They trod the footsteps of that calf.

The years passed on in swiftness fleet,
The road became a village street;
And this, before men were aware,
A city's crowded thoroughfare;
And soon the central street was this
Of a renowned metropolis;
And men two centuries and a half
Trod in the footsteps of that calf.

Each day a hundred thousand rout
Followed the zigzag calf about;
And o'er his crooked journey went
The traffic of a continent.
A hundred thousand men were led
By one calf near three centuries dead.
They followed still his crooked way,
And lost one hundred years a day;
For thus such reverence is lent
To well-established precedent.

A moral lesson this might teach,
Were I ordained and called to preach;
For men are prone to go it blind
Along the calf-paths of the mind,
And work away from sun to sun
To do what other men have done.
They follow in the beaten track,
And out and in, and forth and back,

And still their devious course pursue,
To keep the path that others do.
They keep the path a sacred groove,
Along which all their lives they move.
But how the wise old wood-gods laugh,
Who saw the first primeval calf!
Ah! Many things this tale might teach—
But I am not ordained to preach.
                    -Sam Walter Foss

CHAPTER 1

THE ORDER OF WORSHIP:
SUNDAY MORNINGS SET IN CONCRETE

Custom without truth is error grown old.
-Tertullian

A s a modern church-going Christian, you observe the same perfunctory order of worship every time you go to church. It matters not what stripe of Protestantism to which you belong—be it Baptist, Methodist, Reformed, Presbyterian, Evangelical Free, Church of Christ, Disciples of Christ, CMA, Pentecostal, Charismatic, or non-denominational—your Sunday morning service is virtually identical to that of all other Protestant churches.[1] Even among the so-called "cutting-edge" denominations (like the Vineyard and Calvary Chapel), the variations are minor.

Granted, some churches use contemporary choruses while others use hymns. In some churches, congregants raise their hands. In others, their hands never get above their hips. Some churches observe the Lord's Supper weekly. Others observe it quarterly. In some churches, the liturgy (order of worship) is written out in a

---

[1] There are three exceptions to this point. The Plymouth Brethren (both Open and Closed) have an encased liturgy where there is some open sharing among the congregants at the beginning of the service. Nevertheless, the order of service is the same every week. Old school Quakers have an open meeting where the congregants are passive until someone is "enlightened," after which they share. The other exception is the "high church" Protestants. These are those who retain the "smells and bells" of an elaborate Catholic Mass.

bulletin.[2] In others, the liturgy is unwritten, yet it is just as mechanical and predictable as if it were set to print.

Despite these slight variations, the order of worship is essentially the same in all Protestant churches across the board.

The Sunday Morning Order of Worship

Peel away the superficial alterations that make each church service distinct and you will find the same prescribed liturgy. This is what it looks like:

The Greeting. (As you enter the building, you are greeted by an usher or an appointed greeter—who should be smiling! You are then handed a bulletin or announcement page. Note: if you are part of the Vineyard denomination, you may drink coffee and eat donuts as you are seated.)

Prayer or Scripture Reading. (Usually given by the pastor or song leader.)

The Song Service. (The congregation is led to sing by a professional song leader, choir, or worship team. If you are part of a charismatic-styled church, this will typically last 30 to 45 minutes. Otherwise it will be shorter.)

The Announcements. (Usually given by the pastor or some other church leader.)

---

[2] The word "liturgy" is derived from the Greek word *leitourgia* which means "public service." Christians picked it up to refer to the public ministry to God. A liturgy, therefore, is simply a worship service or a prescribed order of worship. *Leitourgia* referred to the performance of a public task expected of citizens of Ancient Athens. It was the fulfilling of civil obligations. John F. White, *Protestant Worship and Church Architecture* (New York: Oxford University Press, 1964, p. 22); Everett Ferguson, *Early Christians Speak: Faith and Life in the First Three Centuries*, (Abilene: A.C.U. Press, Third Edition, 1999), p. 83; J.G. Davies, *The New Westminster Dictionary of Liturgy and Worship: First American Edition* (Philadelphia: Westminster Press, 1986), p. 314.

The Offering. (Sometimes called "the offertory," it is usually accompanied by special music by the choir, worship team, or a soloist.)

The Sermon. (Typically a 30 to 45-minute oration delivered by the pastor.)[3]

One or more of the Following Post-Sermon Activities:
An after-the-sermon-pastoral prayer,
An altar call,
More singing led by the choir or worship team,
The Lord's Supper,
Prayer for the sick or afflicted.

Closing Announcements (Usually given by the pastor or a lucky "lay-person" who gets to speak.)

The Benediction. (This is the blessing or song that ends the service.)

With some minor rearrangements, this is the unbroken liturgy that 345 million Protestants across the globe observe religiously week after week.[4] And for the last 500 years, no one has seemed to question it.

Look again at the order of worship. Notice that it contains a three-fold structure: 1) singing, 2) the sermon, and 3) closing prayer or song. This order of worship is viewed as sacrosanct in the eyes of most modern Christians. But why? It is simply due to the titanic power of tradition.[5]

---

[3] See Chapter 2 for a complete discussion on the roots of the sermon.

[4] At the time of this writing, there are an estimated 345,855,000 Protestants in the world: 70,164,000 are in North America, and 77,497,000 are in Europe (*The World Almanac and Book of Facts 2003*, New York: World Almanac Education Group, 2003, p. 638).

[5] One scholar defines tradition as "inherited worship practices and beliefs that show continuity from generation to generation" (*Protestant Worship and Church Architecture*, p. 21).

We inherited this liturgy through a consistent yet evolving tradition. And that tradition has set the Sunday morning order of worship in concrete for five centuries . . . never to be moved!

Where Did the Protestant Order of Worship Come From?

Pastors who routinely tell their congregations that "we do everything by the Book" and still perform this ironclad liturgy are simply not correct. (I concede that the lack of truthfulness is due to ignorance rather than overt deception.)

You can scour your Bible from beginning to end, and you will never find anything that resembles it. This is because the first-century Christians knew no such thing. In fact, the Protestant order of worship has about as much Biblical support as does the Roman Catholic Mass![6] Neither of them have any points of contact with the NT.

In *Rethinking the Wineskin*, I describe the meetings of the early church. These meetings were marked by every-member function-ing, spontaneity, freedom, vibrancy, and open participation.[7] It was a fluid gathering, not a static ritual. And it was unpredictable, unlike the modern church service.

---

[6] The medieval Mass is a blending of Roman, Gallic, and Frankish elements (see Edmon Bishop's essay, *The Genius of the Roman Rite* and Monsignor L. Duchesne's *Christian Worship: Its Origin and Evolution*, New York: Society for Promoting Christian Knowledge, 1912, pp. 86-227). The ceremonial aspects of the Mass, such as the incense, candles, and arrangement of the church building were all borrowed from the ceremonial court of the Roman Emperors (Josef A. Jungmann, S.J., *The Early Liturgy: To the Time of Gregory the Great*, Notre Dame: Notre Dame Press, 1959, pp. 132-133, 291-292; M.A. Smith, *From Christ to Constantine*, Downer's Grove: InterVarsity Press, 1973, p. 173).

[7] In Chapter 1 of *Rethinking the Wineskin*, I describe a first-century church meeting in detail. This style of meeting is being observed today on a very small scale. While such gatherings are often considered radical and revolutionary by mainline Christianity, they are no more radical or revolutionary than the first-century church. For a scholarly discussion on the early church meeting, see Robert Banks, *Paul's Idea of Community* (Peabody: Hendrickson, 1994), Chapters 9-11; Robert and Julia Banks, *The Church Comes Home* (Peabody: Hendrickson, 1998), Chapter 2; Eduard Schweizer, *Church Order in the New Testament* (Chatham: W. & J. Mackay, 1961), pp. 1-136.

Further, the first-century church meeting was not patterned after the Jewish synagogue services as some recent authors have suggested.[8] Instead, it was totally unique to the culture.

So where did the Protestant order of worship come from? It has its basic roots in the Catholic Mass.[9] Significantly, the Mass did not originate with the NT. It rather grew out of ancient Judaism and paganism.[10] According to famed historian Will Durant, the Catholic Mass was *"based partly on the Judaic Temple service, partly on Greek mystery rituals of purification, vicarious sacrifice, and participation . . . "*[11]

Gregory the Great (540-604) is the man responsible for shaping the medieval Mass.[12] Gregory was an incredibly superstitious man whose thinking was influenced by magical paganistic concepts. He

---

[8] See Robert Banks *Paul's Idea of Community*, pp. 106-108, 112-117; Paul F. Bradshaw's *The Search for the Origins of Christian Worship* (New York: Oxford University Press, 1992), pp. 13-15, 27-29, 159-160, 186. Bradshaw argues against the idea that first-century Christianity inherited its liturgical practices from Judaism. He points out that this idea began around the 17th century. David Norrington states, "We have little evidence to suggest that the first Christians attempted to perpetuate the style of the synagogue" (David C. Norrington, *To Preach or Not to Preach?*, Carlisle: Paternoster, 1996, p. 48). Moreover, the Jewish synagogue was a human invention. Some scholars believe the synagogue was created during the Babylonian captivity (sixth century B.C.), when worship at the Jerusalem temple was an impossibility. Others believe synagogues emerged afterwards: Either in the third century B.C. or the second century B.C. with the rise of the Pharisees. Even though the synagogue became the center of Jewish life after the Jerusalem temple was destroyed in A.D. 70, there is no Old Testament (or Divine) precedent for such an institution (*Dictionary of Jesus and the Gospels*, Downer's Grove: InterVarsity Press, 1992, pp. 781-82; Alfred Edersheim, *The Life and Times of Jesus the Messiah*, Mclean: Macdonald Publishing Company, p. 431). Furthermore, the architectural inspiration for the synagogue was pagan (*To Preach or Not to Preach?*, p. 28).

[9] The word *Mass*, which means "dismissal" of the congregation (*mission, dismissio*) became, at the end of the fourth century, the word for the worship service that celebrated the Eucharist (Philip Schaff, *History of the Christian Church: Volume 3*, Michigan: Eerdmans, 1910, p. 505).

[10] The story of the origin of the Mass is far beyond the scope of this book. Suffice it to say that the Mass was essentially a blending together of a resurgence of Gentile interest in synagogue worship and pagan influence that dates back to the fourth century (Frank Senn, *Christian Liturgy: Catholic and Evangelical*, Minneapolis: Fortress Press, 1997, p. 54; *The Early Liturgy*, pp. 123, 130-144).

[11] Will Durant, *Caesar to Christ*, New York: Simon & Schuster, 1950, p. 599.

[12] Gregory's major reforms shaped the Catholic Mass into what it was all throughout the medieval period up until the Reformation. Philip Schaff, *History of the Christian Church: Volume 4* (Michigan: Eerdmans, 1910), pp. 387-388.

embodied the medieval mind, which was a cross between heathenism, magic, and Christianity. It is no accident that Durant calls
Gregory *"the first completely medieval man."*[13]

The medieval Mass reflected the mind of its father, Gregory. It
was a blending of pagan and Judaistic ritual sprinkled with
Catholic theology and Christian vocabulary.[14] Durant points out
that the Mass was deeply steeped in pagan magical thinking as
well as Greek drama.[15] He writes, *"The Greek mind, dying, came to
a transmigrated life in the theology and liturgy of the church; the
Greek language, having reigned for centuries over philosophy,
became the vehicle of Christian literature and ritual; the Greek
mysteries passed down into the impressive mystery of the Mass."*[16]

In effect, the Catholic Mass that developed out of the fourth
through sixth centuries was essentially pagan. The Christians stole
from the pagans the vestments of the pagan priests, the use of
incense and holy water in purification rites, the burning of candles
in worship, the architecture of the Roman basilica for their church
buildings, the law of Rome as the basis of "canon law," the title
Pontifex Maximus for the head bishop, and the pagan rituals for the
Catholic Mass.[17]

As various Protestant denominations were born, they all helped
reshape the Catholic liturgy by contributing a unique element to

---

[13] Will Durant, *The Age of Faith*, New York: Simon & Schuster, 1950, pp. 521-524.
[14] Philip Schaff outlines the various Catholic liturgies which climax in Gregory's
liturgy. Gregory's liturgy dominated the Latin church for centuries and was
sanctioned by the Council of Trent. (Philip Schaff, *History of the Christian Church:
Volume 3*, Michigan: Eerdmans, 1910, pp. 531-535). Gregory is also the person that
developed and popularized the Catholic doctrine of "purgatory," although he
extracted it from several speculative comments from Augustine (Justo L. Gonzalez,
The Story of Christianity, Peabody: Prince Press, 1999, p. 247). In effect, Gregory
made Augustine's teachings the foundational theology of the Western church.
"Augustine," says Paul Johnson, "was the dark genius of imperial Christianity, the
ideologue of the Church-State alliance, and the fabricator of the medieval mentality.
Next to Paul, who supplied the basic theology, he did more to shape Christianity than
any other human being" (*A History of Christianity*, New York: Simon & Schuster,
1976, p. 112). Durant says that Augustine's theology dominated Catholic philosophy
until the 13th century. Augustine also gave it a Neo-platonic tinge (*The Age of Faith*,
p. 74).
[15] *Caesar to Christ*, pp. 599-600, 618-619, 671-672; *The Age of Faith*, p. 1027.
[16] *Caesar and Christ*, p. 595.
[17] Ibid., pp. 618-619.

it.[18] It is a complex and enormously vast journey to chronicle. To treat it thoroughly would require a massive volume.[19] In this chapter, we will survey the basic story.

After Gregory established the Mass in the sixth century, it was etched in stone, varying little for over a thousand years.[20] But the liturgical deadlock underwent its first revision when Martin Luther (1483-1546) entered the scene.

Luther's Contribution

In 1520, Luther launched a violent campaign against the Roman Catholic Mass.[21] The high point of the Catholic Mass has always been the Eucharist,[22] also known as "Communion" or "the Lord's Supper." Everything centers on and leads up to that magical

---

[18] James F. White describes nine liturgical traditions within the Protestant camp in his book *Protestant Worship: Traditions in Transition* (Louisville: Westminster/John Knox Press, 1989).

[19] Frank C. Senn has given a technical treatment on the history of both Catholic and Evangelical liturgies in his seminal work *Christian Liturgy: Catholic and Evangelical* (Minneapolis: Fortress Press, 1997). Alongside of Senn's work is Gregory Dix's monster volume *The Shape of the Liturgy* (Continuum Publishing House, 2000). Both books are over 700 pages long!

[20] The modern Mass has changed little for the last 400 years (*Protestant Worship: Traditions in Transition*, p. 17). The form that is used today was issued in the Roman Missal, Sacramentary, and Lectionary of 1970 (*Christian Liturgy*, p. 639). Even so, the Mass of the sixth century resembles the present day Mass (*The Early Liturgy*, p. 298).

[21] This campaign was articulated in Luther's radical treatise, *The Babylonian Captivity of the Church*. This book was a bombshell dropped on the Roman Catholic system challenging the core theology behind the Catholic Mass. In *The Babylonian Captivity*, Luther attacked the following three features of the Mass: 1) The withholding of the cup from the laity, 2) Transubstantiation (the belief that the bread and the wine turn into the *actual* body and blood of Christ), and 3) The concept that the Mass is a human work offered up to God as a sacrifice of Christ. Although Luther rejected transubstantiation, he nevertheless believed that the "real presence" of Christ's body and blood is in, with, and under the elements of bread and wine. This belief is called "consubstantiation." In *Captivity*, Luther also denied the seven sacraments, accepting only three: baptism, penance, and the bread (*Christian Liturgy*, p. 268). Luther later dropped penance as a sacrament.

[22] The word "Eucharist" is derived from the Greek word *eucharisteo* which means "to give thanks." It appears in 1 Corinthians 11:24. There we are told that Jesus took bread, broke it and "gave thanks." Post-apostolic Christians referred to the Lord's Supper as the "Eucharist."

moment when the priest breaks the bread and gives it to the people. To the medieval Catholic mind, the offering of the Eucharist was the re-sacrificing of Jesus Christ. As far back as Gregory the Great (540-604), the Catholic church taught that Jesus Christ is sacrificed anew through the Mass.[23]

Luther railed (often uncouthly) against the mitres and staffs of the Papists and their teaching on the Eucharist. The cardinal error of the Mass, said Luther, was that it was a human "work" based on a false understanding of Christ's sacrifice.[24] So in 1523, Luther set forth his own revisions to the Catholic Mass.[25] These revisions are the foundation for all Protestant worship.[26] The heart of them is this: Luther made preaching, rather than the Eucharist, the center of the gathering.[27]

Accordingly, in the modern Protestant worship service it is the pulpit, rather than the altar-table, that is the central element.[28] (The altar-table is where the Eucharist is placed in Catholic churches.) Luther gets the credit for making the sermon the climax of the Protestant service.[29] Read his words: *"A Christian congregation*

---

[23] Luther penned his liturgical revisions in a treatise called *Form of the Mass*. Justo L. Gonzalez, *The Story of Christianity* (Peabody: Prince Press, 1999), p. 247. Note that most recent Catholic theologians (for the past 70 years) have said that the Mass is a *re-presentation* of the one sacrifice rather than a new sacrifice as did the medieval Catholic church.

[24] The Eucharist was often referred to as an "oblation" or "sacrifice" in the third through fifth centuries (James Hastings Nichols, *Corporate Worship in the Reformed Tradition*, Philadelphia: The Westminster Press, 1968 p. 25). See also *Christian Liturgy*, pp. 270-275. Loraine Boettner has detailed the errors of the medieval Catholic Mass in Chapter 8 of his book *Roman Catholicism* (Phillipsburg: The Presbyterian and Reformed Publishing Company, 1962).

[25] The Latin name for it is *Formula Missae*.

[26] *Protestant Worship: Traditions in Transition*, pp. 36-37.

[27] Ibid., pp. 41-42. While Luther had a very high view of the Eucharist, he stripped the Mass of all sacrificial language, only keeping the Eucharist itself. He was a strong believer in both Word and Sacrament. So his German Mass assumed both holy communion and preaching.

[28] Some "liturgical" churches in the Protestant tradition still have the altar-table somewhere near the pulpit.

[29] Before the medieval age, both the sermon and the Eucharist had a prominent place in the Christian liturgy. However, the sermon fell into serious decline during the medieval period. Many priests were too illiterate to preach, and other elements crowded out the preaching of Scripture. William D. Maxwell, *An Outline of Christian Worship: Its Developments and Forms* (New York: Oxford University Press, 1936),

should never gather together without the preaching of God's Word and prayer, no matter how briefly"[30]. . . *"the preaching and teaching of God's Word is the most important part of Divine service."*[31]

Luther's belief in the centrality of preaching as the mark of the worship service has stuck till this day. Yet it has no Biblical precedent whatsoever.[32] As one historian put it, *"The pulpit is the throne of the Protestant pastor."*[33] It is for this reason that ordained Protestant ministers are routinely called "preachers."[34]

But bracketing these changes, Luther's liturgy varied little from the Catholic Mass.[35] Luther merely tried to save what he thought were the "Christian" elements in the old Catholic order.[36] Consequently, if you compare Luther's order of worship with Gregory's liturgy, it is virtually the same![37] Luther mainly reinterpreted

---

p. 72. Gregory the Great sought to restore the place of the sermon in the Mass. However, his efforts failed. It was not until the Reformation that the sermon was brought to a central place in the worship service (*History of the Christian Church: Volume 4*, pp. 227, 399-402).

[30] "Concerning the Order of Public Worship," *Luther's Works*, LIII, 11. Luther arranged for three services on Sunday morning. They were all accompanied by a sermon (*History of the Church: Volume 7*, p. 488). Roland Bainton counted 2,300 extant sermons preached by Luther in his lifetime (*Here I Stand: A Life of Martin Luther*, Nashville: Abingdon Press, 1950, pp. 348-349).

[31] "The German Mass," *Luther's Works*, LIII, 68.

[32] *Rethinking the Wineskin*, Chapter 1; Chapter 2 of this book.

[33] *History of the Christian Church: Volume 7*, p. 490.

[34] *Protestant Worship: Traditions in Transition*, p. 20.

[35] Luther still followed the historic Western Ordo. The main difference was that Luther eliminated the offertory prayers and the prayers of the Canon after the Sanctus that spoke of offerings. In sum, Luther struck from the Mass everything smacking of "sacrifice." He, along with other Reformers, removed much of the decadent late-medieval elements of the Mass. They did so by rendering the liturgy in the common vernacular, including congregational songs (chants and chorales for the Lutherans; metrical psalms for the Reformed), the centrality of the sermon, and allowing the congregants to participate in holy communion (Frank Senn, *Christian Worship and Its Cultural Setting*, Philadelphia: Fortress Press, 1983, pp. 84, 102).

[36] *History of the Christian Church: Volume 7*, pp. 486-487. The German Reformer Carlstadt (1477-1541) was more radical than Luther. During Luther's absence Carlstadt abolished the entire Mass, destroying the altars along with the pictures.

[37] Frank Senn has the early Catholic liturgy written out in his book (*Christian Liturgy*, p. 139). Luther even retained the word "Mass," which came to mean the entire worship service (p. 486).

many of the Mass' rituals. But he kept the ceremony, believing it was proper.[38]

For instance, Luther retained the act that marked the high moment of the Catholic Mass: When the priest elevated the bread and cup and consecrated them. He merely reinterpreted the meaning of this act.[39] The practice of consecrating the bread and cup by elevating them began in the 13th century. It is a practice mostly built on superstition.[40] Yet it is still observed by many pastors today.

In like manner, Luther did drastic surgery to the Eucharistic prayer, only retaining the "words of institution."[41] The words of institution are the words of 1 Corinthians 11:23ff—*"That the Lord Jesus on the night He was betrayed took bread . . . and said, 'Take and eat, this is my Body' . . ."* Till this day, Protestant pastors religiously recite this text before administering communion.

In the end, Luther's liturgy was nothing more than a truncated version of the Catholic Mass![42] And it was riddled with the same glaring problems: The congregants were still passive-spectators (except that they could now sing), and the entire liturgy was still directed by an ordained clergyman (the pastor had replaced the priest.)

In Luther's own words, *"It is not now nor ever has been our intention to abolish the liturgical service of God completely, but rather to purify the one that is now in use from the wretched accretions which corrupt it . . ."*[43] Tragically, Luther did not realize

---

[38] Luther pointed to the ceremonial in the courts of kings and believed this should be applied to the worship of God (*Christian Worship and Its Cultural Setting*, p. 15). See Chapter 3 of this book for how imperial protocol made its way into the Christian liturgy during the fourth century with the reign of Constantine.

[39] When the Catholic priest held up the sacrament, he was doing so to inaugurate the sacrifice.

[40] *Christian Worship and Its Cultural Setting*, pp. 18-19.

[41] *Protestant Worship: Traditions in Transition*, pp. 41-42; *An Outline of Christian Worship*, p. 75.

[42] Luther retained the basic order of the medieval Mass along with the ceremonial aspects of lights, incense, and vestments (*An Outline of Worship*, p. 77).

[43] *Luther's Works*, LIII, 20.

that new wine cannot be repackaged into old wineskins.[44] At no time did Luther (or any of the other mainstream Reformers) demonstrate a desire to return to the *practices* of the first-century church. These men set out merely to reform the *theology* of the Catholic church.

In sum, the major enduring changes that Luther made to the Catholic Mass were as follows: 1) He performed the Mass in the language of the people, 2) He gave the sermon a central place in the gathering, 3) He introduced congregational singing,[45] 4) He abolished the idea that the Mass was a sacrifice of Christ, and 5) He allowed the congregation to partake of the bread and cup (rather than just the priest as was the Catholic practice). Other than these differences, Luther kept the same order of worship as found in the Catholic Mass!

Still worse, although Luther talked much about the "priesthood of all believers," he never abandoned the practice of an ordained clergy.[46] In fact, so strong was his belief in an ordained clergy that he wrote, *"The public ministry of the Word ought to be established by holy ordination as the highest and greatest of the functions of the church."*[47] Under Luther's influence, the Protestant pastor simply replaced the Catholic priest. And for the most part, there was little practical difference in the way these two offices functioned.[48] This is still the case today as we shall later see.[49]

---

[44] Ironically, Luther insisted that his German Mass should not be adopted legalistically, and if it became outdated it should be discarded (*Christian Worship and Its Cultural Setting*, p. 17). Tragically, this never happened. Traditions die too hard!

[45] A lover of music, Luther made music a key part of the service. *Protestant Worship: Traditions in Transition*, p. 41; *Christian History*, Volume XII, No. 3, Issue 39, pp. 3, 16-19. Luther was a musical genius. So powerful was his gifting in music that the Jesuits said that Luther's songs "destroyed more souls than his writings and speeches." It is not surprising that one of the greatest musical talents in church history happened to be a Lutheran. His name was Johann Sebastian Bach. For details on Luther's musical contribution to the Protestant liturgy see *Christian Liturgy*, pp. 284-287; *Protestant Worship: Traditions in Transition*, pp. 41, 47-48; Will Durant, *The Reformation* (New York: Simon and Schuster, 1957), pp. 778-779.

[46] *Protestant Worship: Traditions in Transition*, p. 41.

[47] "Concerning the Ministry," *Luther's Works*, XL, 11.

[48] The priest administered seven sacraments, while the pastor only administered two (baptism and the Eucharist). However, both priest and pastor were viewed as having the exclusive authority of proclaiming the Word of God. For Luther, the use of clerical robes, candles on the altar, and the attitude of the minister while praying were

What follows is Luther's order of worship.[50] The general outline should look very familiar to you—for it is the taproot of your Sunday morning church service.[51]

Singing
Prayer
The Sermon
Admonition to the people
The Lord's Supper
Singing [52]
Post-communion prayer
The Benediction

Zwingli's Contribution

With the advent of Gutenberg's printing press (about 1450), the bulk production of liturgical books accelerated the liturgical changes that the Reformers attempted to make.[53] Those changes were now set to movable type and printed in mass quantity.

The Swiss Reformer Ulrich Zwingli (1484-1531) made a few of his own reforms that helped shape today's order of worship. He replaced the altar-table with something called "the communion

matters of indifference (*History of the Christian Church: Volume 7*, p. 489). But though he was indifferent about them, he did advise that they be retained (*Christian Liturgy*, p. 282). Hence, they are still with us today.

[49] See Chapter 4.
[50] This liturgy was published in his *German Mass and Order of Service* in the year 1526.
[51] *Christian Liturgy*, pp. 282-283.
[52] Notice that the sermon was both preceded by and followed by singing and prayer. Luther believed that sandwiching the sermon with songs strengthened the sermon and provided a devotional response to it (*Christian Liturgy*, p. 306). Most of the songs sung in Luther's German Mass were versifications of Latin liturgical chants and creeds. (Versification is making verse out of prose.) To Luther's credit, he himself wrote about 36 hymns (*Luther's Works*, LIII). And he was a genius at taking contemporary songs and redeeming them with Christian lyrics. His feeling was, "Why let the devil have all the good tunes?" (Marva J. Dawn, *Reaching Out Without Dumbing Down: A Theology of Worship for the Turn-of-the-Century Culture*, Grand Rapids: Eerdmans, 1995, p. 189).
[53] *Christian Liturgy*, p. 300.

table" from which the bread and wine were administered.[54] He also had the bread and cup carried to the people in their pews using wooden trays and cups.[55]

Most Protestant churches still have such a table. Two candles typically sit upon it—a custom that came directly from the ceremonial court of Roman Emperors![56] And most carry the bread and cup to the people seated in their pews.

Zwingli also recommended that the Lord's Supper be taken quarterly (four times a year). This was in opposition to taking it weekly as other Reformers advocated.[57] Many Protestants imitate the quarterly observation of the Lord's Supper today. Some observe it monthly.

Zwingli is also credited with championing the "memorial" view of the Supper. This view is embraced by mainstream American Protestantism.[58] It is the view that the bread and cup are mere symbols of Christ's body and blood.[59] Nevertheless, aside from these novelties, Zwingli's liturgy was not much different from Luther's.[60] Like Luther, Zwingli emphasized the centrality of preaching. So much so that he and his co-workers preached as often as the television news—fourteen times a week![61]

---

[54] Oscar Hardman, *A History of Christian Worship* (Tennessee: Parthenon Press, 1937), p. 161. On this point, Frank Senn writes, "In Reformed churches, the pulpit dominated the altar so totally that in time the altar disappeared and was replaced by a table used for holy communion only a few times a year. The preaching of the Word dominated the service. This has been taken as a consequence of the so-called rediscovery of the Bible. But the rediscovery of the Bible was the invention of the printing press, a cultural phenomenon" (*Christian Worship and Its Cultural Setting*, p. 45).

[55] *Christian Liturgy*, p. 362; *Protestant Worship: Traditions in Transition*, p. 62.

[56] *The Early Liturgy*, pp. 132-133, 291-292; *From Christ to Constantine*, p. 173.

[57] *Christian Liturgy*, p. 363.

[58] *Protestant Worship: Traditions in Transition*, p. 60.

[59] Zwingli's view was more complex than this. However, his idea of the Eucharist was not as "high" as that of Calvin or Luther (*An Outline of Christian Worship*, p. 81). Zwingli is the father of the modern Protestant view of the Lord's Supper. Of course, his view would not be representative of the "liturgical" Protestant churches, which celebrate both Word and Sacrament weekly.

[60] Zwingli's order of service is listed in *Christian Liturgy*, pp. 362-364.

[61] *Protestant Worship: Traditions in Transition*, p. 61.

The Contribution of Calvin and Company

Reformers John Calvin (1509-1564), John Knox (1513-1572), and Martin Bucer (1491-1551) added to the liturgical molding. These men created their own orders of worship between 1537 and 1562. Even though their liturgies were observed in different parts of the world, they were virtually identical.[62] They merely made a few adjustments to Luther's liturgy. Most notably was the collection of money which followed the sermon.[63]

Like Luther, Calvin stressed the centrality of preaching during the worship service. He believed that each believer has access to God through the preached Word rather than through the Eucharist.[64] Given his theological genius, the preaching in Calvin's Geneva church was intensely theological and academic. It was also highly individualistic, a mark that never left Protestantism.[65]

Calvin's Geneva church was held up as the model for all Reformed churches. Thus its order of worship spread far and wide. This accounts for the cerebral character of most Protestant churches today, particularly the Reformed and Presbyterian brand.[66]

---

[62] These liturgies were used in Strasbourg, Germany (1537), Geneva, Switzerland (1542), and Scotland (1562).

[63] The collection was alms for the poor (*Christian Liturgy*, pp. 365-366). Calvin wrote, "No assembly of the church should be held without the Word being preached, prayers being offered, the Lord's Supper being administered, and alms given" (*Corporate Worship in the Reformed Tradition*, p. 29). Although Calvin desired to have the Lord's Supper weekly, his Reformed churches followed Zwingli's practice of taking it quarterly (*Protestant Worship: Traditions in Transition*, pp. 65, 67).

[64] *Dictionary of Pentecostals and Charismatic Movements* (Grand Rapids: Zondervan, 1988), p. 904. The "Word" in Reformed usage meant the Bible and the preached word as conveying the incarnated Word. Both the sermon and Scripture-reading were connected and were viewed as the "Word" (*Corporate Worship in the Reformed Tradition*, p. 30). The idea that the preaching of the Bible is the very "Word of God" appears in the Confessio Helvetica Posterior of 1566.

[65] The rugged individualism of the Renaissance influenced the message of the Reformers. They were a product of their times. The gospel they preached was centered on individual needs and personal development. It was not communitarian as was the message of the first-century Christians. This individualistic emphasis was picked up by the Puritans, Pietists, and Revivalists, and it pervaded all areas of American life and thought (*Christian Worship and Its Cultural Setting*, pp. 100, 104; John Mark Terry, *Evangelism: A Concise History*, Nashville: Broadman & Holman Publishers, 1994, p. 125; *Rethinking the Wineskin*, Chapter 4).

[66] *Protestant Worship: Traditions in Transition*, p. 65.

Because musical instruments were not explicitly mentioned in the NT, Calvin did away with pipe organs and choirs.[67] All singing was *a capella*. (Some modern Protestants, like the Church of Christ, still follow Calvin's rigid non-instrumentalism.) This changed in the mid-19th century when Reformed churches began using instrumental music and choirs.[68] However, the Puritans (English Calvinists) continued in the spirit of Calvin, condemning both instrumental music and choir singing.[69]

Probably the most damaging feature of Calvin's liturgy is that he led most of the service from his pulpit![70] Christianity has never recovered from this. Today, it is the pastor that is the MC and CEO of the Sunday morning church service—just as the priest is the MC and CEO of the Catholic Mass!

Another feature that Calvin contributed to the order of worship is the somber attitude that the congregation is taught to adopt when they enter the building. That atmosphere is one of a profound sense of self-abasement before a sovereign and austere God.[71]

Martin Bucer is equally credited with fostering this attitude. At the beginning of every service, he had the Ten Commandments uttered to create a sense of veneration.[72] Out of this mentality grew some rather outrageous practices. Puritan New England was noted for fining children who smiled in church! Add to this the creation of the "Tithingman" who would wake up sleeping congregants by poking them with a heavily-knobbed staff![73]

Such thinking is a throw-back to the late medieval view of piety.[74] Yet it was embraced and kept alive by Calvin and Bucer.

---

[67] Ibid., p. 66. Zwingli, a musician himself, shared Calvin's conviction that music and choirs ought not to be part of the church service (p. 62).

[68] Ibid., p. 76. For Calvin, all songs had to include the words of Old Testament Scripture, so hymns were excluded (p. 66).

[69] Ibid., p. 126.

[70] Ibid., p. 67. This was also the practice of Calvin's contemporary, Martin Bucer (*Protestant Worship and Church Architecture*, p. 83).

[71] Horton Davies, *Christian Worship: Its History and Meaning* (New York: Abingdon Press, 1957), p. 56.

[72] *Protestant Worship: Traditions in Transition*, p. 74.

[73] *Searching Together*, Vol. 11, No. 4, 1982, pp. 38-39.

[74] The medievals equated somberness with holiness and moroseness with godliness. By contrast, the early Christians were marked by an attitude of gladness and joy (Acts 2:46; 8:8; 13:52; 15:3; 1 Pet. 1:8).

While many modern Pentecostals and Charismatics broke with this tradition, it is mindlessly followed in most churches today. The message is: "Be quiet and reverent, for this is the house of God!"[75]

One further practice that the Reformers retained from the Mass was the practice of the clergy walking to their allotted seats at the beginning of the service while the people stood singing. This practice started in the fourth century when the bishops walked into their magnificent basilica churches. It was a practice copied straight from the pagan imperial court ceremony![76] When the Roman magistrates entered into the court room, the people would stand singing. This practice is still observed today in many Protestant churches. Yet no one ever questions it.

As Calvinism spread throughout Europe, Calvin's Geneva liturgy was adopted in most Protestant churches. It was transplanted and took root in multiple countries.[77] Here is what it looks like:[78]

Prayer
Confession
Singing (Psalm)
Prayer for enlightenment of the Spirit in the preaching
The Sermon

---

[75] By contrast, the Psalms beckon God's people to enter His gates with joy, praise, and thanksgiving (Ps. 100, et al.).

[76] *Christian Worship and Its Cultural Setting*, pp. 26-27. This so-called "entrance rite" included psalmody (introit), the litany prayer (Kyrie), and a song of praise (Gloria). It was borrowed from the imperial court ceremony (*The Early Liturgy*, pp. 292, 296). As Constantine saw himself as God's vicar on earth, God came to be viewed as the Emperor of heaven. Thus the Mass turned into a ceremonial performed before God and before his representative, the bishop—just like the ceremonial performed before the Emperor and his magistrate. The bishop, clad in his garments of a high magistrate, entered the church building in solemn procession preceded by candles. He was then seated on his special throne—the *sella curulis* of a Roman official. The fourth-century church had borrowed both the ritual and flavor of Roman officialdom in its worship (Richard Krautheimer, *Early Christian and Byzantine Architecture*, Middlesex: Penguin Books, 1986, p. 40; *Christian Liturgy*, p. 184).

[77] The Geneva liturgy was "a fixed Reformed liturgy used without variation or exception not only for the celebration of the sacraments but for ordinary Sunday worship as well"(*Protestant Worship: Traditions in Transition*, p. 69).

[78] James Mackinnon, *Calvin and the Reformation* (New York: Russell and Russell, 1962), pp. 83-84. For a more detailed version of the Geneva liturgy, see *Christian Liturgy*, pp. 365-366.

Collection of alms
General prayer
Communion (at the appointed times) while Psalm is sung
Benediction

It should be noted that Calvin sought to model his order of worship after the writings of the early church fathers[79]—particularly those who lived in the third through sixth centuries.[80] This accounts for his lack of clarity on the character of the first-century church meeting. The early fathers of the third through sixth centuries were intensely liturgical, heady, and ritualistic.[81] They did not have a first-century Christian mindset.[82] They were also theoreticians more than practitioners.

To put it another way, the church fathers of this period represent nascent (early) Catholicism. And that is what Calvin took as his main model for establishing a new order of worship![83] It is no wonder that the so-called "Reformation" brought very little reform in the way of church practice.[84] As was the case with Luther's

---

[79] Hughes Oliphant Old, *The Patristic Roots of Reformed Worship* (Zurich: Theologischer Veriag, 1970), pp. 141-155. Calvin also took the post-apostolic fathers as his model for church government. Hence, he embraced a single pastorate (*Calvin and the Reformation,* p. 81).

[80] James Hastings Nichols, *Corporate Worship in the Reformed Tradition,* p. 14.

[81] The church fathers were greatly influenced by their Greco-Roman culture. Many of them, in fact, were pagan philosophers and orators before they became Christians. As already stated, this is why their church services reflected a blending of pagan culture and Jewish synagogue forms. Further, recent scholarship has shown that the writings of the fathers on Christian worship were written later than assumed and have been reshaped by various layers of tradition (*The Search for the Origins of Christian Worship,* Chapter 3).

[82] The church fathers were heavily influenced by paganism and Neo-platonism. Will Durant, *Caesar to Christ* (New York: Simon & Schuster, 1950), pp. 610-19, 650-51. See also Durant's *The Age of Faith* (New York: Simon & Schuster, 1950), pp. 63, 74, 521-24.

[83] Since this study focuses on the unscriptural contributions of the Reformers, listing their positive contributions is beyond the scope of this book. Nevertheless, let it be known that the author is well aware that Luther, Zwingli, Calvin, et al. contributed many positive practices and beliefs to the Christian faith. At the same time, they failed to bring us to a complete reformation.

[84] The Protestant Reformation was mainly an intellectual movement (*Protestant Worship: Traditions in Transition,* p. 37). While the theology was radical compared to that of Roman Catholicism, it hardly touched ecclesiastical practice. Those who

order of worship, the liturgy of the Reformed church *"did not try to change the structures of the official [Catholic] liturgy but rather it tried to maintain the old liturgy while cultivating extra-liturgical devotions. "*[85]

The Puritan Contribution

The Puritans were Calvinists from England.[86] They embraced a rigorous biblicism and sought to adhere tightly to the NT order of worship.[87] The Puritans felt that Calvin's order of worship was not Biblical enough. Consequently, when pastors bellow about "doing everything by the Word of God," they are echoing Puritan sentiments. But the Puritan effort to restore the NT church meeting turned into a dramatic failure.

The forsaking of clerical vestments, idols, ornaments, and clergymen writing their own sermons (as opposed to reading homilies) were positive contributions that the Puritans gave us.[88] However, because of their emphasis on spontaneous prayer, the Puritans also bequeathed to us the long "pastoral prayer" that precedes the sermon.[89] A pastoral prayer in a Sunday morning Puritan service could easily last an hour or more![90]

The sermon reached its zenith with the American Puritans. They felt it was almost supernatural. And they punished church members who missed the Sunday morning sermon![91] New England residents

---

went further in their reforms, letting it touch their practice of the church, are referred to as the "Radical Reformation." For a discussion on the Radical Reformers, see *The Pilgrim Church* by E.H. Broadbent (Gospel Folio Press, 1999); *The Reformers and Their Stepchildren* by Leonard Verduin (Eerdmans, 1964); *The Radical Reformation* by George H. Williams (The Westminster Press, 1962); *The Torch of the Testimony* by John Kennedy (Christian Books, 1984).

[85] *The Patristic Roots of Reformed Worship*, p. 12.

[86] *Christian Liturgy*, p. 510.

[87] *Protestant Worship: Traditions in Transition*, p. 118.

[88] *Protestant Worship: Traditions in Transition*, pp. 119, 125; *Christian Liturgy*, p. 512.

[89] *Protestant Worship: Traditions in Transition*, p. 129.

[90] *Christian History*, Volume XIII, No. 1, Issue 41, p. 2.

[91] One Puritan leader wrote that "the preaching of the Word is the Scepter of Christ's Kingdom, the glory of a nation, and the chariot upon which life and salvation comes riding." A Puritan might hear 15,000 hours of preaching in his lifetime.

who failed to attend Sunday worship were fined or put in stocks![92] (Next time your pastor threatens you with God's unbridled wrath for missing church, be sure to thank the Puritans.)

It is worth noting that in some Puritan churches the laity was allowed to speak at the end of the service. Immediately after the sermon, the pastor would sit down and answer the congregation's questions.[93] Congregants would also be allowed to give testimonies.[94] But with the advent of Frontier- Revivalism, this practice faded away, never again to be adopted by mainstream Christianity.[95]

All in all, the Puritan contribution in shaping the Protestant liturgy did little in releasing God's people to function under Christ's Headship. Like the liturgical reforms that preceded them, the Puritan order of worship was highly predictable. It was written out in detail and followed uniformly in every church.[96]

What follows is the Puritan liturgy.[97] Compare it to the liturgies of Luther and Calvin and you will notice that the central features did not change.

Call to worship
Opening prayer
Reading of Scripture
Singing of the Psalms
Pre-sermon prayer
The sermon
Post-sermon prayer

---

[92] *Christian History*, Volume XIII, No. 1, Issue 41, pp. 2, 23.

[93] *Protestant Worship: Traditions in Transition*, p. 126.

[94] Doug Adams, *Meeting House to Camp Meeting* (Austin: The Sharing Company, 1981), p. 13.

[95] Ibid., p. 14.; *Protestant Worship: Traditions in Transition*, p. 130.

[96] *Protestant Worship: Traditions in Transition*, pp. 120, 127.

[97] *Christian Liturgy*, pp. 514-515. The Puritan's basic liturgy is contained in a work called *A Directory of the Public Worship of God* written in 1644 (*Protestant Worship: Traditions in Transition*, p. 127). This was a revision of the Anglican *Book of Common Prayer* which was first drafted in 1549. The *Directory* was used by English (not Scottish) Presbyterians and Congregationalists.

(When communion is observed, the minister exhorts the congregation, blesses the bread and cup, and passes them to the people.)

In time, the Puritans spawned their own off-shoot denominations.[98] Some of them were part of the "Free Church"[99] tradition. The Free Churches created what is called the "hymn-sandwich."[100] Here is what it looks like:

Three hymns
Scripture reading
Choir music
Unison prayers
Pastoral prayer
The sermon
The offering
The benediction

Does this look familiar to you? I assure you, you cannot find it in the NT.

Methodist and Frontier-Revival Contributions

18th century Methodists brought to the Protestant order of worship an emotional dimension. People were invited to sing loudly with vigor and fervor.[101] In this way, the Methodists were the forerunners of the Pentecostals.

Running on the heels of the Puritans, the Methodists spiced up the pastor's Sunday morning pre-sermon prayer. The Methodist clerical prayer was painfully long and universal in its scope. It swallowed up all other prayers, covering the waterfront of

[98] The descendants of Puritanism are the Baptists, Presbyterians, and Congregationalists (*Protestant Worship: Traditions in Transition*, p. 129).
[99] The so-called "Free Church" tradition includes Puritans, Separatists, Baptists, Quakers in the 17th and 18th centuries, Methodists in the late 18th century, and Disciples of Christ in the early 19th century (*Meeting House to Camp Meeting*, p. 10).
[100] *Protestant Worship: Traditions in Transition*, p. 133.
[101] Ibid., p. 153.

confession, intercession, and praise. But more importantly, it was always offered up in Elizabethan English (i.e., *Thee, Thou, Thy,* etc.)![102]

Even today, in the 21st century, the Elizabethan pastoral prayer lives and breathes.[103] A raft of modern pastors still pray in this outdated language—even though it has been a dead dialect for 400 years! Why? Because of the thoughtless power of tradition.

The Methodists also popularized the Sunday evening worship service.[104] The discovery of incandescent gas as a means of lighting enabled John Wesley (1703-1791) to make this innovation popular.[105] Today, many Protestant churches have a Sunday evening service—even though it is typically poorly attended.

The 18th and 19th centuries brought a new challenge to American Protestantism. It was the pressure to conform to the ever popular American Frontier-Revivalist services.[106] In the 18th and 19th centuries, these services greatly influenced the order of worship for scores of churches. Eventually, they were injected into the bloodstream of American Protestantism.[107] Let us look at the enduring changes the Frontier-Revivalists made.

First, the Frontier-Revivalists changed the goal of preaching. They preached exclusively with one aim: To convert lost souls. To the mind of a Frontier-Revivalist, there was nothing beyond

---

[102] Ibid., p. 164.

[103] Ibid., p.183. The "pastoral prayer before the sermon" was prescribed in detail in the *Westminster Directory of Worship*.

[104] Horton Davies, *Worship and Theology in England: 1690-1850* (Princeton: Princeton University Press, 1961), p. 108. Evening prayer services were common in the Catholic church since the fourth century. And Sunday vespers (evening services) were a stable part of cathedral and parish liturgical life for many centuries. However, the Methodists are noted for bringing into the Protestant faith the Sunday evening worship service.

[105] *Worship and Theology in England*, p. 108.

[106] *Protestant Worship: Traditions in Transition*, p. 91.

[107] Ibid., p. 171; Iain H. Murray, *Revival and Revivalism: The Making and Marring of American Evangelicalism* (Carlisle: Banner of Truth Trust, 1994).

salvation involved in God's plan.[108] This emphasis finds its seeds in the innovative preaching of George Whitefield (1714-1770).[109]

Whitefield was the first modern evangelist to preach to outdoor crowds in the open-air.[110] He is the man that shifted the emphasis in preaching from God's plans for *the church* to His plans for *the individual*. The popular notion that "God loves you and has a wonderful plan for your life" was first introduced by Whitefield.[111]

Second, Frontier-Revivalist music spoke to the soul and sought to elicit an emotional response to the salvation message.[112] All the great revivalists had a musician on their team for this purpose.[113] Worship began to be viewed as primarily individualistic, sub-

---

[108] American revivalism gave birth to the "missionary society" at the end of the 18th century. This included the Baptist Missionary Society (1792), the London Missionary Society (1795), the General Methodist Missionary Society (1796), and the Church Missionary Society (1799). Kim Tan, *Lost Heritage: The Heroic Story of Radical Christianity* (Godalming: Highland Books, 1996), p. 195.

[109] Whitefield is called "the father of American revivalism." Whitefield's central message was "the new birth" of the individual Christian. With this he led the Great Awakening (1740-1741) in New England. In 45 days, Whitefield preached 175 sermons. A superb orator, his voice could be heard by 30,000 people in one meeting. As many as 50,000 would come to hear him speak. Remarkably, it is said that Whitefield's voice could be heard at a range of one mile without amplification. And his oratorical powers were so great that he could make an audience weep with his pronunciation. Positively, Whitefield is credited for recovering the lost practice of itinerant ministry. He also shared credit with the Puritans for restoring extemporaneous prayer and preaching (*A Brief History of Preaching*, p. 165; *Christian History*, Volume XII, No. 2, Issue 38; *Christian History*, Volume IX, No. 4, Issue 28, p. 47; *Who's Who in Christian History*, Tyndale, 1992, pp. 716-17; *Evangelism: A Concise History*, pp. 100, 110, 124-125).

[110] *Worship and Theology in England*, p. 146; *Christian History*, Volume IX, No. 4, Issue 28, p. 46; *Christian History*, Volume VIII, No. 3, Issue 23, p. 17.

[111] *Christian History*, Volume XII, No. 2, Issue 38, p. 44; *Christian History*, Volume IX, No. 4, Issue 28, p. 47. The Great Awakening under Whitefield stamped American Protestantism with a individualistic-revivalistic character from which it has never recovered.

[112] *Christian Liturgy*, pp. 562-65; *Protestant Worship and Church Architecture*, pp. 8,19

[113] Finney used Thomas Hastings. Moody used Ira B. Sankey. Billy Graham continued the tradition by using Cliff Barrows and George Beverly Shea (*Christian Liturgy*, p. 600). Music was extremely instrumental in furthering the goals of revivalism. George Whitefield and John Wesley are credited for being the first to employ music to induce conviction and a readiness to hear the gospel (*Evangelism: A Concise History*, p. 110).

jective, and emotional.[114] This shift in emphasis was picked up by the Methodists, and it began to penetrate many other Protestant subcultures.

Taking their cue from the camp meetings of the revivalists, Methodist services became a means to an end. The goal shifted from worshiping God and instructing believers to the making of individual converts. Sermons moved from discussing "real-life" matters to proclaiming the gospel to the lost. All of humanity was divided into two hopelessly polarized camps: Lost or saved, converted or unconverted, regenerated or damned.[115]

The theology of revivalism showed no understanding of God's eternal purpose or His plan for the church.[116] Methodist choral music was designed to soften the hard hearts of sinners.[117] Lyrics began to reflect the individual salvation experience as well as personal testimony.[118] Charles Wesley (1707-1788) is credited for being the first to write invitational hymns.[119]

Pastors who exclusively gear their Sunday morning sermons toward winning the lost still reflect the revivalist influence.[120] This influence has pervaded the majority of today's television and radio evangelism. Many Protestant churches (not just Pentecostal and Charismatic) begin their services with rousing songs to prepare people for the emotionally-targeted sermon. But few people know that this tradition began with the Frontier-Revivalists little more than a century ago.

Third, the Methodists and the Frontier-Revivalists gave birth to the "altar call." This novelty began with the Methodists in the 18th

---

[114] *Protestant Worship and Church Architecture*, p. 11.

[115] Ibid., p. 180.

[116] For a summary of the eternal purpose, see *Rethinking the Wineskin*, Chapter 7.

[117] *Protestant Worship: Traditions in Transition*, pp. 165, 184-85.

[118] Ibid., pp. 164-65.

[119] R. Alan Streett, *The Effective Invitation* (Old Yappan: Fleming H. Revell Co., 1984), p. 190. Charles Wesley wrote over 6,000 hymns. Charles was the first hymn writer to introduce a congregational style of singing that expressed the feelings and thoughts of the *individual* Christian.

[120] The Baptists are the most noted for making the winning of the lost the goal of the Sunday morning service. Revivalism's call to make "personal decisions" for Christ both reflected and appealed to the cultural ideology of American individualism just as the "new measures" reflected and appealed to American pragmatism. *Evangelism: A Concise History* , pp. 170-171.

century.[121] The practice of inviting people who wanted prayer to stand to their feet and walk to the front to receive prayer was given to us by a Methodist evangelist named Lorenzo Dow.[122] Later, in 1807 in England, the Methodists created the "mourner's bench."[123] Anxious sinners now had a place to mourn for their sins when they were invited to walk down the sawdust trail. This method reached the United states a few years later and was given the name the "anxious bench" by Charles Finney (1792-1872).[124] The "anxious bench" was located in the front where preachers stood on an erected platform.[125] It was there that both sinners and needy saints were called forward to receive the minister's prayers.[126] Finney raised the "altar call" to a fine art. His method was to ask those who wished to be saved to stand up and come forward. Finney made this method so popular that "after 1835, it was an indispensable fixture of modern revivals."[127]

Finney later abandoned the anxious seat and simply invited sinners to come forward into the aisles and kneel at the front of the platform to receive Christ.[128] Aside from popularizing the altar call, Finney is credited with inventing the practice of praying for persons by name, mobilizing groups of workers to visit homes, and

---

[121] *Revival and Revivalism*, pp. 185-190.

[122] *The Effective Invitation*, pp. 94-95. Reverend James Taylor was among the first to call inquirers to the front of his church in 1785 in Tennessee. The first recorded use of the altar in connection with a public invitation occurred in 1799 at a Methodist camp meeting at Red River, Kentucky. See also *Protestant Worship: Traditions in Transition*, p. 174.

[123] Finney was an innovator in the business of winning souls and starting revivals. Employing his so-called "new measures," he argued that there existed no normative forms of worship in the NT. But whatever was successful in leading sinners to Christ was approved (*Christian Liturgy*, p. 564; *Protestant Worship: Traditions in Transition*, pp. 176-177).

[124] *The Effective Invitation* p. 95. Finney began using this method exclusively following his famous Rochester, New York crusade of 1830. The first historically traceable use of the phrase "anxious seat" comes from Charles Wesley: "Oh, that blessed anxious seat." For a thorough critique on the anxious bench see J.W. Nevin's *The Anxious Bench* (Chamgersburg: Wipf & Stock, 1843).

[125] *Protestant Worship: Traditions in Transition*, p. 181; *Christian History*, Volume VII, No. 4, Issue 20, pp. 7, 19.

[126] *Christian History*, Volume VIII, No. 3, Issue 23, p. 30; *Christian History*, Volume VII, No. 4, Issue 20, p. 7; *Christian Liturgy*, p. 566.

[127] *Revival and Revivalism*, pp. 226, 241-243, 277.

[128] *The Effective Invitation*, p. 96.

displacing the routine services of the church with special services every night of the week.

In time, the "anxious bench" in the outdoor camp meeting was replaced by the "altar" in the church building. The "sawdust trail" was replaced by the church aisle. And so was born the famous "altar-call."[129]

Perhaps the most dominating element that Finney gave to modern Christianity was pragmatism. By pragmatism, I mean the belief that if something works, it should be embraced. Finney believed that the NT did not teach any prescribed forms of worship.[130] He taught that the sole purpose of preaching was to win converts. Any devices were acceptable that helped accomplish that goal.[131] Under Finney, 18th-century revivalism was turned into a science and brought into mainstream churches.[132]

Modern Christianity has never recovered from this unspiritual ideology. Pragmatism, not Biblicism or spirituality, governs the activities of most modern churches. ("Seeker-sensitive" churches have excelled the best at following in Finney's footsteps.) Pragmatism is harmful because it teaches "the end justifies the means." If the end is considered "holy," any "means" are acceptable.

It is for these reasons that Charles Finney has been called *"the most influential liturgical Reformer in American history."*[133] To the

---

[129] *Dictionary of Pentecostals and Charismatic Movements*, p. 904. For further study, see Gordon L. Hall's *The Sawdust Trail: The Story of American Evangelism* (Philadelphia: Macrae Smith Company, 1964). The "sawdust trail" later became equated with the dust-covered aisle of the evangelist's tent. This usage ("hit the sawdust trail") was popularized by the ministry of Billy Sunday (1862-1935). See *Evangelism: A Concise History*, p. 161.

[130] *Protestant Worship: Traditions in Transition*, p. 177.

[131] *Pastor's Notes: A Companion Publication to Glimpses*, Volume 4, No. 2 (Worcester: Christian History Institute, 1992), p. 6.

[132] *Protestant Worship and Church Architecture*, p. 7.

[133] *Protestant Worship: Traditions in Transition*, p. 176. Finney believed that his revivalist methods which worked in his camp meetings could be imported into the Protestant churches to bring revival there. This notion was popularized and put into the Protestant mindset via his 1835 book *Lectures on Revival* (Minneapolis: Bethany House Publishers, 1989). This book sold 1200 copies the day it became available in bookstores (*Pastor's Notes: A Companion Publication to Glimpses*, Volume 4, No. 2, p. 6). Iain Murray points out that the camp meetings under the Methodists were a precursor to Finney's systematic evangelistic techniques (*Revival and Revivalism*, pp. 184-185).

Protestant mind, *doctrine* must be vigorously checked with Scripture before it is accepted. But with church *practice,* anything goes as long as it works to win converts!

In all of these ways, American Frontier-Revivalism turned church into a preaching-station. It reduced the experience of the *ekklesia* into an evangelistic mission.[134] It normalized Finney's revivalist methods and created pulpit personalities as the dominating attraction for church. It also made the church an individualistic affair rather than a corporate one.

Put differently, the goal of the Frontier-Revivalists was to bring *individual* sinners to an *individual* decision for an *individualistic* faith.[135] As a result, the goal of the early church—*mutual* edification and *every-member* functioning to *corporately* manifest Jesus Christ before principalities and powers—was altogether lost.[136] Ironically, John Wesley, an early revivalist, understood the dangers of the revivalist movement. He wrote, *"Christianity is essentially a social religion . . . to turn it into a solitary religion is indeed to destroy it."*[137]

The final tweak that Frontier-Revivalism added to the Protestant order of worship was tacking the so-called "altar call" onto the end of the hymn-sandwich. This is the liturgy that dominates American Protestantism today. Amazingly, it has changed little from Luther's invention of the *German Mass* four centuries beforehand.

With Albert Blake Dick's (1856-1934) invention of stencil duplicating in 1884, the order of worship began to be printed in

---

[134] Properly conceived, the goal of preaching is not the salvation of souls. It is the birth of the church. As one scholar put it, "Conversion can only be the means; the goal is the extension of the visible church" (*Dictionary of Mission: Theology, History, Perspective*, Maryknoll: Orbis Books, 1998, p. 431). Scholar D.J. Tidball has echoed the same thought saying, "Paul's primary interest was not in the conversion of individuals but in the formation of Christian communities" (*Dictionary of Paul and His Letters*, Downers Grove: InterVarsity Press, 1993, p. 885). The Frontier-Revivalists had no concept of the *ekklesia*.

[135] *Protestant Worship and Church Architecture*, pp. 121-124.

[136] See 1 Cor. 12-14; Eph. 1-3; *Rethinking the Wineskin*, Chapter 7.

[137] "Sermon on the Mount IV," *Sermons on Several Occasions* (London: Epworth Press, 1956), p. 237.

bulletins.[138] Thus was born the famous "Sunday morning bulletin."[139]

The Staggering Influence of D.L. Moody

The seeds of the "revivalist gospel" were spread throughout the Western world by the mammoth influence of D.L. Moody (1837-1899).[140] Moody's gospel, like Whitefield's, had but one center—salvation for the sinner. All other ends were secondary.[141] Moody's preaching technique was dominated by this single interest. He invented the *solo* hymn that followed the pastor's sermon.[142] The invitational solo hymn was sung by a soloist until George Beverly Shea suggested it be handled by a choir. Shea encouraged Billy Graham to employ a choir to sing songs like "Just as I am" as people came forward to receive Christ.[143]

Moody gave us door-to-door witnessing and evangelistic advertising/campaigning.[144] He gave us the "gospel song" or "gospel hymn."[145] And he popularized the "decision card," an invention of Absalom B. Earle (1812-1895).[146]

---

[138] Ibid., p. 132. See http://www.officemuseum.com/copy_machines.htm for details on Dick's mimeograph stencil invention.

[139] *Early Christians Speak*, p. 84. Written liturgies first came into being in the fourth century. But they were not put into bulletin form until the 19th century.

[140] Moody traveled more than one million miles and preached to more than 100 million people. This was in a day without airplanes, microphones, television, or the Internet. Like Whitefield, Moody preached an individualistic gospel. His theology was encapsulated in the three R's: Ruined by sin, redeemed by Christ, and regenerated by the Spirit. Moody saw nothing beyond this (*Christian History*, Volume IX, No. 1, Issue 25; *Who's Who in Christian History*, Tyndale, 1992, pp. 483-485; *Evangelism: A Concise History*, pp. 151-152).

[141] H. Richard Niebuhr and Daniel D. Williams, *The Ministry in Historical Perspectives* (San Francisco: Harper and Row Publishers, 1956), p. 256.

[142] *The Effective Invitation*, pp. 193-194

[143] Ibid., p. 197.

[144] *Evangelism: A Concise History*, pp. 153-154, 185.

[145] David P. Appleby, *History of Church Music* (Chicago: Moody Press, 1965), p. 142.

[146] *The Effective Invitation*, p. 97. "Each person who came forward signed a card to indicate his pledge to live a Christian life and to show a church preference. This portion of the card was retained by the personal worker, so some form of follow-up could be worked out. Another portion of the card was given to the new Christian as a guide for Christian living" (pp. 97-98).

In addition, Moody was the first to ask those who wanted to be saved to stand up from their seats and be led in a "Sinner's Prayer."[147] Some 50 years later, Billy Graham upgraded Moody's technique. He introduced the practice of asking the audience to bow their heads, close their eyes (*"with no one looking around"*), and raise their hands in response to the salvation message.[148] (All of these methods have met fierce opposition by those who argue that they are psychologically manipulative.)[149]

For Moody, the church was just a voluntary association for the saved.[150] So staggering was his influence that by 1874 it could be said that the church is "not a great corporate body," but "only a company of individuals."[151] This emphasis was picked up by every revivalist who followed him.[152] And it eventually entered into the marrow and bones of evangelical Christianity.

It is also worth noting that Moody was heavily influenced by the Plymouth Brethren teaching on the end time. This was the teaching that Christ may return at any second before the great tribulation.

---

[147] Ibid., p. 98. For more information on the "Sinner's Prayer," see Chapter 8.

[148] Ibid., pp. 112-113. In his 45th year of ministry, Graham had preached to 100 million people in 85 different countries (*Pastor's Notes: A Companion Publication to Glimpses,* Volume 4, No. 2, Worcester: Christian History Institute, 1992, p. 7).

[149] Ian Murray, *The Invitational System* (Edinburgh: Banner of Truth, 1967). Murray distinguishes between "revival" which is an authentic, spontaneous work of God's Spirit and "revivalism" which are the human methods of obtaining (at least in appearance) the signs of conviction, repentance, and rebirth. The use of psychological and social pressures to bring converts is part of "revivalism" (pp. xvii-xix). See also Jim Ehrhard, *The Dangers of the Invitational System* (Christian Communicator's Worldwide, 1999).

[150] *The Ministry in Historical Perspectives,* p. 256.

[151] Sandra Sizer, *Gospel Hymns and Social Religion* (Philadelphia: Temple University Press, 1978), p. 134.

[152] Moody along with Great Awakening preachers like George Whitefield strongly appealed to the emotions. They were influenced by the philosophy of Romanticism, the body of thought stressing the will and emotions. This was a reaction to the stress on reason that marked earlier Christian thinking which was shaped by the Enlightenment (*Christian History,* Volume IX, No. 1, Issue 25, p. 23). The Awakening preachers' emphasis was the individual's heart-felt response to God. Conversion came to be viewed as the paramount goal of Divine activities. As J. Stephen Lang and Mark A. Noll point out, "Because of the preaching of the Awakening, the sense of *religious self* intensified. The principle of individual choice became forever ingrained in American Protestantism and is still evident today among evangelicals and many others" (*Christian History*, Volume IV, No. 4, pp. 9-10).

(This teaching is also called "pre-tribulational dispensationalism").[153] Pretribulational dispensationalism gave rise to the idea that Christians must save as many souls as quickly as possible before the world ends.[154] With the founding of the *Student Volunteer Movement* by John Mott in 1888, a related idea sprang forth: "The evangelization of the world in one generation."[155] The "in one generation" watchword still lives and breathes today in the modern church.[156] Yet it does not map well with the mindset of the first-century Christians.[157]

The Pentecostal Contribution

Beginning around 1906, the Pentecostal movement gave us a more emotional expression of congregational singing. This included the lifting of one's hands, dancing in pews, clapping, speaking in tongues, and the use of tambourines. The Pentecostal expression chimed well with its emphasis on the ecstatic working of the Holy Spirit.

What few people realize is that if you removed the emotional features from a Pentecostal church service, it would look just like a Baptist liturgy. Thus no matter how loudly a Pentecostal claims that they are following NT patterns, Pentecostals and Charismatics follow the same order of worship as do all other Protestants. A Pentecostal is merely allowed more room to move in his pew!

---

[153] John Nelson Darby spawned this teaching (see *Time,* July 1, 2002, pp. 41-48). The origin of Darby's pretribulational doctrine is both fascinating and shocking. See Dave MacPherson's *The Incredible Cover-Up* (Medford: Omega Publications, 1975) for a full discussion on it.

[154] *Christian History,* Volume IX, No. 1, Issue 25, pp. 23-24.

[155] *Concise Dictionary of Christianity in America* (Downers Grove: InterVarsity Press, 1995), p. 330.

[156] Example: The *AD 2000 and Beyond* movement, etc.

[157] The apostles stayed in Jerusalem for many years before they "went into the utter most parts of the earth" as Jesus predicted. They were in no hurry to evangelize the world. Equally, the church in Jerusalem did not evangelize anyone for the first eight years of its life. They too were in no hurry to evangelize the world. Finally, there is not the faintest whisper in any of the NT epistles where an apostle tells a church to evangelize because "the hour is late and the days are few." The early Christians were in no hurry to evangelize the world.

Another interesting feature of Pentecostal worship occurs during the song service. Sometimes the singing will be punctuated by an occasional utterance in tongues, an interpretation of tongues, or word of "prophecy." But such utterances rarely last more than a minute or two. Such a pinched form of open participation cannot accurately be called "Body ministry." The Pentecostal tradition also gave us solo or choral music (often tagged as "special music") that accompanies the offering.[158]

As in all Protestant churches, the sermon is the climax of the Pentecostal meeting. However, in the garden-variety Pentecostal church, the pastor will sometimes "feel the Spirit moving." At such times he will suspend his sermon until the following week. The congregation will then sing and pray for the rest of the service. To a Pentecostal, this is the pinnacle of a great church service.

The way that these special services are commonly reported is fascinating. Congregants typically describe this break in the normal liturgy by saying, *"The Holy Spirit led our meeting this week. Pastor Buxman did not get to preach."* Interestingly, no one ever thinks to ask, *"Isn't the Holy Spirit supposed to lead all our meetings?"* Hmmm . . .

Even so, as a result of being born in the afterglow of Frontier-Revivalism, Pentecostal worship is highly subjective and individualistic.[159] In the mind of the Pentecostal, worshipping God is not a corporate affair, but a solo experience. With the pervasive influence of the Charismatic movement, this individualistic worship mindset has infiltrated the vast majority of Protestant traditions.[160]

Many Adjustments, No Vital Change

Our study of the liturgical history of the Lutherans (16th century), Reformed (16th century), Puritans (16th century),

---

[158] *Protestant Worship: Traditions in Transition*, p. 204.

[159] *Protestant Worship and Church Architecture*, p. 129.

[160] The Great Awakening of the 18th century set the tone for an individualistic faith, something foreign to the first-century church. America was fast becoming a nation of rugged individualists, so this new emphasis sat well with the country (*Evangelism: A Concise History*, pp. 122-123).

Methodists (18th century), Frontier-Revivalists (18th-19th centuries), and Pentecostals (20th century) uncovers one inescapable point: For the last 500 years, the Protestant order of worship has undergone minimal change![161]

At bottom, all Protestant traditions share the same tragic features in their order of worship: They are officiated and directed by a clergyman, they make the sermon central, and the people are passive and not permitted to minister.[162]

The Reformers did a great deal in changing the *theology* of Roman Catholicism. But in terms of actual *practice*, they made minor rearrangements to the liturgical furniture. Despite the many stripes of Protestant churches that have appeared on the canvas of church history, the Sunday morning order of worship continues to be etched in stone. The result: God's people have never broken free from the liturgical straightjacket that they inherited from Roman Catholicism![163]

---

[161] Frank Senn's *Christian Liturgy* compares scores of various liturgies down through the ages. Anyone who compares them will readily spot their common features.

[162] Senn compares five modern written liturgies side by side: Roman Catholic Missal, Lutheran Book of Worship, Book of Common Prayer, Methodist, and Book of Common Worship. The similarities are shocking! (*Christian Liturgy*, pp. 646-647).

[163] It should be noted that some scholars have tried to tease out of the writings of the church fathers a unified, monolithic liturgy that was observed by all the churches. But recent scholarship has shown that the writings of the fathers are pluriform rather than uniform. This means that none of their writings can be universalized to represent what was happening in all the churches at a given time (See *The Search for the Origins of Christian Worship*, pp. 67-73, 158-183). Furthermore, archeological findings have demonstrated that the writings of the church fathers do not provide an accurate view of the second and third century church. The church fathers were the theologians of their day. They do not give us a peek into the beliefs or practices of the garden-variety Christians of those times. NT professor Graydon F. Snyder's *Ante Pacem: Church Life Before Constantine* (Mercer University Press, 1985) is a study of the archeological evidence that contradicts the portrait that the church fathers give of church life before Constantine. According to one seminary writer, "Snyder raises the question, do the writings of the intellectuals in early Christianity give us adequate portrait of the church of their times? The question has only to be asked for the obvious answer 'no' to be heard on our lips. Do the intellectuals of any age tell it like it is in the trenches? Do Barth, Tillich, or even the Niebuhrs describe in any way what popular twentieth-century American Christianity has been like? We all know they don't, and yet we have assumed that the New Testament and the so-called 'Patristic' theologians give us accurately a description of Christianity of the first three centuries. In part, of course, this has been assumed because we have thought they are the only sources we have, and to a large extent this is true, as far as *literary*

The Reformation did little to change the structure of the Catholic Mass.[164] As one author put it, *"The Reformers accepted in substance the ancient Catholic pattern of worship*[165]*... the basic structures of their services were almost universally taken from the late medieval orders of various sorts . . . "*[166]

The Reformers produced a half-baked reform of the Catholic liturgy. Their main contribution was in changing the central focus. In the words of one scholar, *"Catholicism increasingly followed the path of the [pagan] cults in making a rite the center of its activities, and Protestantism followed the path of the synagogue in placing the book at the center of its services . . . "*[167] Unfortunately, neither Catholicism nor Protestantism were successful in making Jesus Christ the center of their gatherings.

Yes, the book replaced the Eucharist, and the pastor replaced the priest. But there is still a man directing God's people, rendering them as silent spectators. The centrality of the Author of the book was never restored either. Hence, the Reformers dramatically failed to put their finger on the nerve of the original problem: A clergy-led worship service attended by a passive laity.[168] It is not surprising, then, that the Reformers viewed themselves as re-formed Catholics.[169]

---

documents are concerned" (*Chicago Theological Seminary Register*, Fall 1985, Vol. 75, No. 3, p. 26).

[164] The Reformers translated and adapted the Mass, but they took very little creative responsibility in changing it (*Corporate Worship in the Reformed Tradition*, p. 13).

[165] Ibid., p. 21.

[166] Ibid., p. 13. "Much of traditional [i.e., Catholic] theological terminology and concepts are truly part of the Lutheran approach as well as they were part of the Roman Catholic approach" (Kenan B. Osborne, *Priesthood: A History of Ordained Ministry in the Roman Catholic Church*, New York: Paulist Press, 1988, p. 223).

[167] Robert Banks, *Paul's Idea of Community*, Peabody: Hendrickson, 1994, p. 108; Edwin Hatch, *The Influence of Greek Ideas and Usages Upon the Christian Church* (Peabody: Hendrickson, 1895), pp. 308-309.

[168] Chapter 3 discusses the influence of fourth-century church architecture on the active clergy and the passive congregation. In this vein, Horton Davies writes, "The passing of three or four centuries shows a great alteration in the character of Christian worship . . . In the fourth century, worship is not celebrated in private houses, but in stately cathedrals and magnificent churches; not in free and simple forms of service, but in fixed and ordered worship" (*Christian Worship: It's History and Meaning*, p. 26).

[169] *Corporate Worship in the Reformed Tradition*, p. 155.

What is Wrong With This Picture?

It is painfully clear that the Protestant order of worship did not originate with the Lord Jesus, the apostles, or the NT Scriptures.[170] This in itself does not make it wrong. It just means that it has no Biblical basis.

The use of chairs and pile carpets in Christian gatherings has no Biblical support either. And both were invented by pagans.[171] Nonetheless, who would claim that sitting in chairs or using carpets is "wrong" simply because they are post-biblical inventions authored by pagans?

The fact is that we do many things in our culture that have pagan roots. Consider our accepted calendar. The days of our week and the months of our year are named after pagan gods.[172] But using the accepted calendar does not make us pagans.

Yet the Sunday morning order of worship is a different matter. Aside from being unscriptural and heavily influenced by paganism (which runs contrary to what is preached from the pulpit), it is spiritually harmful.[173]

---

[170] Some liturgical scholars, like Anglican Gregory Dix, have tried to argue that the NT contains a primitive model of the Mass. However, a careful examination of their arguments shows that they are merely reading their present tradition back into the Biblical text (*The Search for the Origins of Christian Worship*, Chapter 2).

[171] The earliest known chairs were made in Egypt. For thousands of years, they were used only by royalty, nobility, priests, and the wealthy. Chairs did not come into common use among the general populace until the 16th century ("Chairs," *Encarta Encyclopedia*, Microsoft, 1999 Edition). Pile carpets were developed in India in the 11th century and spread throughout the rest of the Eastern world ("Floor and Floor Coverings," *Encarta Encyclopedia*, Microsoft, 1998 Edition).

[172] The seven-day week originated in ancient Mesopotamia and became part of the Roman calendar in A.D. 321. January is named after the Roman god Janus; March is named after the Roman god Mars; April comes from *Aprilis*, the sacred month of Venus; May is named for the goddess Maia; and June is named for the goddess Juno; Sunday celebrates the sun god; Monday is the day of the moon goddess; Tuesday is named after the warrior god *Tiw*; Wednesday is named after the Teutonic god *Wotan*; Thursday is named after the Scandinavian god *Thor;* Friday is named after the Scandinavian goddess *Frigg*; and Saturday is named after Saturn, the Roman god of agriculture (Source: *Months of the Year* at www.ernie.cummings.net/calendar.htm).

[173] David Norrington makes the point that although there is nothing intrinsically wrong with the church embracing ideas from the surrounding culture, because they are pagan they are often contrary to Biblical faith. Thus syncretism and acculturation are frequently harmful to the church (*To Preach or Not to Preach?* p. 23).

First, the Protestant order of worship represses mutual participation and the growth of Christian community. It puts a chokehold on the functioning of the Body of Christ by silencing its members. There is absolutely no room for you to give a word of exhortation, share an insight, start or introduce a song, or spontaneously lead a prayer. You are forced to be a muted, staid pewholder!

Like every other poor, miserable "layman," you may only open your mouth during the congregational singing. (Of course, if you happen to be a Pentecostal/Charismatic, you may be permitted to give a one-minute ecstatic utterance. But then you must sit down and be quiet.)

Even though open-sharing in a church meeting is completely Scriptural,[174] you would be breaking the liturgy if you dared try something so outrageous! You would be considered "out of order" and asked to behave yourself or leave.

Second, the Protestant order of worship strangles the Headship of Jesus Christ.[175] The entire service is directed by a man. Where is the freedom for our Lord Jesus to speak through His Body at will? Where in the liturgy may God give a brother or a sister a word to share with the whole congregation? The order of worship allows for no such thing. Jesus Christ has no freedom to express Himself through His Body at His discretion. He is held captive by our liturgy! He too is rendered a passive spectator!

Granted, Christ may be able to express Himself through one or two members of the church—usually the pastor and the music leader. But this is a very limited expression. The Lord is stifled from manifesting Himself through the other members of the Body. Consequently, the Protestant liturgy distorts the Body of Christ into a monstrosity. It turns it into one huge tongue (the pastor) and

---

acculturation are frequently harmful to the church (*To Preach or Not to Preach?* p. 23).

[174] 1 Corinthians 14:26. The NT teaches that all Christians are to use their gifts as functioning priests to edify one another when they gather together (Rom. 12:3, 6; 1 Cor. 12:7; Eph. 4:7; Heb. 10:24-25; 13:15-16; 1 Pet. 2:5, 9).

[175] In the words of Arthur Wallis, "Liturgies, whether ancient or modern, written or unwritten, are a human device to keep the religious wheels turning by doing what is customary, rather than exercising faith in the immediate presence and operation of the Spirit."

many little ears (the congregation)! This does violence to Paul's vision of the Body of Christ where every member functions in the church meeting for the common good.[176]

Third, for many Christians, the Sunday morning service is shamefully boring. It is without variety or spontaneity. It is highly predictable, highly perfunctory, and highly mechanical. There is little in the way of freshness or innovation.

The Sunday morning order of worship is a one-stringed violin that has remained frozen in immobility for five centuries. It is the same dog and pony show every week. Put bluntly, the order of worship embodies the ambiguous power of the rote. And the rote very quickly decays into the routine, which in turn becomes tired, meaningless, and ultimately invisible.

"Seeker-sensitive" churches have recognized the sterile nature of the modern church service. In response, they have incorporated a vast array of media and theatrical modernizations into the liturgy. This is done to market worship to the unchurched. Employing the latest electronic technology, "seeker-sensitive" churches have been successful at swelling their ranks. As a result, they have garnered the largest market share of any Protestant tradition in America.

But despite the added entertainment it affords, the "seeker-sensitive" movement has been unable to break free from the unmovable, unimaginative, uncreative, inflexible, mindlessly ritualistic, *pro forma* Protestant liturgy. The service is still held captive by the pastor, the three-fold "hymn-sandwich" remains intact, and the congregants continue to be muted spectators (only they are a tad more entertained in their spectating).[177]

Fourth, the Protestant liturgy that you quietly sit through every Sunday, year after year, actually hinders spiritual transformation. It does so because: 1) It encourages passivity, 2) It limits functioning, and 3) It implies that putting in one hour per week is the key to the victorious Christian life.

Every Sunday you attend the service to be bandaged and recharged, like all other wrecked soldiers. However, this never gets

---

[176] 1 Corinthians 12:1ff.

[177] See Chapter 11 of *Rethinking the Wineskin* for a critique of the "seeker-sensitive" movement.

accomplished. The reason is quite simple. The NT never links sitting through an ossified ritual that we mislabel "church" as having anything to do with spiritual transformation. We grow by functioning, not by passively watching and listening.

Face it. The Protestant order of worship is unscriptural, impractical, and unspiritual. It has no analog in the NT. Rather, it finds its roots in the culture of fallen man.[178] It rips at the heart of primitive Christianity which was informal and free of ritual. Five centuries after the Reformation, the Protestant order of worship still varies little from the Catholic Mass—a religious ritual which is a fusion of pagan and Judaistic elements.

As one liturgical scholar put it, *"The history of Christian worship is the story of the give and take between cult and culture. As the gospel was preached in different times and places, missionaries brought with them the forms and styles of worship with which they were familiar . . . As a result, the practices of the popular mystery cults were sometimes employed by the church . . ."*[179]

In my book *Rethinking the Wineskin*, I describe a first-century styled church meeting. I am no armchair liturgist. What I have written concerning open meetings under the Headship of Christ is not fanciful theory. I have participated in such meetings for the last fifteen years.

Such meetings are marked by incredible variety. They are not bound to a one-man, pulpit-dominated pattern of worship. There is a great deal of spontaneity, creativity, and freshness. The overarching hallmark of these meetings is the visible Headship of Christ and the free-yet-orderly functioning of the Body of Christ.

In closing, the NT is not silent with respect to how we Christians are to meet. Shall we, therefore, opt for man's tradition when it clearly runs contrary to God's thought for His church? Shall we continue to undermine the functioning Headship of Christ for the sake of our sacrosanct liturgy? Is the church of Jesus Christ the pillar and ground of truth or the defender of man's tradition?[180]

---

[178] The purpose of the first-century church meeting was not for evangelism, sermonizing, worship, or fellowship. It was rather for mutual edification through manifesting Christ corporately (*Rethinking the Wineskin*, Chapter 1).

[179] *Christian Worship and Its Cultural Setting*, pp. 38, 40.

[180] 1 Tim. 3:15.

The only sure way to thaw out God's frozen people is to make a dramatic break with the Sunday morning ritual. The other option is to be guilty of our Lord's bone-rattling words: *"Full well do you reject the commandment of God that you may keep your own tradition."*[181]

---

[181] Mark 7:8. See also Matt. 15:2-6; Mark 7:9-13; Col. 2:8.

Son of man, show the house to the house . . . that they may be ashamed . . .
  -Ezekiel, the prophet

CHAPTER 2

THE SERMON: PROTESTANTISM'S MOST SACRED COW

Christianity did not destroy paganism; it adopted it.
-Will Durant

We now come to one of the most sacrosanct church practices of all: The sermon. Remove the sermon, and the Protestant order of worship becomes nothing more than a songfest. Remove the sermon, and attendance at the Sunday morning service is doomed to drop down to single digits.[1]

The sermon is the bedrock of the Protestant liturgy. For 500 years, it has functioned like clockwork. Every Sunday morning, the pastor climbs into his pulpit and delivers an inspirational oration to a passive, pew-warming audience.[2] So central is the sermon that it is the very reason why most Christians go to church. In fact, the entire service is typically judged by the quality of the sermon. Ask a person how church was last Sunday and you will invariably get a description of the sermon. It sounds like this:

Question: *"How was church last week?"*

Answer: *"Oh, it was wonderful. Pastor Peckman spoke about the importance of giving seed-faith offerings to increase our income; it was really great. It inspired me to offer my entire paycheck next week."*

---

[1] Sometimes the attendance drops *because* of the sermon . . . if it happens to be boring.

[2] "Nothing is more characteristic of Protestantism than the importance it attaches to preaching." H. Richard Niebuhr and Daniel D. Williams, *The Ministry in Historical Perspectives* (San Francisco: Harper and Row Publishers, 1956), p. 110.

In short, the modern Christian mindset equates the sermon with Sunday morning worship.[3] But it does not end there.

Most Christians are addicted to the sermon. They come to church with an empty bucket expecting the preacher to fill it up with a "feel-good" message. For the typical Christian, the sermon is the chief means of spiritual sustenance. It ranks above prayer, reading the Scriptures, and fellowship with other believers. And if we are dead-level honest, it even ranks above fellowship with Jesus Christ (at least in practice)!

Remove the sermon and you have eliminated the most important source of spiritual nourishment for most believers (so it is thought). Yet the stunning reality is that the sermon has no root in Scripture! Rather, it was borrowed from pagan culture, nursed and adopted into the Christian faith. That is a startling statement, is it not? But there is more.

The sermon actually detracts from the very purpose for which God designed the church gathering. And it has very little to do with genuine spiritual growth. I will prove these words in this chapter.

The Sermon and the Bible

Doubtlessly, someone reading what I have just written will retort: *"People preached all throughout the Bible. Of course the sermon is Scriptural!"*

Granted, the Scriptures do record men and women preaching. However, there is a world of difference between the Spirit-inspired preaching described in the Bible and the modern sermon. This difference is virtually always overlooked because we have been unwittingly conditioned to read our modern-day practices back into the Scripture. So we mistakenly embrace today's pulpiteerism as being Biblical. Let me unfold that a bit. The modern Christian sermon has the following features:

---

[3] In France, the Protestant church service is called *aller 'a sermon* (*Protestant Worship: Traditions in Transition* (Louisville: Westminster/John Knox Press, 1989), p. 20.

- It is a regular occurrence—delivered faithfully from the pulpit at least once a week.
- It is delivered by the same person—typically the pastor.[4]
- It is delivered to a passive audience; it is essentially a monologue.
- It is a cultivated form of speech, possessing a specific structure. It typically contains an introduction, three to five points, and a conclusion.

Contrast this with the kind of preaching mentioned in the Bible. In the Old Testament, men of God preached and taught. But their speaking did not map to the modern sermon. Here are the features of Old Testament preaching and teaching:

- Active participation and interruptions by the audience were common.[5]
- They spoke extemporaneously and out of a present burden, rather than from a set script.
- There is no indication that Old Testament prophets or priests gave *regular* speeches to God's people.[6] Instead, the nature of Old Testament preaching was sporadic, fluid, and open for audience participation. Preaching in the ancient synagogue followed a similar pattern.[7]

Come now to the NT. The Lord Jesus did not preach a regular sermon to the same audience.[8] His preaching and teaching took

---

[4] Occasionally, the pastor may allow for guest speakers, who are usually other professional ministers.

[5] David C. Norrington, *To Preach or Not to Preach? The Church's Urgent Question* (Carlisle: Paternoster Press, 1996), p. 3.

[6] Ibid., p. 3

[7] Ibid., p. 4. The only difference in synagogue preaching is that a message delivered on a Biblical text was a *regular* occurrence. Even so, some synagogues allowed for any member to preach to the people who wished to do so. This, of course, is in direct contradiction to the modern sermon where only religious "specialists" are allowed to address the congregation.

[8] The Lord's so-called "Sermon on the Mount" was given that name in the post-apostolic period. Augustine was the first to give Matt. 5-7 this name in his book *The Lord's Sermon the Mount* in A.D. 395. But the passage was not generally referred to as "the Sermon on the Mount" until the 16th century (*Dictionary of Jesus and the*

many different forms. And He delivered His messages to many different audiences. (Of course, He concentrated most of His teaching on His disciples. Yet the messages He brought to them were consistently spontaneous and informal.[9])

Following the same pattern, the apostolic preaching recorded in Acts possessed the following features:

* It was sporadic.[10]
* It was delivered on special occasions in order to deal with specific problems.
* It was extemporaneous and without rhetorical structure.[11]
* It was most often dialogical (meaning it included feedback and interruptions from the audience) rather than monological (a one-way discourse).[12]

In like manner, the NT letters show that the ministry of God's Word came from the entire church in their regular gatherings.[13] This "every-member" functioning was also conversational[14] and marked by interruptions.[15] Equally so, the exhortations of the local elders were normally impromptu.[16]

Gospels, Downer's Grove: InterVarsity Press, 1992, p. 736; J.D. Douglas, *Who's Who in Christian History*, Wheaton: Tyndale House Publishers, 1992, p. 48). Even so, the so-called "Sermon the Mount" is a poor fit with the modern sermon in both style and rhetoric.

[9] *To Preach or Not to Preach?*, pp. 5-7.

[10] Ibid., pp. 7-12. Norrington analyzes the speeches in the NT and contrasts them with the modern-day sermon.

[11] The spontaneous and non-rhetorical character of the apostolic messages delivered in Acts is evident upon close inspection. See for instance Acts 2:14-35; 7:1-52; 17:22-34, et al.

[12] Jeremy Thomson, *Preaching as Dialogue: Is the Sermon a Sacred Cow?* (Cambridge: Grove Books, 1996), pp. 3-8. The Greek word often used to described first-century preaching and teaching is *dialegomai* (Acts 17:2,17; 18:4,19; 19:8,9; 20:7,9; 24:25). This word means a two-way form of communication. Our English word "dialogue" is derived from it. In short, apostolic ministry was more dialogue than it was monological sermonics (William Barclay, *Communicating the Gospel*, Sterling: The Drummond Press, 1968, pp. 34-35).

[13] 1 Cor. 14:26, 31; Rom. 12:4ff.; Eph. 4:11ff.; Heb. 10:25.

[14] 1 Cor. 14:29.

[15] 1 Cor. 14:30.

[16] Alan Kreider, *Worship and Evangelism in Pre-Christendom* (Oxford: Alain/GROW Liturgical Study, 1995), p. 37

In a word, the modern sermon delivered for Christian consumption is foreign to both Old and New Testaments. There is absolutely nothing in Scripture to indicate its existence in the early Christian gatherings."[17]

Where Did the Christian Sermon Come From?

The earliest recorded Christian source for regular sermonizing is found during the late second century.[18] Clement of Alexandria (150-215) lamented the fact that sermons did so little to change Christians.[19] Yet despite its recognized failure, the sermon became a standard practice among believers by the fourth century.[20]

This raises a thorny question. If the first-century Christians were not noted for their sermonizing, from whom did the post-apostolic Christians pick up the sermon? The answer is telling: The Christian sermon was borrowed straight from the pagan pool of Greek culture!

To find the headwaters of the sermon, we must go back to the fifth century B.C. with a group of wandering teachers called sophists.[21] The sophists are credited for inventing rhetoric (the art of persuasive speaking). They recruited disciples and demanded payment for delivering their orations.[22]

The sophists were expert debaters. They were masters at using emotional appeals, physical appearance, and clever language to "sell" their arguments.[23] In time, the style, form, and oratorical skill of the sophists became more prized than their accuracy.[24] This

---

[17] *To Preach or Not to Preach?*, p. 12.

[18] Ibid., p. 13. The first recorded Christian sermon is contained in the so-called *Second Letter of Clement* dated between A.D. 100 and A.D. 150. Yngve Brilioth, *A Brief History of Preaching* (Philadelphia: Fortress Press, 1965), pp. 19-20.

[19] *To Preach or Not to Preach?*, p. 13.

[20] Edwin Hatch, *The Influence of Greek Ideas and Usages Upon the Christian Church* (Peabody: Hendrickson, 1895), p. 109.

[21] Douglas J. Soccio, *Archetypes of Wisdom: An Introduction to Philosophy* (Belmont: ITP Wadsworth Publishing Company, 1998), pp. 56-57.

[22] Ibid.

[23] Ibid.

[24] We get our words "sophistry" and "sophistical" from the sophists. Sophistry refers to specious and fallacious (bogus) reasoning used to persuade (*Archetypes of Wisdom*, p. 57). The Greeks celebrated the orator's style and form over the accuracy of the

spawned a class of men who became masters of fine phrases, "cultivating style for style's sake."[25] The truths they preached were abstract rather than truths that were practiced in their own lives. They were experts at imitating *form* rather than *substance*.[26]

The sophists identified themselves by the special clothing they wore.[27] Some of them had a fixed residence where they gave regular sermons to the same audience. Others traveled to deliver their polished orations.[28] (They made a good deal of money when they did.)[29] Sometimes the Greek orator would enter his speaking forum "already robed in his pulpit-gown."[30] He would then mount the steps to his professional chair to sit before he brought his sermon.[31]

To make his points, he would quote Homer's verses.[32] (Some orators studied Homer so well that they could repeat him by heart.)[33] So spell-binding was the sophist, that he would often incite his audience to clap their hands during his discourse. If his speaking was very well received, some would call his sermon "inspired."[34]

The sophists were the most distinguished men of their time. So much so that some lived at public expense. Others had public statues erected in their honor.[35]

(Does all this not remind you of many modern-day preachers?)

About a century later, the Greek philosopher Aristotle (384-322 B.C.) gave to rhetoric the three-point speech. *"A whole,"* said

---

content of his sermon. Thus a good orator could use his sermon to sway his audience to believe what he knew to be false. To the Greek mind, winning an argument was a greater virtue than distilling truth. Unfortunately, an element of sophistry has never left the Christian fold (*To Preach or Not to Preach?*, pp. 21-22; *The Influence of Greek Ideas*, p. 113).

[25] *The Influence of Greek Ideas*, p. 113.
[26] Ibid.
[27] Ibid., pp. 91-92.
[28] Ibid.
[29] Ibid., p. 112.
[30] Ibid., p. 92.
[31] Ibid.
[32] Ibid., p. 54.
[33] Ibid., p. 56.
[34] Ibid., p. 96.
[35] Ibid., pp. 97-98

Aristotle, *"must have a beginning, a middle, and an end."*[36] In time, Greek orators implemented Aristotle's three-point principle into their discourses.

The Greeks were intoxicated with rhetoric.[37] So the sophists faired well. When Rome took over Greece, the Romans fell under the Greek spell of being obsessed with rhetoric.[38] Consequently, Greco-Roman culture developed an insatiable lust to hear someone give an eloquent oration. This was so fashionable that a "serm-onette" from a professional philosopher after dinner was a regular form of entertainment.[39]

The ancient Greeks and Romans viewed rhetoric as one of the greatest forms of art.[40] Accordingly, the orators in the Roman Empire were lauded with the same glamorous status that Americans assign to movie stars and professional athletes. They were the shining stars of their day.

Orators could bring a crowd to a frenzy simply by their powerful speaking skills. Teachers of rhetoric, the leading science of the era, were the pride of every major city.[41] The orators they produced were given celebrity status. In short, the Greeks and Romans were addicted to the pagan sermon—just like many modern Christians are addicted to the "Christian" sermon.

The Arrival of a Polluted Stream

How did the Greek sermon find its way into the Christian church? Around the third century a vacuum was created when mutual ministry faded from the Body of Christ.[42] At this time the traveling worker who spoke out of a spontaneous burden left the pages of church history.[43] To fill his absence, the clergy-caste

---

[36] Aristotle, *On Poetics*, Chapter 7. Although Aristotle was speaking about writing "Plot" or "Fable," his principle was nonetheless applied to delivering speeches.

[37] The love of speech was second nature to the Greeks. "They were a nation of talkers" (*The Influence of Greek Ideas*, p. 27).

[38] *To Preach or Not to Preach?*, p. 21.

[39] *The Influence of Greek Ideas*, p. 40.

[40] *A Brief History of Preaching*, p. 26.

[41] *Christian History*, Volume XIII, No. 4, Issue 44, p. 7.

[42] *To Preach or Not to Preach?*, p. 24.

[43] *The Influence of Greek Ideas*, pp. 106-107, 109.

began to emerge. Open meetings began to die out, and church gatherings became more and more liturgical.[44]

During the third century, the clergy-laity distinction was widening at breakneck speed. A hierarchical structure began to take root, and there grew up the idea of the "religious specialist."[45] In the face of these changes, the functioning Christian had trouble fitting into this evolving ecclesiastical structure.[46] There was no place for him to exercise his gifts. By the fourth century, the church had become fully institutionalized and the functioning of God's people froze.

As this was happening, many pagan orators were becoming Christians. As a result, pagan philosophical ideas unwittingly made their way into the Christian community.[47] Some of the new converts at this time happened to be former pagan philosophers and orators.[48] Regrettably, many of these men became the theologians of the early Christian church. They are known as the "church fathers," and some of their writings are still with us.[49]

Thus the pagan notion of a trained professional speaker who delivers orations for a fee moved straight into the Christian bloodstream. Note that the concept of the "paid teaching specialist" did not come from Judaism. It came from Greece. It was the custom of Jewish rabbis to take up a trade so as to not charge a fee for their teaching.[50]

The upshot of the story is that these former pagan orators (now turned Christian) began to use their Greco-Roman oratorical skills for Christian purposes. They would sit in their official chair[51] and *"expound the sacred text of Scripture, just as the sophist would*

---

[44] *To Preach or Not to Preach?*, pp. 24-25.

[45] Ibid., pp. 24-25; See Chapter 4 of this book.

[46] Ibid., p. 25.

[47] Ibid., p. 22.

[48] *From Christ to Constantine*, p. 115.

[49] Among them are Tertullian, Cyprian, Arnobius, Lactantius, and Augustine (*To Preach or Not to Preach?* p. 22). See also *The Influence of Greek Ideas*, pp. 7-9, 109; Richard Hanson, *Christian Priesthood Examined* (Guildford and London: Lutterworth Press, 1979), p. 53.

[50] F.F. Bruce, *Paul: Apostle of the Heart Set Free* (Grand Rapids: Eerdmans, 1977), p. 220. The noted Jewish rabbi Hillel said, "He who makes a worldly crown of the Torah shall waste away" (pp. 107-108).

[51] *The Influence of Greek Ideas,* p. 110.

supply an exegesis[52] of the near-sacred text of Homer . . . "[53] If you compare a third-century pagan sermon with a sermon given by one of the church fathers, you will find both the structure and the phraseology to be shockingly similar.[54]

So a new style of communication was being birthed in the Christian church—a style that emphasized polished rhetoric, sophisticated grammar, flowery eloquence, and monologue. It was a style that was designed to entertain and show off the speaker's oratorical skills. It was Greco-Roman rhetoric.[55] And only those who were trained in it were allowed to address the assembly![56] (Sound familiar?)

One scholar put it this way: *The original proclamation of the Christian message was a two-way conversation . . . but when the oratorical schools of the Western world laid hold of the Christian message, they made Christian preaching something vastly different. Oratory tended to take the place of conversation. The greatness of the orator took the place of the astounding event of Jesus Christ. And the dialogue between speaker and listener faded into a monologue.*[57]

In a word, the Greco-Roman sermon replaced prophesying, open sharing, and Spirit-inspired teaching.[58] The sermon became the elitist privilege of church officials, particularly the bishops.[59] Such people had to be educated in the schools of rhetoric to learn

---

[52] An exegesis is an interpretation and explanation of a Biblical text.

[53] *To Preach or Not to Preach?*, p. 22.

[54] *The Influence of Greek Ideas*, p. 110.

[55] A student who studied rhetoric completed his studies when he could talk off-hand on any subject that was presented to him. Logic, in the form of debate, was common in the study of rhetoric. Every student learned how to argue and argue well. Logic was natural to the Greek mind. But it was logic divorced from practice and built on theoretical arguments. This entire mindset seeped into the Christian faith early on (*The Influence of Greek Ideas*, pp. 32-33).

[56] Ibid., p. 108. Hatch writes, " . . . with the growth of organization there grew up also, not only a fusion of teaching and exhortation, but also the gradual restriction of the liberty of addressing the community to the official class."

[57] Wayne E. Oates, *Protestant Pastoral Counseling* (Philadelphia: Westminster Press), 1962, p. 162.

[58] Ibid., p. 107.

[59] *A Brief History of Preaching*, p. 26.

how to speak.[60] Without such education, a Christian was not permitted to speak to God's people.

As early as the third century, Christians called their sermons by the same name that Greek orators called their discourses. They called them *homilies*.[61] Today, one can take a seminary course called *homiletics* to learn how to preach. Homiletics is considered a *"science, applying rules of rhetoric, which go back to Greece and Rome."*[62]

Put another way, neither homilies (sermons) nor homiletics (the art of sermonizing) have a Christian origin. They were stolen from the pagans. A polluted stream made its entrance into the Christian faith and poisoned its waters. And that stream flows just as strongly today as it did in the fourth century.

Chrysostom and Augustine

John Chrysostom (347-407) was one of the greatest Christian orators of his day.[63] (Chrysostom means "golden-mouthed.")[64] Never had Constantinople heard "sermons so powerful, brilliant, and frank" as those preached by Chrysostom.[65] Chrysostom's preaching was so compelling that people would sometimes shove their way toward the front to hear him better.[66]

Naturally endowed with the orator's gift of gab, Chrysostom learned how to speak under the leading sophist of the fourth

---

[60] Ibid., p. 27.

[61] *The Influence of Greek Ideas*, p. 109; Yngve Brilioth, *A Brief History of Preaching* (Philadelphia: Fortress Press, 1965), p. 18.

[62] J.D. Douglas, *Encyclopedia of Religious Knowledge* (Grand Rapids: Baker Book House, 1991), p. 405.

[63] On his death-bed, Libanius (Chrysostom's pagan tutor) said that he would have been his worthiest successor "if the Christians had not stolen him" (*The Influence of Greek Ideas*, p. 109).

[64] Tony Castle, *Lives of Famous Christians* (Ann Arbor: Servant Books, 1988), p. 69; *The Influence of Greek Ideas*, p. 6. John was nicknamed golden-mouth (*Chrysostomos*) because of his eloquent and uncompromising preaching (*Christian History*, Volume XIII, No. 4, Issue 44, p. 7).

[65] Will Durant, *The Age of Faith* (New York: Simon & Schuster, 1950), p. 63.

[66] *Christian History*, Volume XIII, No. 4, Issue 44, p. 3. Of the sermons that Chrysostom preached, more than 600 survive.

century, Libanius.[67] Chrysostom's pulpit eloquence was unsurpassed. So powerful were his orations that his sermons would often get interrupted by congregational applause. Chrysostom once gave a sermon condemning the applause as unfitting in God's house.[68] But after he finished preaching it, the congregation loved the sermon so much they applauded.[69] This story illustrates the untamable power of Greek rhetoric.

We can credit both Chrysostom and Augustine (354-430), a former professor of rhetoric,[70] for making pulpit oratory part and parcel of the Christian faith.[71] In Chrysostom, the Greek sermon reached its zenith. The Greek sermon style indulged in rhetorical brilliance, the quoting of poems, and focused on impressing the audience. Chrysostom emphasized that *"the preacher must toil long on his sermons in order to gain the power of eloquence."*[72]

In Augustine, the Latin sermon reached its heights.[73] The Latin sermon style was more down to earth than the Greek style. It focused on the "common man" and was directed to a simpler moral point. Zwingli took John Chrysostom as his model in preaching, while Luther took Augustine as his model.[74] Both Latin and Greek styles included a verse-by-verse commentary form as well as a paraphrasing form.[75]

Even so, Chrysostom and Augustine stood in the lineage of the Greek sophists. They gave us polished Christian rhetoric. They

---

[67] *Christian History*, Volume XIII, No. 4, Issue 44, p. 7; Philip Schaff, *History of the Christian Church: Volume 3*, (Michigan: Eerdmans, 1910), pp. 933-941; *The Age of Faith*, p. 9. Chrysostom imbibed rhetoric from Libanius, but he was also a student of pagan philosophy and literature (*The Age of Faith*, p. 63).

[68] The enthusiastic applause from an audience to a sophist's homily was a Greek custom.

[69] *History of the Christian Church: Volume 3*, p. 938.

[70] *The Age of Faith*, p. 65.

[71] *To Preach or Not to Preach?*, p. 23.

[72] H. Richard Niebuhr and Daniel D. Williams, *The Ministry in Historical Perspectives* (San Francisco: Harper and Row Publishers, 1956), p. 71.

[73] *A Brief History of Preaching*, pp. 31, 42.

[74] Frank C. Senn, *Christian Liturgy: Catholic and Evangelical* (Minneapolis: Fortress Press, 1997), p. 366. Both Lutheran and Reformed preaching tended to be a verse-by-verse exposition. This was characteristic of the patristic fathers like Chrysostom and Augustine.

[75] Private Email from Professor John McGuckin, 9/29/02.

gave us the "Christian" sermon. Biblical in content, but Greek in style.[76]

The Reformers, the Puritans, and the Great Awakening

During medieval times, the Eucharist dominated the Roman Catholic Mass, and preaching took a backseat. But with the coming of Martin Luther (1483-1546), the sermon was again given prominence in the worship service.[77] Luther improperly conceived the church to be the gathering of the people who *listen* to the Word of God being spoken to them. For this reason, he once called the church building a *Mundhaus* (mouth or speech-house)![78]

Taking his cue from Luther, John Calvin (1509-1564) argued that the preacher is the "mouth of God."[79] (Ironically, both men vehemently railed against the idea that the Pope was the Vicar of Christ.) It is not surprising that many of the Reformers had studied rhetoric and were deeply influenced by the Greco-Roman sermons of Augustine, Chrysostom, Origen, and Gregory the Great.[80]

Thus the flaws of the church fathers were reduplicated by the Reformers and the Protestant subcultures that were created by them. This was especially true of the Puritans.[81] In fact, the modern

---

[76] *To Preach or Not to Preach?*, p. 23
[77] *Protestant Worship: Traditions in Transition*, pp. 46-47.
[78] *The Ministry in Historical Perspectives*, p. 114.
[79] *Preaching as Dialogue*, pp. 9-10.
[80] Hughes Oliphant Old, *The Patristic Roots of Reformed Worship* (Zurich: Theologischer Veriag, 1970), p. 79ff.
[81] The evolution of sermon content from the Reformation to the present day is a lengthy story that is beyond the scope of this book. Suffice it to say that sermons during the Enlightenment period degenerated into barren moral discourses. They became instruments for improving human society. The Puritans brought back the verse-by-verse expositional preaching that began with the church fathers. Some Puritan pastors exposited every verse in the Bible. Social justice themes became prominent in 19th-century Methodism. And with the advent of frontier revivalism, preaching in evangelical churches was dominated by a salvation call. The Puritans also made contributions to modern sermonic rhetoric. The Puritan sermon was written out ahead of time into a tidy four-part outline with a detailed organizational structure. The four-part outline that all Puritan preachers used consisted of text (the reading of a Scripture), doctrine (theological statement), uses (proving and illustrating the doctrine), and application (*Protestant Worship*, pp. 53, 121, 126, 166, 183; *Christian History*, Volume XIII, No. 1, Issue 41, pp. 24-25).

evangelical preaching tradition finds its most recent roots in the Puritan movement of the 17th century and the Great Awakening of the 18th century.

The Puritans borrowed their preaching style from Calvin. What was that style? It was the systematic exposition of Scripture. It was a style taken from the early church fathers and which became popular during the Renaissance. Renaissance scholars would provide a sentence-by-sentence commentary on a writing from classical antiquity. Calvin was a master at this form. Before his conversion, he employed this style on a commentary by the pagan author Seneca. When he was converted and turned to sermonizing, he applied the same analytical style to the Bible.[82]

Following the path of their father John Calvin, the Puritans centered all their church services around a systematic teaching of the Bible. As they sought to Protestantize England (purifying it from the flaws of Anglicanism), the Puritans centered all of their church services around highly structured, methodical, logical, verse-by-verse expositions of Scripture. Their stress was that Protestantism was a religion of "the Book."[83] (Ironically, "the Book" knows nothing of a sermon!)

The Puritans also invented a form of preaching called "plain-style." This style was rooted in the memorization of sermon notes. Their dividing, sub-dividing, and analyzing of a Biblical text raised the sermon to a fine science.[84] This form is still used today by countless pastors. In addition, the Puritans gave us the one-hour sermon,[85] the practice of congregants taking notes on the sermon, the tidy four-part sermon outline, and pastor's use of crib notes while delivering his oration.[86]

Another influence, the Great Awakening, is responsible for the kind of preaching that was common in early Methodist churches

---

[82] Meic Pearse and Chris Matthews, *We Must Stop Meeting Like This* (E Sussex: Kingsway Publications, 1999), pp. 94-95.

[83] Ibid., pp. 92-93.

[84] Ibid.

[85] Although some Puritan sermons lasted 90 minutes.

[86] *Protestant Worship: Traditions in Transition,* pp. 53, 121, 126, 166, 183; *Christian History,* Volume XIII, No. 1, Issue 41, pp. 24-25. The ghosts of Puritan preaching are still with us today. Every time you hear a Protestant pastor sermonize, underneath you will find the Puritan sermon style which has its roots in pagan rhetoric.

and is still used in modern Pentecostal churches. Strong outbursts of emotion, screaming, running up and down the platform, are all carry-overs from this tradition.[87]

Summing up the origin of the modern sermon, we can say the following: Christianity had taken Greco-Roman rhetoric, baptized it, and wrapped it in swaddling clothes. The Greek homily made its way into the Christian church around the second century, and reached its height in the pulpit orators of the fourth century—namely Chrysostom and Augustine.[88]

The Christian sermon took a backseat from the fifth century till the Reformation, when it became encased and enshrined as *the* central focus of the Protestant worship service. Yet for 500 years, most Christians have never questioned its origin or its effectiveness.[89]

How Sermonizing Harms the Church

Though revered for five centuries, the conventional sermon has contributed to the malfunction of the church in a number of ways.

First, the sermon makes the preacher the virtuoso performer of the church service. As a result, congregational participation is hampered at best and precluded at worst. The sermon turns the church into a preaching station. The congregation degenerates into a group of muted spectators who watch a performance. There is no room for interrupting or questioning the preacher while he is delivering his discourse. The sermon freezes and imprisons the functioning of the Body of Christ. It fosters a docile priesthood by allowing hand-waving[90] pulpiteers to dominate the church gathering week after week.

Second, the sermon stalemates spiritual growth. Because it is a one-way affair, it blunts curiosity and produces passivity. The sermon lames the church from functioning. It suffocates mutual

---

[87] *We Must Stop Meeting Like This*, p. 95.
[88] *A Brief History of Preaching*, p. 22.
[89] The 19th-century historian Edwin Hatch is one of the first to challenge the sermon.
[90] The term "hand-waving" is derived from stage magic. The magician waves his hands and creates a rabbit out of thin air. In the same way, the sermon sells itself as the major facilitator of Christian growth. But this idea is both false and deceptive.

ministry. It smothers open participation. This causes the spiritual growth of God's people to take a nosedive.[91]

As Christians, we must function if we will grow.[92] We do not grow by sitting like a pillar of salt as one man preaches us under the pew week after week. In fact, one of the goals of NT-styled preaching and teaching is to get you to function.[93] It is to encourage you to open your mouth in the church meeting.[94] The conventional sermon hinders this very process.

Third, the sermon preserves the unbiblical clergy mentality. It creates an excessive and pathological dependence on the clergy. The sermon makes the preacher the religious specialist—the only one having anything worthy to say. Everyone else is treated as a second-class Christian—a silent pew-warmer. (While this is not usually voiced, it is the reality.)[95]

How can the pastor learn from the other members of the Body of Christ when they are muted? How can the church learn from the pastor when its members cannot ask him questions during his oration?[96] How can the brothers and sisters learn from one another if they are gagged from speaking in the meetings?

The sermon makes "church" both distant and impersonal.[97] It deprives the pastor of receiving spiritual sustenance from the church. And it deprives the church of receiving spiritual nourishment from one another. For these reasons, the sermon is one of the biggest roadblocks to a functioning priesthood![98]

Fourth, rather than equipping the saints, the sermon deskills them. It matters not how loudly ministers drone on about "equip-

---

[91] *Rethinking the Wineskin*, Chapter 1.

[92] Mark 4:24-25; Heb. 10:24-25.

[93] Eph. 4:11-16. This passage also points out that functioning is necessary for spiritual maturity.

[94] See 1 Cor. 12-14. The meeting that is described in this passage is clearly a church gathering.

[95] Some pastors have been known to give voice to the mindless idea that "all that sheep do is say 'baa' and eat grass."

[96] Ruel L. Howe, *Partners in Preaching: Clergy and Laity in Dialogue* (New York: Seabury Press, 1967), p. 36.

[97] George W. Swank, *Dialogical Style in Preaching* (Valley Forge: Hudson Press, 1981), p. 24.

[98] Kevin Craig, "Is the Sermon Concept Biblical," *Searching Together* (Dresser: Word of Life Church, 1986, Vol. 15:1-2), p. 22.

ping the saints for the work of the ministry," the truth is that preaching sermons equips no one for spiritual service.[99] In reality, God's people are just as addicted to hearing sermons as preachers are addicted to preaching them. (I am aware that some Christians do not appreciate being preached under the table every week. But most seem to enjoy it.)[100] By contrast, NT-styled preaching and teaching equips the church so that it can function without the presence of a clergyman.[101]

Fifth, the modern sermon is completely impractical. Most preachers are experts at that which they have never experienced. Whether it be abstract/theoretical, devotional/inspirational, demanding/compelling, or entertaining/amusing, the sermon fails to put the hearers into a direct, practical experience of what has been preached. Thus the typical sermon is a swimming lesson on dry land! It lacks any practical value. Much is preached, but nothing ever lands. Most of it is aimed at the frontal lobe. Modern pulpiteerism fails to get beyond merely disseminating information to the role of equipping believers for both experiencing and utilizing that which they have heard.

In this regard, the sermon mirrors its true father—Greco-Roman rhetoric. Greco-Roman rhetoric was bathed in abstraction.[102] It *"involved forms designed to entertain and display genius rather than instruct or develop talents in others."*[103] The modern polished sermon can warm the heart, inspire the will, and stimulate the mind. But it rarely if ever shows the team *how* to leave the huddle!

---

[99] While many pastors talk about "equipping the saints" and "liberating the laity," promises to free the flaccid laity and equip the church for ministry virtually always prove to be empty. So long as the pastor is still dominating the church service by his sermonics, God's people are not free to function. Therefore, "equipping the saints" is typically empty rhetoric.

[100] For those of us who regard the sermon to be exotically boring, we understand the feeling of being "preached to death." The quote by Sydney Smith captures the sentiment: "He deserves to be preached to death by wild curates!"

[101] Consider Paul's method of preaching to an infant church then leaving it on its own for long periods of time. For details, see Gene Edwards' *How to Meet in Homes* (Sargent: Seedsowers, 1999).

[102] "Is the Sermon Concept Biblical," p. 25.

[103] *To Preach or Not to Preach?*, p. 23.

In all of these ways, the sermon fails to promote spiritual growth. Instead, it intensifies the impoverishment of the church.[104] The sermon acts like a momentary stimulant. Its effects are short-lived at best.

Let us be honest. There are scores of Christians who have been sermonized for decades, and they are still babes in Christ.[105] We Christians are not transformed by hearing sermons. We are transformed by regular encounter with the Lord Jesus Christ.[106] Those who minister, therefore, are called to make their ministry intensely practical. They are called to not only reveal Christ, but to show their hearers *how* to experience, know, follow, and serve Him.

If a preacher cannot bring his hearers into a living spiritual experience of that which he is ministering, the results of his message will be short-lived. Therefore, the church needs less pulpiteers and more spiritual facilitators. It is in dire need of those who can proclaim Christ and know how to deploy God's people to experience *Him* who has been preached.[107]

We need a restoration of the first-century practice of mutual exhortation and mutual ministry.[108] For the NT hinges spiritual transformation upon these two things.[109] Granted, the gift of teaching is present in the church. But teaching is to come from all

---

[104] Clyde H. Reid, *The Empty Pulpit* (New York: Harper & Row, 1967), pp. 47-49.

[105] Alexander R. Hay, *The New Testament Order for Church and Missionary* (New Testament Missionary Union, 1947), pp. 292-293, 414.

[106] One may encounter Christ either in glory or in suffering (2 Cor. 3:18; Heb. 12:1ff.).

[107] Acts 3:20; 5:42; 8:5; 9:20; Gal 1:6; Col. 1:27-28. Whether one is preaching (*kerygma*) to unbelievers or teaching (*didache*) believers, the message to both believer and unbeliever alike is Jesus Christ (C.H. Dodd, *The Apostolic Preaching and Its Developments*, London: Hodder and Stoughton, 1963, p. 7ff). Speaking of the early church, Michael Green writes, "They preached a person. Their message was frankly Christocentric. Indeed, the gospel is referred to simply as Jesus or Christ: 'He preached Jesus to him . . . ' Jesus the man, Jesus crucified, Jesus risen, Jesus exalted to the place of power in the universe . . . Jesus who meantime was present among His people in the Spirit . . . The risen Christ was unambiguously central in their message" (*Evangelism in the Early Church,* Houder and Stoughton, 1970, p. 150).

[108] See *Rethinking the Wineskin,* Chapter 1.

[109] Heb. 3:12-13; 10:24-26a. Notice the emphasis on "one another" in these passages. It is *mutual* exhortation that the author has in view.

the believers[110] as well as from those who are specially gifted to teach.[111] We move far outside of Biblical bounds when we allow teaching to take the form of a conventional sermon and relegate it to a class of professional orators.

Wrapping It Up

The pulpit sermon is not the equivalent of the preaching that is found in the Scriptures.[112] It cannot be found in the Judaism of the Old Testament, the ministry of Jesus, or the life of the primitive church.[113] What is more, Paul told his Greek converts that he refused to be influenced by the communication patterns of his pagan contemporaries.[114]

The sermon is a sacred cow that was conceived in the womb of Greek rhetoric. It was born into the Christian community when ex-pagans-now-turned-Christians began to bring their oratorical styles of speaking into the church. By the third century, it became common for Christian leaders to deliver a sermon. By the fourth century it became the norm.[115]

Christianity has absorbed its surrounding culture.[116] When your pastor mounts his pulpit wearing his clerical costume and delivers his sacred sermon, he is playing out the role of the ancient Greek orator.

Nevertheless, despite the fact that the sermon does not have a shred of Biblical merit to support its existence, it continues to be uncritically admired in the eyes of most modern Christians. It has become so entrenched in the Christian mind that most Bible-believing pastors and "laymen" fail to see that they are affirming and perpetuating an unscriptural practice out of sheer tradition. The sermon has become permanently embedded in a complex

---

[110] 1 Cor. 14:26,31.

[111] Eph. 4:11; Jam. 3:1.

[112] "Preacher and Preaching: Some Lexical Observations," *Journal of the Evangelical Theological Society* (December, 1981, Vol. 24, No. 4).

[113] *To Preach or Not to Preach?*, p. 69.

[114] 1 Cor. 1:17,22; 2:1-5.

[115] *To Preach or Not to Preach?*, p. 69.

[116] George T. Purves, "The Influence of Paganism on Post-Apostolic Christianity," *The Presbyterian Review* (No. 36, October, 1988), pp. 529-554.

organizational structure that is far removed from first-century church life.[117]

In view of all that we have discovered about the modern sermon, consider these penetrating questions:

How can a man preach a sermon on being faithful to the Word of God when he is preaching a sermon!? And how can a Christian passively sit in a pew and affirm the priesthood of all believers when he is passively sitting in a pew!? To put a finer point on it, how can you, dear Christian, claim to uphold the Protestant doctrine of *sola Scriptura* ("by the Scripture only") and still support the pulpit sermon?

As one author so eloquently put it, *"The sermon is, in practice, beyond criticism. It has become an end in itself, sacred—the product of a distorted reverence for 'the tradition of the elders'. . . it seems strangely inconsistent that those who are most disposed to claim that the Bible is the Word of God, the 'supreme guide in all matters of faith and practice' are amongst the first to reject Biblical methods in favor of the 'broken cisterns' of their fathers (Jer. 2:13)."*[118] To put it another way, there is no room in the church's corral for sacred cows like the sermon!

---

[117] For a detailed discussion of the unscriptural nature of the modern organizational structure of the Protestant church, see my book, *Who is Your Covering?* Chapters 1-3. Also see Chapter 4 of this book.

[118] *To Preach or Not to Preach?*, pp. 102, 104.

And my speech and my preaching was not with enticing words of man's wisdom, but in demonstration of the Spirit and of power: That your faith should not stand in the wisdom of men, but in the power of God.
  -Paul of Tarsus

CHAPTER 3

THE CHURCH BUILDING: INHERITING THE EDIFICE COMPLEX

In the process of replacing the old religions, Christianity became a religion.
-Alexander Schmemann

The modern Christian has a love affair with brick and mortar. The edifice complex is so ingrained in our thinking that if a group of believers begins to meet together, their first thoughts are toward securing a building. For how can a group of Christians rightfully claim to be a church without a building? (So the thinking goes.)

The "church" building is so connected with the idea of church that we unconsciously equate the two. Just listen to the vocabulary of the average Christian today:

"Wow honey, did you see that beautiful church we just passed?"

"Heavens to Betsy, that is the largest church I have ever seen! I wonder what the electric bill costs to keep it going?"

"Our church is too small. I'm developing claustrophobia. We need to extend the balcony."

"The church is chilly today; I am freezing my buns off in here!"

"We have gone to church every Sunday this past year except for the Sunday when Aunt Rotunda dropped the microwave oven on her toe."

Or how about the vocabulary of the average pastor:

"Isn't it wonderful to be in the house of God today?"

"We must show reverence when we come into the sanctuary of the Lord."

Or how about the mother who tells her happy child (in subdued tones), *"Wipe that smile off your face, you're in church now! We behave ourselves in the house of God!"*

To put it bluntly, none of these thoughts have anything to do with NT Christianity. They rather reflect the thinking of other religions—primarily Judaism and paganism.[1]

Temples, Priests, and Sacrifices

Ancient Judaism was centered on three elements: The temple, the priesthood, and the sacrifice. When Jesus came, He ended all three, fulfilling them in Himself. He is the Temple[2] who embodies a new and living house made of *living* stones—"without hands."[3] He is the Priest[4] who has established a new priesthood.[5] And He is the perfect and finished Sacrifice.[6]

Consequently, the temple, the priesthood, and the sacrifice of Judaism all passed away with the coming of Jesus Christ.[7] Christ is the fulfillment and the reality of it all.[8] In Greco-Roman

---

[1] As earlier stated, a mixture of Judaism and mystery pagan religion heavily influenced the shape of the church after the apostolic age. Ilion T. Jones, *A Historical Approach to Evangelical Worship* (New York: Abingdon Press, 1954), pp. 94, 97.

[2] John 1:14 (the Greek word for "dwelt" literally means "tabernacled"); 2:19-21.

[3] Mark 14:58; Acts 7:48; 1 Cor. 3:16; 2 Cor. 5:1, 6:16; Eph. 2:21-22; Heb. 3:6-9, 9:11, 24; 1 Tim. 3:15.

[4] Heb. 4:14; 5:5,6,10; 8:1.

[5] 1 Pet. 2:9; Rev. 1:6.

[6] Heb. 7:27; 9:14,25-28; 10:12; 1 Pet. 3:18. Hebrews continually stresses that Jesus offered Himself "once, for all time" emphasizing the fact that He need not be sacrificed again. The sacrifice of Christ on Calvary was all-sufficient.

[7] Stephen's message in Acts 7 indicates that "the temple was merely a man-made house originating with Solomon; it had no connection with the tent of meeting that Moses had been commanded to set up on a Divinely revealed pattern and that had continued until David's time" (Harold W. Turner, *From Temple to Meeting House: The Phenomenology and Theology of Places of Worship*, The Hague: Mouton Publishers, 1979, pp. 116-117). See also the Lord's contrasting word in Mark 14:58 that the temple of Solomon (and Herod) was made "with hands," while the temple that He would raise up would be made "without hands." Stephen uses the same wording in Acts 7:48 . . . God does not dwell in temples "made with hands." In other words, our heavenly Father is not a temple-dweller!

[8] Col. 2:16-17. That Christ came to fulfill the shadows of the Jewish law is the central theme of the book of Hebrews. The NT writers all affirm that God does not require any holy sacrifices nor a mediating priesthood. All has been fulfilled in Jesus—the

paganism,[9] these three elements were also present: Pagans had their temples,[10] their priests, and their sacrifices.[11]

It was only the Christians who did away with all of these elements.[12] It can be rightly said that Christianity was the first non-temple based religion ever to emerge. In the minds of the early Christians, it is the *people* that constitute a sacred space, not the architecture. The early Christians understood that they them-selves—corporately—were the temple of God and the house of God.[13]

Strikingly, nowhere in the NT do we find the terms "church" (*ekklesia*), "temple," or "house of God" used to refer to a building. To the ears of a first-century Christian, calling a building an *ekklesia* (church) would be like calling a woman a skyscraper![14]

The first recorded use of the word *ekklesia* (church) to refer to a Christian meeting place was penned around A.D. 190 by Clement of Alexandria (150-215).[15] Clement is the first person to use the phrase "go to church"—which was a foreign thought to the first-

---

Sacrifice and the Mediating Priest.

[9] Paganism dominated the Roman Empire until around the fourth century. But many of its elements were absorbed by the Christians in the third and fourth centuries. The term "pagan" was an invention of the Christian apologists in an attempt to group non-Christians into a convenient package. At bottom, a "pagan" is a country-dweller; an inhabitant of the *pagus* or rural district. Because Christianity primarily spread in the cities, the country bumpkins, or "pagans," were regarded as those who believed in the old gods (*Christians and the Holy Places*, p. 301).

[10] Ernest H. Short dedicates an entire chapter to the architecture of Greek temples in his book *A History of Religious Architecture* (London: Philip Allen & Co., 1936), Chapter 2. David Norrington states, "Religious buildings were, nonetheless, an integral part of Graeco-Roman religion" (David C. Norrington, *To Preach or Not to Preach? The Church's Urgent Question*, Carlisle: Paternoster Press, 1996, p. 27). Pagans also had "holy" shrines. Michael Grant, *The Founders of the Western World: The History of Greece and Rome* (New York: Charles Scribner's Sons, 1991), pp. 232-234.

[11] Robin Lane Fox, *Pagans and Christians* (New York: Alfred Knopf, 1987), pp. 39, 41-43, 71-76, 206.

[12] *Christian History*, Volume XII, No. 1, Issue 37, p. 3.

[13] 1 Cor. 3:16; Gal. 6:10; Eph. 2:20-22; Heb. 3:5; 1 Tim. 3:15; 1 Pet. 2:5; 4:17. All of these passages refer to God's people, not to a building. In the words of Arthur Wallis, "In the Old Testament, God had a sanctuary for His people; in the New, God has His people as a sanctuary."

[14] According to the NT, the church is the most beautiful girl in the world: John 3:29; 2 Cor. 11:2; Eph. 5:25-32; Rev. 21:9.

[15] Clement of Alexandria, *The Instructor*, Book III, Ch. 11.

century believers.[16] (You cannot go to something you are! Throughout the NT, *ekklesia* always refers to an assembly of people, not a place.)[17]

Even so, Clement's reference to "going to church" is not a reference to attending a special building for worship. It rather refers to a private home that the second-century Christians used for their meetings.[18] Christians did not erect special buildings for worship until the Constantinian era in the fourth century.[19] Neither did they have a special priestly caste that was set apart to serve God. Instead, *every* believer recognized that he or she was a priest unto God.

---

[16] Adolf Von Harnack states of the first and second century Christians, "One thing is clear—the idea of a special place for worship had not yet arisen. The Christian idea of God and of Divine service not only failed to promote this, but excluded it, while the practical circumstances of the situation retarded its development" (*To Preach or Not to Preach?* p. 28).

[17] Robert Saucey, *The Church in God's Program*, p. 12; A.T. Robertson, *A Grammar of the Greek New Testament in the Light of Historical Research*, p. 174. The English word "church" along with the Scottish word *kirk* and the German word *kirche* are all derived form the Greek word *kuriakon* which means "belonging to the Lord." The English word "church" comes from the Old English *cirice* or *circe* which is derived from the Greek word *kuriakon*. In time, it took on the meaning of "God's house" and was convoluted to refer to a building. The translators of the English Bible did us a huge injustice by translating *ekklesia* into "church." *Ekklesia,* in all of its 114 appearances in the NT, always means an assembly of people (*The Church in God's Program*, pp. 11,16). William Tyndale should be commended because in his translation of the NT, he refused to use the word "church" to translate *ekklesia*. Instead, he translated it more correctly as "congregation." Unfortunately, the translators of the KJV chose not to follow Tyndale's superior translation in this matter and resorted to "church" as a translation of *ekklesia*. They rejected the correct translation of *ekklesia* as "congregation" because it was the terminology of the Puritans ("The Translators to the Reader" from the Preface to the 1611 translation in G. Bray, *Documents of the English Reformation*, Cambridge: James Clarke, 1994, p. 435).

[18] *The Instructor*, Book III, Ch. 11. Clement writes, "Woman and man are to go to church decently attired."

[19] Graydon F. Snyder, *Ante Pacem: Archaeological Evidence of Church Life Before Constantine* (Mercer University Press/Seedsowers, 1985), p. 67. Snyder states, "There is no literary evidence nor archaeological indication that any such home was converted into an extant church building. Nor is there any extant church that certainly was built prior to Constantine." In another work Snyder writes, "The first churches consistently met in homes. Until the year 300 we know of no buildings first built as churches (*First Corinthians: A Faith Community Commentary,* Macon: Mercer University Press, 1991, p. 3).

The early Christians also did away with sacrifices. For they understood that the true and final Sacrifice (Christ) had come. The only sacrifices they offered were the spiritual sacrifices of praise and thanksgiving.[20]

When Roman Catholicism evolved in the fourth to the sixth centuries, it absorbed the religious practices of both paganism and Judaism. It set up a professional priestcraft. It erected sacred buildings.[21] And it turned the Lord's Supper into a mysterious sacrifice.

Following the path of the pagans, Catholicism adopted the practice of burning incense and having vestal (sacred) virgins.[22] Thankfully, the Protestants dropped the sacrificial use of the Lord's Supper, the burning of incense, and the vestal virgins. But they retained the priestly caste (the clergy) as well as the sacred building.

From House Churches to Holy Cathedrals

The early Christians believed that Jesus is the very presence of God. They believed that the Body of Christ, the church, constitutes a temple.

When the Lord Jesus was on earth, He made some radically negative statements about the Jewish temple.[23] The chief one being that it would be destroyed![24]

While Jesus was pointing to the temple that existed in the architectural sense, He was really speaking of His Body. Jesus said that after the temple was destroyed, He would raise it up in three

---

[20] Heb. 13:15; 1 Pet. 2:5.

[21] "According to Canon Law, a church is a sacred building dedicated to Divine worship for the use of all the faithful and the public exercise of religion" (Peter F. Anson, *Churches: Their Plans and Furnishings*, Milwaukee: Bruce Publishing Co., 1948, p. 3).

[22] *Pagans and Christians*, pp. 71, 207, 27, 347, 355. Fox states that "in modern Christianity, there are more than 1.6 million adults vowed to virginity" (p. 355). They are called nuns and priests.

[23] Stephen also spoke negatively about the temple. Both Jesus and Stephen were charged with the same exact crime—speaking against the temple (Mark 14:58; Acts 6:13-14).

[24] John 2:19-21. Significantly, the veil of the temple was rent in half when Jesus died (Matt. 27:50-51).

days. Significantly, He was referring to the real temple—the church—which He raised up in Himself on the third day.

Since Christ has risen, we Christians have become *the* temple of God.[25] It is for this reason that the NT always reserves the word "church" (*ekklesia*) for the people of God. It never uses this word to refer to a building of any sort.

Jesus' act of clearing the temple signified that the "temple worship" of Judaism was being replaced by Himself.[26] With His coming, the Father would no longer be worshipped in a mountain or a temple. He would instead be worshipped in spirit and in reality.[27]

When Christianity was born, it was the only religion on earth that had no sacred objects, no sacred persons, and no sacred spaces.[28] Although surrounded by Jewish synagogues and pagan temples, the early Christians were the only religious people on earth that did not erect sacred buildings for their worship.[29] The Christian faith was born in homes, out in courtyards, along roadsides, and in living rooms.[30]

---

[25] At His resurrection, Christ became a "life-giving spirit"(1 Cor. 15:45). Therefore, He can take up residence in the believers thus making them His house.

[26] John 2:12-22. See Oscar Cullman, *Early Christian Worship* (London: SCM Press, 1969), pp. 72-73, 117.

[27] John 4:23. The NT Christians believed that the church, the community of the believers, was the temple. And that worship was not spatially located nor extracted from the totality of life. Thus in their minds there did not exist the idea of a "holy place." The Christians' "holy place" is as omnipresent as their ascended Lord! Worship is not something that happens in a certain place at a certain time. It is a lifestyle (J.G. Davies, *The Secular Use of Church Buildings*, New York: The Seabury Press, 1968, pp. 3-4).

[28] James D.G. Dunn, "The Responsible Congregation, 1 Corinthians 14:26-40," in Charisma and *Agape* (Rome: Abbey of St. Paul before the Wall, 1983), pp. 235-236.

[29] The third century Christian apologist Minucius Felix stated, "We have no temples and no altars" (*The Octavius of Minucius Felix,* Chapter 32). See also Robert Banks, *Paul's Idea of Community* (Peabody: Hendrickson Publishers, 1994), pp. 8-14, 26-46.

[30] Acts 2:46; 8:3; 20:20; Rom. 16:3,5; 1 Cor. 16:19; Col. 4:15; Phm. 1:12; 2 John 10. It should be noted that on occasion, the Christians used *already existing* buildings for special and temporary purposes. Solomon's porch and the school of Tyrannus are examples (Acts 5:12; 19:9). Their normal church meetings, however, were always set in a private home.

For the first three centuries, the Christians did not have any special buildings.[31] As one scholar put it, *"The Christianity that conquered the Roman Empire was essentially a home-centered movement."*[32] Some have argued that this was by force. But that is not true.[33] It was a conscious choice on their part.[34]

As Christian congregations grew in size, they began to remodel their homes to accommodate their growing numbers.[35] One of the most outstanding finds of archeology is the house of Dura-Europos in modern Syria. This is the earliest identifiable Christian meeting place.[36] It was simply a private home remodeled as a Christian gathering place around A.D. 232.[37]

The house at Dura Europos was essentially a house with a wall torn out between two bedrooms to create a large living room.[38]

---

[31] *Ante Pacem*, p. 166. John A.T. Robinson has written "In the first three centuries the church had no buildings . . . " (*The New Reformation*, Philadelphia: The Westminster Press, 1965), p. 89.

[32] Robert Banks, *The Church Comes Home* (Peabody: Hendrickson Publishers, 1998), pp. 49-50. The house at Dura Europos was destroyed in A.D. 256. According to Frank Senn, "Christians of the first several centuries lacked the publicity of the pagan cults. They had no shrines, temples, statues, or sacrifices. They staged no public festivals, dances, musical performances, or pilgrimages. Their central ritual involved a meal that had a domestic origin and setting inherited from Judaism. Indeed, Christians of the first three centuries usually met in private residences that had been converted into suitable gathering spaces for the Christian community . . . This indicates that the ritual bareness of early Christian worship should not be taken as a sign of primitiveness, but rather as a way of emphasizing the spiritual character of Christian worship" (*Christian Liturgy*, p. 53).

[33] Some have argued that the pre-Constantine Christians were poor and could not own property. But this is false. Under the persecution of Emperor Valerian (253-260), for example, all property owned by Christians was seized (Philip Schaff, *History of the Christian Church: Volume 2*, Michigan: Eerdmans, 1910, p. 62). L. Michael White points out that the early Christians had access to higher socioeconomic strata. Also, the Greco-Roman environment of the second and third century was quite open to many groups adapting private buildings for communal and religious use (*Building God's House in the Roman World*, pp. 142-143).

[34] *Toward a House Church Theology* (Atlanta: New Testament Restoration Foundation, 1998), pp. 29-42.

[35] *Ante Pacem*, p. 67. These restructured homes are called *domus ecclesiae*.

[36] Everett Ferguson, *Early Christians Speak: Faith and Life in the First Three Centuries* (Abilene: A.C.U. Press, Third Edition, 1999), pp. 46, 74.

[37] Ibid., p. 46. L. Michael White, *Building God's House in the Roman World* (Baltimore: John Hopkins University Press, 1990), Vol. 1, pp. 16-25.

[38] James F. White, *Protestant Worship and Church Architecture* (New York: Oxford University Press, 1964), pp. 54-55.

With this modification, the house could house about 70 people.[39]

Remodeled houses like Dura Europos cannot rightfully be called "church buildings." They were simply refurbished homes to accommodate larger assemblies.[40] Further, these homes were never called "temples," the term that both pagans and Jews used for their sacred spaces. Christians did not begin calling their buildings "temples" until the 15th century![41]

The Creation of the Sacred Spaces and Objects

In the late second and third centuries a shift occurred. The Christians began to adopt the pagan view of reverencing the dead.[42] Their focus was the memory of the martyrs.[43] So prayers *for* the saints (which later devolved into prayers *to* them) began.[44]

The Christians picked up from the pagans the practice of having meals in honor of the dead.[45] Both the Christian funeral and the funeral dirge came straight out of paganism in the third century.[46]

---

[39] *Christian History*, Volume XII, No. 1, Issue 37, p. 33.

[40] *To Preach or Not to Preach?*, p. 25. In addition to remodeling private homes, Alan Kreider states that "by the mid-third century, congregations were growing in numbers and wealth. So Christians who met in *insulae* (islands), multi-storied blocks containing shops and housing, unobtrusively began to convert private spaces into domestic complexes tailored to fit congregational needs. They knocked out walls to unite apartments, thereby creating the varied spaces, large and small, that were required by the lives of their growing communities" (*Worship and Evangelism in Pre-Christendom*, Oxford: Alain/GROW Liturgical Study, 1995, p. 5).

[41] *From Temple to Meeting House*, p. 195. The Renaissance theorists Alberti and Palladio studied the temples of ancient Rome and began using the term "temple" to refer to the Christian church building. Later, Calvin referred to Christian buildings as temples, adding it to the Reformation vocabulary (p. 207). See also *The Secular Use of Church Buildings* pp. 220-222 for the thinking that led up to the Christian use of the term "temple" as a reference to a church building.

[42] *Ante Pacem*, pp. 83, 143-144, 167.

[43] *Christian History*, Volume XII, No. 1, Issue 37, p. 2.

[44] Ibid., p. 31.

[45] *Ante Pacem*, p. 65; Johannes Quasten, *Music and Worship in Pagan & Christian Antiquity* (Washington D.C.: National Association of Pastoral Musicians, 1983), pp. 153-154, 168-169.

[46] *Music and Worship in Pagan & Christian Antiquity*, pp. 162-168. Tertullian (160-225) demonstrates the relentless efforts of the Christians to do away with the pagan custom of the funeral procession. Yet the Christians succumbed to it. Christian funeral rites, which drew heavily from pagan forms, begin to appear in the third century (David W. Bercot, ed., *A Dictionary of Early Christian Beliefs*, Peabody:

Third-century Christians had two places for their meetings: Their private homes and the cemetery.[47] They met in the cemetery because they wished to be close to their dead brethren.[48] It was their belief that to share a meal at a cemetery of a martyr was to commemorate him and to worship in his company.[49]

Since the bodies of the "holy" martyrs resided there, Christian burial places came to be viewed as "holy spaces."[50] The Christians then began to build small monuments over these spaces—especially over the graves of famous saints.[51] Building a shrine over a burial place and calling it "holy" was also a pagan practice.[52]

In Rome, the Christians began to decorate the catacombs (underground burial places)[53] with Christian symbols. So art became associated with sacred spaces. Clement of Alexandria (150-215) was one of the first Christians advocating the visual arts in worship.[54]

(Parenthetically, the cross as an artistic reference for Christ's death cannot be found prior to the time of Constantine.[55] The

---

Hendrickson, 1998, p. 80; Everett Ferguson, ed., *Encyclopedia of Early Christianity*, New York: Garland Publishing, 1990, p. 163). Praying for the dead seems to have been born around the second century. Tertullian tells us that it was a common practice in his day (*The Oxford Dictionary of the Christian Church,* Third Edition, p. 456). See also Frank Senn's *Christian Worship and Its Cultural Setting* (Philadelphia: Fortress Press, 1983), p. 41.

[47] *Ante Pacem*, p. 83.

[48] *Christian History*, Volume XII, No. 1, Issue 37, p. 35; *From Temple to Meeting House,* pp. 168-172.

[49] *Christian History*, Volume XII, No. 1, Issue 37, p. 35; Josef A. Jungmann, S.J., *The Early Liturgy: To the Time of Gregory the Great* (Notre Dame: Notre Dame Press, 1959), p. 141.

[50] *Protestant Worship and Church Architecture*, p. 60.

[51] These monuments would later be transformed into magnificent church buildings.

[52] *The Early Liturgy,* p. 178; *From Temple to Meeting House,* pp. 164-167.

[53] Philip Schaff, *History of the Christian Church: Volume 2* (Michigan: Eerdmans, 1910), p. 292. "The use of catacombs lasted about three centuries, from the end of the second to the end of the fifth" (*Ante Pacem*, p. 84). Contrary to popular belief, there is not a shred of historical evidence that Roman Christians hid in the catacombs to escape persecution. They met there to be close to the dead saints (*Christian History*, Volume XII, No. 1, Issue 37, p. 35).

[54] *Christian History*, Volume XII, No. 1, Issue 37, p. 30.

[55] *Ante Pacem*, p. 27. "Jesus does not suffer or die in pre-Constantinian art. There is no cross symbol, nor any equivalent" (p. 56). Philip Schaff says that following Constantine's victory over Maxentius in A.D. 312, crosses were seen on helmets, bucklers, crowns, etc. (*History of the Christian Church: Volume 2,* p. 270).

crucifix, an artistic representation of the Savior attached to the cross, made its first appearance in the fifth century.[56] The custom of making the "sign of the cross" with one's hands dates back to the second century.)[57]

At about the second century, the Christians began to venerate the bones of the saints, regarding them as holy and sacred. This eventually gave birth to relic collecting.[58] Reverence for the dead was the most powerful community-forming force in the Roman Empire.[59] Now the Christians were absorbing it into their own faith.[60]

In the late second century there was a shift in how the Lord's Supper was viewed. The Supper had devolved from a full meal to a stylized ceremony called "Holy Communion."[61]

By the fourth century, this trend became ridiculous. The cup and the bread were seen as producing a sense of awe, dread, and mystery. So much so that the churches in the East placed a canopy over the altar-table[62] where the bread and cup sat.[63] (In the 16th century, rails were placed upon the altar-table.[64] The rails signified that the altar-table was a holy object only to be handled by holy persons—i.e., the clergy!)[65]

---

[56] *Ante Pacem*, p. 165.

[57] *History of the Christian Church: Volume 2*, pp. 269-270.

[58] A relic is the material remains of a saint after his death as well as any sacred object which has been in contact with his body. The word "relic" comes from the Latin word *reliquere*, meaning "to leave behind." The first evidence of the veneration of relics appears around A.D. 156 in the *Martyrium Polycarpi*. In this document, the relics of Polycarp are considered more valuable than precious stones and gold (*The Oxford Dictionary of the Christian Church*, Third Edition, p. 1379; Father Michael Collins and Matthew A. Price, *The Story of Christianity* (DK Publishing, 1999), p. 91; *The Early Liturgy*, pp. 184-187.

[59] *Ante Pacem*, p. 91.

[60] *From Temple to Meeting House*, pp. 168-172.

[61] See Chapter 8 for details.

[62] This is the table where the holy communion was placed. The altar-table signifies what is offered to God (the altar) and what is given to man (the table). *Protestant Worship and Church Architecture*, p. 40. Side altars did not come into use until Gregory the Great (*The History of Christianity: Volume 3*, p. 550).

[63] *Protestant Worship and Church Architecture*, p. 63.

[64] Ibid., p. 42.

[65] In the fourth century, the laity was forbidden to go to the altar. Edwin Hatch, *The Growth of Church Institutions* (Hodder and Stoughton, 1895), pp. 214-215.

So by the third century, the Christians not only had sacred spaces. They also had sacred objects. (They would soon develop a sacred priesthood.) In all of this, the second and third-century Christians began to assimilate the magical mindset that characterized pagan thinking.[66] All of these factors made the Christian terrain ready for the man who would be responsible for creating church buildings.

Constantine—Father of the Church Building

The story of Constantine (285-337) fills a dark page in the history of Christianity. Church buildings began with him.[67] The story is astonishing.

By the time Constantine emerged on the scene, the atmosphere was ripe for Christians to escape their despised, minority status. The temptation to be accepted was just too great to resist and the Constantinian snowball began to roll.

In A.D. 312, Constantine became Caesar of the Western Empire.[68] By 324, he became Emperor of the entire Roman Empire. Shortly afterward, he began ordering the construction of church buildings. He did so to promote the popularity and acceptance of Christianity. If the Christians had their own sacred

---

[66] Norman Towar Boggs, *The Christian Saga* (New York: The Macmillan Company, 1931), p. 209.

[67] *A Historical Approach to Evangelical Worship,* p. 103; *History of the Christian Church: Volume 3,* p. 542. Schaff's opening words are telling: "After Christianity was acknowledged by the state and empowered to hold property, it raised houses of worship in all parts of the Roman Empire. There was probably more building of this kind in the fourth century than there has been in any period, excepting perhaps the nineteenth century in the United States . . ." See also *To Preach or Not to Preach?,* p. 29. Norrington points out that as the bishops of the fourth and fifth centuries grew in wealth, they funneled it into elaborate church building programs. Everett Ferguson writes, "Not until the Constantinian age do we find specially constructed buildings, at first simple halls and then the Constantinian basilicas." Before Constantine, all structures used for church gatherings were "houses or commercial buildings modified for church use" (*Early Christians Speak*, p. 74).

[68] In A.D. 312, Constantine defeated the western Emperor Maxentius at the battle of Milvian Bridge. Constantine claimed that on the eve of the battle, he saw a sign of the cross in the heavens and was converted to Christ (Ken Connolly, *The Indestructible Book,* Grand Rapids: Baker Books, 1996, pp. 39-40)

buildings—as did the Jews and the pagans—their faith would be regarded as legitimate.

It is important to understand Constantine's mindset—for it was the womb that gave birth to the church building. Constantine's thinking was dominated by superstition and paganistic magic. Even after he became Emperor, he allowed the old pagan institutions to remain as they were.[69]

Following his conversion to Christianity, Constantine never abandoned sun-worship. He kept the sun on his coins.[70] And he set up a statue of the sun-god which bore his own image in the Forum of Constantinople (his new capital).[71] Constantine also built a statue of the mother-goddess Cybele. (Though he presented her in a posture of Christian prayer.)[72]

(Historians continue to debate whether or not Constantine was a genuine Christian. The fact that he is reported to have had his eldest son, his nephew, and his brother-in-law executed does not help to strengthen the case for his conversion.[73] But we will not probe that nerve too deeply here.)

In A.D. 321, Constantine decreed that Sunday would be a day of rest—a legal holiday.[74] It appears that Constantine's intention in doing this was to honor the god Mithras, the Unconquered Sun.[75]

---

[69] This includes the temples, priestly offices, college of pontiffs, vestal virgins, and the title (reserved for himself) *Pontifex Maximus* (chief of the pagan priests). Monsignor Louis Duchesne, *Early History of the Christian Church: From Its Foundation to the End of the Fifth Century* (London: John Murray, 1912), pp. 49-50; M.A. Smith, *From Christ to Constantine* (Downer's Grove: InterVarsity Press, 1973), p. 172.

[70] Paul Johnson, *A History of Christianity* (New Your: Simon & Schuster, 1976), p. 68.

[71] Ibid., 68.

[72] Ibid.

[73] He is also charged with the death of his second wife, though some historians believe this is a false rumor. Joan E. Taylor, *Christians and the Holy Places: The Myth of Jewish-Christian Origins* (Oxford: Clarendon Press, 1993), p. 297; *History of the Christian Church: Volume 3*, pp. 16-17; Ramsay MacMullen, *Christianizing the Roman Empire: A.D. 100-400* (London: Yale University Press, 1984), pp. 44-58.

[74] Kim Tan, *Lost Heritage: The Heroic Story of Radical Christianity* (Godalming: Highland Books, 1996), p. 84.

[75] Constantine seems to have thought that the Unconquered Sun (a pagan god) and Christ were somehow compatible (Justo L. Gonzalez, *The Story of Christianity*, Peabody: Prince Press, 1999), pp. 122-123).

(He described Sunday as "the day of the sun."[76]) To further demonstrate his affinity with sun worship, excavations of St. Peter's in Rome uncovered a mosaic of Christ as the Unconquered Sun.[77]

Almost to his dying day, Constantine "still functioned as the high priest of paganism."[78] In fact, he retained the pagan title *Pontifex Maximus*, which means chief of the pagan priests![79] (In the 15th century, this same title became the honorific title for the Catholic Pope!)[80]

Constantine used pagan as well as Christian rituals and decorations in dedicating his new capital, Constantinople.[81] And he used pagan magic formulas to protect crops and heal diseases.[82]

Further, all historical evidence indicates that Constantine was an egomaniac. When he built the new "Church of the Apostles," he built monuments to the 12 apostles. The 12 monuments surrounded a single tomb, which layed at the center. That tomb was reserved for Constantine himself—thus making himself the 13th and chief apostle![83] Thus Constantine not only continued the pagan practice of honoring the dead,[84] he also sought to be included as one of the significant dead![85]

Constantine also strengthened the pagan notion of the sacredness of objects and places.[86] Largely due to his influence, relic-

---

[76] *Christian History*, Volume XII, No. 1, Issue 37, p. 20.

[77] Ibid.; *The Early Liturgy*, p. 136.

[78] *The Story of Christianity* (Gonzalez), p. 123.

[79] *Pagans and Christians*, p. 666; *Caesar to Christ*, pp. 63,656.

[80] *The Oxford Dictionary of the Christian Church*, Third Edition, p. 1307.

[81] Constantine dedicated the new city on May 11, 330. He adorned it with treasures taken from heathen temples throughout the East. Robert M. Grant, *Early Christianity and Society* (San Francisco: Harper and Row Publishers, 1977), p. 155.

[82] *Caesar to Christ*, p. 656.

[83] *A History of Christianity*, p. 69; *Early History of the Christian Church*, p. 69. In the Eastern Church, Constantine is actually named the 13th apostle and is venerated as a saint (*The Oxford Dictionary of the Christian Church*, Third Edition, p. 405; *Christians and the Holy Places*, p. 303).

[84] *Christians and the Holy Places*, p. 316.

[85] *Ante Pacem*, p. 93.

[86] *Christians and the Holy Places*, p. 308; *The Secular Use of Buildings*, pp. 222-237.

mongering became common in the church.[87] By the fourth century, obsession with relics got so bad that some Christian leaders spoke out against it saying, *"A heathen observance introduced in the churches under the cloak of religion . . . the work of idolaters."*[88]

Constantine is also noted for bringing to the Christian faith the idea of the "holy site" which was based on the model of the pagan shrine.[89] Because of the aura of "sacredness" that the fourth-century Christians attached to Palestine, it became known as "the Holy Land" by the sixth century.[90]

Still more startling is that after Constantine's death, he was declared to be "divine." (This was the custom for all pagan Emperors who died before him.)[91] It was the Senate who declared him to be a pagan god at his death.[92] And no one stopped them from doing this.

At this point, a word should be said about Constantine's mother, Helena. This woman was most noted for her obsession with relics. In A.D. 326, Helena made a pilgrimage to the Holy Land.[93] In A.D. 327 in Jerusalem, she reportedly found the cross and nails that were used to crucify Jesus.[94] It is reported that Constantine promoted the idea that the bits of wood that came from Christ's

---

[87] The notion that relics had magical power cannot be credited to the Jews, for they believed that any contact with a dead body was a pollution. This idea was completely pagan (*The Christian Saga*, p. 210).

[88] *A History of Christianity*, p. 106. This is a quote from Vigilantius.

[89] *Christians and the Holy Places*, pp. 317, 339-341.

[90] Ibid., p. 341.

[91] *The Christian Saga*, p. 202.

[92] *The Story of Christianity* (Gonzalez), p. 123.

[93] *The Oxford Dictionary of the Christian Church*, Third Edition, p. 1379. Helena made her pilgrimage to the Holy Land immediately following the execution of Constantine's son and the "suicide" of his wife (*Pagans and Christians*, pp. 670-671, 674).

[94] Oscar Hardman, *A History of Christian Worship* (Tennessee: Parthenon Press, 1937). Helena gave Constantine two of these nails: One for his diadem and the other for his horse's bit (*A History of Christianity*, p. 106; *Early History of the Christian Church*, pp. 64-65). "The cross was said to have miraculous powers, and pieces of wood claiming to come from it were found all over the Empire" (*The Story of Christianity*, Gonzalez, p. 126). The legend of Helena's discovery of the cross originated in Jerusalem in the second half of the fourth century and rapidly spread over the entire Empire.

cross possessed spiritual powers![95] Truly, a pagan magical mind was at work in Emperor Constantine. Behold, the father of the church building.

Constantine's Building Program

Following Helena's trip to Jerusalem in A.D. 327, Constantine began erecting the first church buildings throughout the Roman Empire.[96] In so doing, he followed the path of the pagans in constructing temples to honor God.[97]

Interestingly, he named his church buildings after saints—just as the pagans named their temples after gods. Constantine built his first church buildings upon the cemeteries where the Christians held meals for the dead saints.[98] That is, he built them over the bodies of dead saints.[99] Why? Because for at least a century beforehand, the burial places of the saints were considered "holy spaces."[100]

Many of the largest buildings were built over the tombs of the martyrs.[101] This practice was based on the idea that the martyrs had the same powers that they had once ascribed to the gods of paganism.[102] Although pagan, the Christians adopted this view hook, line, and sinker.

The most famous Christian "holy spaces" were: St. Peter's on the Vatican hill (built over the supposed tomb of Peter),[103] St. Paul's outside the walls (built over the supposed tomb of Paul),[104]

---

[95] *Christians and the Holy Places*, p. 308; *The Christian Saga*, pp. 206-207.

[96] Some of these church buildings were erected at public expense (*Pagans and Christians*, pp. 667-668).

[97] *Christians and the Holy Places*, p. 309.

[98] *Ante Pacem*, p. 65. These places are referred to as *martyria*.

[99] Ibid., p. 92; *Christian History*, Volume XII, No. 1, Issue 37, p. 35.

[100] *Christians and the Holy Places*, pp. 340-341. As J.G. Davies says, "As the first Christians had no holy shrines, the need for consecration did not arise. It was only in the fourth century, with the peace of the church, that the practice of dedicating buildings began (*The Secular Use of Buildings*, pp. 9, 250).

[101] *A History of Religious Architecture*, p. 62.

[102] *A History of Christianity*, p. 209.

[103] *Ante Pacem*, p. 109. St. Peter's was 835 feet long (*Christian History*, Volume XII, No. 1, Issue 37, p. 35).

[104] *The Oxford Dictionary of the Christian Church*, Third Edition, p. 1442.

the dazzling and astonishing church of the Holy Sepulcher in Jerusalem (built over the supposed tomb of Christ),[105] and the church of the Nativity in Bethlehem (built over the supposed cave of Jesus' birth).[106] Constantine built nine churches in Rome and many others in Jerusalem, Bethlehem, and Constantinople.[107]

Behold the roots of the "sacred" church building, dear Christian. It is wholly pagan. It was invented by a former pagan who still had a pagan mind. And it was built on the pagan idea that the dead create a sacred space. Please remember that the next time you hear a church building referred to as God's "holy" and "sacred" house!

Exploring the First Church Buildings

Because the church building was regarded as sacred, congregants had to undergo a purification ritual before entering. So in the fourth century, fountains were erected in the courtyard so the Christians could wash-up before they entered the building.[108]

Constantine's church buildings were spacious and magnificent edifices that were said to be "worthy of an Emperor." They were so splendid that his pagan contemporaries observed that these "huge buildings imitated" the structure of pagan temples![109] This should come as no surprise. Constantine profusely decorated the new church buildings with pagan art![110]

---

[105] Edward Norman, *The House of God: Church Architecture, Style, and History* (London: Thames and Hudson, 1990), pp. 38-39.

[106] Ibid., p. 31.

[107] *Protestant Worship and Christian Architecture*, p. 56; *Building God's House in the Roman World*, p. 150; *Early Christianity and Society*, pp 152-155.

[108] *From Temple to Meeting House*, p. 185.

[109] This is a quote from the anti-Christian writer Porphyry (*The Secular Use of Church Buildings*, p. 8). Porphyry said that the Christians were inconsistent because they criticized pagan worship, yet erected buildings that imitated pagan temples! (*Building God's House in the Roman World*, p. 129).

[110] *The Story of Christianity* (Gonzalez), p. 122. According to Professor Harvey Yoder, Constantine built the original church of Hagia Sophia (the church of wisdom) on the site of a pagan temple and imported 427 pagan statues from across the Empire to decorate it ("From House Churches to Holy Cathedrals," Lecture given in Harrisburg, VA, Oct., 1993).

The church edifices built under Constantine were patterned exactly after the model of the basilica.[111] The basilica was the common government building.[112] And it was designed after Greek pagan temples.[113]

Basilicas served the same function as high school auditoriums do today. They were wonderful for seating passive and docile crowds that watch a performance. This was one of the reasons why Constantine chose the basilica model.[114]

He also favored it because of his fascination with sun worship. Basilicas were designed so that the sun fell upon the speaker as he faced the congregation.[115] Like the temples of the Greeks and Romans, the Christian basilicas were built with a facade (front) facing east.[116]

Let us explore the inside of the Christian basilica. It was an exact duplicate of the Roman basilica that was used for Roman magistrates and officers. Christian basilicas possessed an elevated platform where the clergy ministered. The platform was usually

---

[111] *The Founders of the Western World*, p. 209. The first basilica was the church of St. John Lateran built from an imperial palace donated in A.D. 314 (*Building God's House in the Roman World*, p. 18). "Constantine, when deciding what the pioneer church of St. John Lateran was to be like, chose the basilica as a model, thereby establishing it as standard for Rome's Christian places of worship" (Lionel Casson, *Everyday Life in Ancient Rome*, Baltimore: The Johns Hopkins University Press, 1998, p. 133).

[112] *Christian History*, Volume XII, No. 1, Issue 37, p. 19; *The House of God*, p. 24; *The Early Liturgy*, p. 123. The word basilica comes from the Greek word *basileus* which means "king." "The Christian architects adapted the pagan plan, installing an altar near the large, rounded recess, or apse, at one end of the edifice, where the king or judge sat; the bishop was now to take the place of the pagan dignitary." Father Michael Collins and Matthew A. Price, *The Story of Christianity* (DK Publishing, 1999), p. 64.

[113] *Protestant Worship and Christian Architecture*, p. 56. One Catholic scholar states, "Long before the Christian epoch, various pagan sects and associations had adapted the basilica type of building to worship" (*The Early Liturgy*, p. 123; *From Temple to Meeting House*, pp. 162-163. Furthermore, Gregory Dix points out that Constantine's churches in Jerusalem and Bethlehem, built between A.D. 320 and 330, were modeled on Syrian pagan sanctuaries (*The Shape of the Liturgy*, New York: The Seabury Press, 1982, p. 26).

[114] Michael Gough, *The Early Christians* (London: Thames and Hudson, 1961), p. 134.

[115] *The Early Christians*, p. 134.

[116] *The Early Liturgy*, p. 137.

elevated by several steps.[117] There was also a rail or screen that separated the clergy from the laity.[118]

In the center of the building was the altar. It was either a table (the altar-table) or a chest covered with a lid.[119] The altar was considered the most holy place in the building for two reasons. First, it often contained the relics of the martyrs.[120] (After the fifth century, the presence of a relic in the church altar was essential to make the church legitimate.)[121] Second, upon the altar sat the Eucharist (the bread and the cup).

The Eucharist, now viewed as a sacred sacrifice, was offered upon the altar.[122] Because they were regarded as "holy men," no one but the clergy was allowed to receive the Eucharist within the altar rails![123]

In front of the altar stood the bishop's chair which was called the *cathedra*.[124] The term *ex cathedra* is derived from this chair. *Ex cathedra* means "from the throne."[125] The bishop's chair, or "throne" as it was called, was the biggest and most elaborate seat in the building. It replaced the seat of the judge in the Roman basilica.[126] And it was surrounded by two rows of chairs reserved for the elders.[127]

---

[117] *Protestant Worship and Church Architecture*, p. 57.

[118] Ibid., pp. 57, 73-74. "The church building in this view was no longer the house of the people of God for their common worship, but the House of God which they were allowed to enter with due reverence. They must remain in the nave (where the congregants sit or stand) and refrain from entering the chancel (the clergy platform) which was for the choir or the sanctuary reserved for the priesthood" (*From Temple to Meeting House*, p 244; *The Growth of Church Institutions*, pp. 219-220).

[119] Altars were first made of wood. Then, beginning in the sixth century, they were made of marble, stone, silver, or gold (*The History of Christianity: Volume 3*, p. 550).

[120] *Ante Pacem*, p. 93; *Protestant Worship and Church Architecture*, p. 58; William D. Maxwell, *An Outline of Christian Worship: Its Developments and Forms* (New York: Oxford University Press, 1936), p. 59.

[121] *A History of Christianity*, p. 204.

[122] *The History of Christianity: Volume 3*, pp. 549-550. In the Protestant church building, the pulpit is in the foreground and the altar-table is in the background.

[123] Ibid., p. 551.

[124] *A History of Religious Architecture*, p. 64.

[125] *The Oxford Dictionary of the Christian Church*, Third Edition, p. 302.

[126] *Protestant Worship and Church Architecture*, p. 57.

[127] *The Secular Use of Church Buildings*, p. 11; *The Shape of the Liturgy*, p. 28.

The sermon was preached from the bishop's chair.[128] The power and authority rested in the chair. The chair was covered with a white linen cloth. The elders and deacons sat on either side of it in a semi-circle.[129] The hierarchical distinction embedded in the basilican architecture was unmistakable.

Interestingly, most modern church buildings have special chairs for the pastor and his staff situated on the platform behind the pulpit. (Like the bishop's throne, the pastor's chair is usually the largest of them all!) All of this is a clear carry over from the pagan basilica.

In addition to all of this, Constantine did not destroy pagan temples on a large scale. Neither did he close them.[130] In some places, existing pagan temples were emptied of their idols and converted into Christian edifices.[131] The Christians used materials stripped from pagan temples and built new church buildings on pagan temple sites.[132]

Major Influences on Worship

The church building brought significant changes to Christian worship. Because the Emperor was the number one "lay-person" in the church, a simple ceremony was not sufficient. In order to honor him, the pomp and ritual of the imperial court was adopted into the Christian liturgy.[133]

It was the custom of the Roman Emperors to have lights carried before them whenever they appeared in public. The lights were

---

[128] *Protestant Worship and Church Architecture*, p. 59.

[129] *The Shape of the Liturgy*, p. 28.

[130] *Early Christianity and Society*, p. 155.

[131] *The House of God*, pp. 23-24.

[132] *Christian History*, Volume XII, No. 1, Issue 37, p. 19. Gregory the Great (540-604) is the first to prescribe the use of holy water and Christian relics to purify pagan temples for Christian use. Bede, *A History of the Christian Church and People* (New York: Dorset Press, 1985), pp. 86-87 (Book I, Chapter 30). These pages contain instructions from Gregory the Great on how pagan temples were to be sanctified for Christian use. See also John Mark Terry, *Evangelism: A Concise History* (Nashville: Broadman & Holman Publishers, 1994), pp. 48-50; *The Secular Use of Church Buildings*, p. 251.

[133] Ibid., p. 20; *Protestant Worship and Church Architecture*, p. 56.

accompanied by a basin of fire filled with aromatic spices.[134] Taking his cue from this custom, Constantine introduced candles and the burning of incense as part of the church service. And they were brought in when the clergy entered the room![135]

Under Constantine's reign, the clergy, who had first worn everyday clothes, began dressing in special garments. What were those special clothes? They were the garments of Roman officials. Further, various gestures of respect toward the clergy were introduced in the church that were comparable to the gestures that were used to honor Roman officials.[136]

The Roman custom of beginning a service with processional music was adopted as well. For this purpose, choirs were developed and brought into the Christian church.[137] Worship became more professional, dramatic, and ceremonial.

All of these features were borrowed from the Greco-Roman culture and carried straight into the Christian church.[138] Fourth-century Christianity was being profoundly shaped by Greek paganism and Roman imperialism.[139] The upshot of it all was that there was an immediate loss of intimacy and open participation. The professional clergy performed the acts of worship while the laity looked on as spectators.[140]

As one Catholic scholar readily admits, with the coming of Constantine *"various customs of ancient Roman culture flowed into the Christian liturgy . . . even the ceremonies involved in the ancient worship of the Emperor as a deity found their way into the church's worship, only in their secularized form."*[141]

---

[134] *The Early Liturgy*, p. 132.

[135] Richard Krautheimer, *Early Christian and Byzantine Architecture* (Middlesex: Penguin Books, 1986), pp. 40-41. Krautheimer gives a vivid description of the parallels between the Roman imperial service and the Christian liturgy under Constantine.

[136] *The Early Liturgy*, pp. 129-133.

[137] See Chapter 6 for a full discussion on the origin of the choir.

[138] *The Story of Christianity* (Gonzalez), p. 125.

[139] Kenneth Scott Latourette traces the strong influence of Greco-Roman paganism into the Christian faith in his book *A History of Christianity* (New York: Harper and Brothers, 1953), pp. 201-218.

[140] *Protestant Worship and Church Architecture*, p. 56.

[141] *The Early Liturgy*, pp. 130, 133.

Constantine brought peace for all Christians.[142] Under his reign, the Christian faith had become legitimate. In fact, it had risen to a status greater than Judaism and paganism.[143]

For these reasons, the Christians saw Constantine's rise to Emperor as an act of God. Here was God's instrument that had come to their rescue. Christianity and Roman culture were now melded together.[144]

The Christian building demonstrates that the church, whether she wanted it or not, had entered into a close alliance with pagan culture.[145] As Will Durant put it, *"Pagan isles remained in the spreading Christian sea."*[146] This was a tragic shift from the primitive simplicity that the church of Jesus Christ first knew.

The first-century Christians saw themselves as set over against the world and avoided any contact with paganism. This all changed during the fourth century when the church emerged as a public institution in the world and began to *"absorb and Christianize pagan religious ideas and practices."*[147] As one historian put it, *"church buildings took the place of temples; church endowments replaced temple lands and funds."*[148] Under Constantine, tax exempt status was granted for all church property.[149]

Consequently, the story of the church building is the sad saga of Christianity borrowing from heathen culture. A borrowing that has

---

[142] Historians call the period of Constantine's reign "the Peace." The Peace actually came with the Edict of Galerian in A.D. 311. It was then popularized by the Edict of Milan in A.D. 313. These edicts stopped Diocletian's vicious persecution of the Christians that was launched in A.D. 303. Just 11 years after the Edict of Milan, Constantine, the first Christian Emperor, became sole ruler of the Roman Empire (*The Story of Christianity* (Gonzalez), pp. 106-107; *Caesar to Christ*, p. 655).

[143] Adolf Von Harnack estimates that there were three to four million Christians in the Empire at the beginning of Constantine's reign. *The Mission and Expansion of Christianity in the First Three Centuries, Volume 2* (New York: G.P. Putnam's Sons, 1908), p. 325. Others estimate it was only four or five percent of the Empire's population (*Christians and the Holy Places*, p. 298).

[144] *A History of Christianity*, p. 126; *Christian History*, Volume XII, No. 1, Issue 37, p. 19.

[145] *The Early Liturgy*, p. 123.

[146] Will Durant, *The Age of Faith* (New York: Simon & Schuster, 1950), p. 8.

[147] *The Search for the Origins of Christian Worship*, p. 65.

[148] *Early Christianity and Society*, p. 163.

[149] Constantine granted tax exempt status in A.D. 323 (*Caesar and Christ*, p. 656).

radically transformed the face of our faith.[150] To put it bluntly, the church buildings of the Constantinian and post-Constantinian era essentially became holy shrines.[151] The Christians embraced the concept of the temple. They imbibed the pagan idea that there exists a special place where God dwells in a special way. And that place is made "with hands."[152]

As with other pagan customs that were absorbed into the Christian faith (the liturgy, the sermon, clerical vestments, the hierarchical leadership structure, etc.), third and fourth-century Christians incorrectly attributed the origin of the church building to the Old Testament.[153] But this was misguided thinking.

The church building was borrowed straight from pagan culture as we have seen. *"Dignified and sacramental ritual had entered the church services by way of the mysteries [the pagan cults], and was justified, like so many other things, by reference to the Old Testament."*[154]

To use the Old Testament as a justification for the church building is not only inaccurate, but self-defeating. The old Mosaic economy of sacred priests, sacred buildings, sacred rituals, and sacred objects has been forever destroyed by the cross of Christ. In addition, it has been replaced by a non-hierarchical, non-ritualistic, non-liturgical organism called the *ekklesia* (church).[155]

---

[150] *Christian History*, Volume XII, No. 1, Issue 37, p. 20.

[151] *From Temple to Meeting House*, pp. 167, 180. Constantine built Christian shrines at the sites of Biblical-historical locations (*Pagans and Christians*, p. 674).

[152] Contrast this with Mark 14:58, Acts 7:48, 2 Cor. 5:1, Heb. 9:11, and Heb. 9:24.

[153] *To Preach or Not to Preach?*, p. 29. J.D. Davies writes, "When Christians began to build their great basilicas, they turned for guidance to their Bible and were soon applying all that was said about the Jerusalem Temple to their new edifices, seemingly ignorant of the fact that in so doing they were behaving contrary to the NT outlook." Davies goes on to say that the cult of the saints [revering dead saints] and its steady penetration of church buildings finally set its seal upon the outlook of the church as a holy place, "towards which Christians should adopt the same attitude as Jews to the Jerusalem Temple and pagans to their shrines" (*The Secular Use of Church Buildings*, pp. 16-17). Oscar Hardman writes, "the Roman system of administration and the architecture of its larger houses and public halls lent suggestive guidance to the church in the grading of its hierarchy and the subsequent defining of spheres of jurisdiction, and in the building of its places of worship" (*A History of Christian Worship*, pp. 13-14).

[154] *The Christian Saga*, p. 209.

[155] Mark 14:58; Acts 7:48; 17:24; Gal. 4:9; Col. 2:14-19; 1 Pet. 2:4-9; Heb. 3-11.

The Evolution of Church Architecture

Following the Constantinian era, church buildings passed through various different stages. (They are too complex for us to detail here.) To quote one scholar, *"Changes in church architecture are the result of mutation rather than a steady line of evolution."*[156] These mutations did little to change the dominant architectural features that fostered a monopolizing clergy and an inert congregation.[157]

Let us quickly survey the evolution of church architecture:

- After Constantine, Christian architecture passed from the basilica phase to the Byzantine phase.[158] Byzantine churches had wide central domes and decorative icons and mosaics.[159]

- Byzantine architecture was followed by Romanesque architecture.[160] Romanesque buildings were characterized by a three-story elevation, massive pillars supporting round arches, and colorful interior.[161] This form of building arose shortly after Charlemagne became Emperor of the Holy Roman Empire on Christmas day A.D. 800.

- Following the Romanesque period was the Gothic era of the 12th century. Gothic architecture gave rise to the spell-binding Gothic cathedrals with their cross-ribbed vaults, pointed arches, and flying buttresses.[162] The term "cathedral" is derived from *cathedra*. It is the building that houses the *cathedra*, the

---

[156] *Protestant Worship and Church Architecture*, p. 51.

[157] Ibid., p. 57.

[158] For details see Richard Krautheimer, *Early Christian and Byzantine Architecture* (Middlesex: Penguin Books, 1986).

[159] For details see *The House of God*, pp. 51-71. The Hagia Sophia (the Church of Holy Wisdom), which opened in AD 360 and was rebuilt in AD 415, is touted by the Eastern church to be the perfect embodiment of a church building.

[160] For details see *A History of Religious Architecture,* Chapter 10.

[161] For details see *The House of God*, pp. 104-135.

[162] For details see *A History of Religious Architecture,* Chapter 11-14 and Otto Van Simon's classic volume *The Gothic Cathedral: Origins of Gothic Architecture & the Medieval Concept of Order* (Princeton: Princeton University Press, 1988).

bishop's chair.[163] It is the church which contains the "throne" of the bishop![164]

Colored glass was first introduced to church buildings in the sixth century with Gregory of Tours (538-593).[165] The glass was set into the narrow windows of some Romanesque churches. Suger (1081-1151), abbot of St. Denis, took colored glass to another level. He adorned the glass with sacred paintings.[166] He thus became the first to use stained-glass windows in church buildings, placing them in his Gothic cathedrals.[167]

Great panels of colored glass came to fill the walls of Gothic churches to emit brilliant, bright colored light.[168] Rich and dark colors were also employed to create the effect of the new Jerusalem. The stained-glass windows of the 12th and 13th centuries have rarely been equaled in their beauty and quality. With their dazzling colors, stained-glass windows effectively created a soulish sense of majesty and splendor. They induced feelings associated with the worship of a mighty, fear-inspiring God.[169]

As is the case with the Constantine basilicas, the root of the Gothic cathedral is completely pagan. Gothic architects relied heavily on the teachings of the pagan Greek philosopher Plato. Plato taught that sound, color, and light have lofty mystical meanings. They can induce moods and help bring one closer to the "Eternal Good."[170] The Gothic designers took Plato's teachings and

---

[163] *Early Christian and Byzantine Architecture*, p. 43.

[164] *The Oxford Dictionary of the Christian Church*, Third Edition, p. 302. Frank Senn explains how the Gothic structure scattered the congregation and reflected the compartmentalization of the clergy from the laity (*Christian Liturgy*, pp. 212-216).

[165] *The Age of Faith*, p. 856.

[166] *The Gothic Cathedral*, p. 122. Frank Senn writes, "More space between the pillars could be filled in with larger windows, which gave a lightness and a brightness to the new buildings that the old Romanesque buildings lacked. The windows could be filled with stained-glass, which could tell the Biblical stories or employ the theological symbols that were previously painted on the walls (*Christian Liturgy*, p. 214).

[167] Ibid., p. 857.

[168] *The Age of Faith*, p. 856.

[169] *The House of God*, pp. 153-154; *Exploring Churches*, pp. 66-67.

[170] *The Gothic Cathedral*, pp. 22-42, 50-55, 58, 188-191, 234-235. Von Simon shows how the metaphysics of Plato shaped Gothic architecture. Light and luminosity reach their perfection in Gothic stained-glass windows. Numbers of perfect proportions harmonize all elements of the building. Light and harmony are images of heaven; they

set them to brick and stone. They created awe-inspiring lighting to elicit a sense of overwhelming splendor and worship.[171]

Color is one of the most powerful emotive factors available. Thus the Gothic stained-glass windows were employed skillfully to create a sense of mystery and transcendence. Drawing inspiration from the grandiose statues and towers of ancient Egypt, Gothic architecture sought to recapture the sense of the sublime through its exaggerated heights.[172]

It was said of the Gothic structure that *"the whole building seems chained to earth in fixed flight . . . It rises like an exhalation from the soil . . . No architecture so spiritualizes, refines and casts heavenward the substance which it handles."*[173] It was the ultimate symbol of heaven joining the earth.[174]

So with its cunning use of light, color, and excessive height, the Gothic cathedral fostered a sense of mystery, transcendence, and awe.[175] All of these features were borrowed from Plato and passed off as Christian.[176]

Basilica, Romanesque, and Gothic church buildings are a human attempt to duplicate that which is heavenly and spiritual.[177] In a very real way, the church building throughout history reflects

---

are the ordering principles of creation. Plato taught that light is the most notable of natural phenomena—the closest to pure form. The Neo-platonists conceived light as a transcendental reality that illuminates our intellect to grasp truth. The Gothic design was essentially a blending together of the visions of Plato, Augustine, and Denis, the pseudo-Areopagite (a noted Neo-platonist).

[171] *Protestant Worship and Church Architecture*, p. 6.

[172] Neil Carter, "The Story of the Steeple," Unpublished manuscript, 2001. The full text can be accessed at www.christinyall.com/steeple.html

[173] *From Temple to Meeting House*, p. 190.

[174] The baroque architecture of the 17th and 18th centuries followed the path of the Gothic in inducing the senses with its harmonious richness and decoration (*Exploring Churches*, pp. 75-77). J.G. Davies states that in the West during the Middle Ages, cathedrals were regarded as models of the cosmos (*The Secular Use of Church Buildings*, p. 220).

[175] *Protestant Worship and Church Architecture*, p. 131.

[176] For a detailed discussion of the historical specificities of Gothic architecture, see Will Durant's *The Age of Faith*, Chapter 32. Although antiquated, Gothic architecture made a reappearance among Protestants with the Gothic revival in the mid-19th century. But Gothic construction ceased after World War II (*Protestant Worship and Church Architecture*, pp. 130-142; *The House of God*, pp. 252-278).

[177] *Christian Liturgy*, p. 604.

man's misguided need to sense the Divine with his human hands and eyes. It reveals the fact that by the fourth century, the Christian community lost touch with those heavenly realities that cannot be perceived by the senses, but which can only be registered by the human spirit.[178]

Worse still, the main message of Gothic architecture is: "God is transcendent and unreachable—so be awed at His majesty." But such a message defies the message of the gospel which says that God is very accessible. So much so that He has taken up residence inside of us!

The Protestant Church Building

In the 16th century, the Reformers inherited the aforementioned building tradition. In a short period of time, thousands of medieval cathedrals became their property.[179]

Most of the Reformers were former priests. Hence, they had been unwittingly conditioned by the thought patterns of medieval Catholicism.[180] So even though the Reformers did some re-modeling to their newly acquired church buildings, they made little functional change in the architecture.[181]

Even if the Reformers wanted to bring radical changes to the practice of the church, the masses were not ready for it.[182] Martin Luther was quite clear that the church was not a building or an

---

[178] See 1 Cor. 2:9-16.
[179] *Protestant Worship and Church Architecture*, p. 64. The first Protestant church building was the castle at Torgua built in 1544 for Lutheran worship. There was no chancel, and the altar had become a simple table (*From Temple to Meeting Place*, p. 206).
[180] *Protestant Worship and Church Architecture*, p. 78.
[181] *A Historical Approach to Evangelical Worship*, pp. 142-143, 225. Interestingly, the 19th and 20th centuries have seen a major revival of medieval architecture among all Protestant bodies (*Protestant Worship and Church Architecture*, p. 64).
[182] *Protestant Worship and Church Architecture*, p. 79.

institution.[183] Yet it would have been impossible for him to overturn more than a millennium of confusion on the subject.[184]

The central architectural change that the Reformers made reflected their theology. They made the pulpit the dominant center of the building rather than the altar-table.[185] The kernel truth of the Reformation was the idea that people could not know God nor grow spiritually unless they heard preaching. Thus when the Reformers inherited existing church buildings, they adapted them toward that end.[186]

The Steeple

Ever since the inhabitants of Babel erected a tower to "reach to the heavens," civilizations have followed suit by building structures with pointed tops.[187] The Babylonians and Egyptians built obelisks and pyramids which reflected their belief that they were

---

[183] "Of all the great teachers of Christianity, Martin Luther perceived most clearly the difference between the *Ecclesia* of the New Testament and the institutional church, and reacted most sharply against the *quid pro quo* which would identify them. Therefore he refused to tolerate the mere word 'church:' he called it an obscure ambiguous term. In his translation of the Bible, he rendered *ecclesia* by 'congregation' . . . he realized that the New Testament *ecclesia* is just not an 'it,' 'a thing,' an 'institution,' but rather a unity of persons, a people, a communion . . . Strong as was Luther's aversion to the word 'church,' the facts of history prove stronger. The linguistic usage of both the Reformation and the post-Reformation era had to come to terms with the so powerfully developed idea of the church, and consequently all the confusion dependent upon the use of this 'obscure ambiguous' word penetrated Reformation theology. It was impossible to put the clock back one millennium and a half. The conception 'church' remained irrevocably moulded by this historical process of 1500 years . . . " (Emil Brunner, *The Misunderstanding of the Church*, London: Lutterworth Press, 1952, pp. 15-16).

[184] Martin Luther, *Luther's Works* (Philadelphia: Fortress Press, 1965), pp. 53-54.

[185] *Protestant Worship and Church Architecture*, p. 82.

[186] *Exploring Churches*, pp. 72-73. The altar-table was moved from the lofty position of "altar" and moved down the chancel (clergy platform) steps, giving it a position of less prominence. The pulpit was moved closer to the nave where the people sat, so as to make the sermon a fixed part of the service.

[187] See Gen. 11:3-9. The story of the steeple is based on Neil Carter's "The Story of the Steeple," Unpublished manuscript, 2001. The full text can be accessed at www.christinyall.com/steeple.html

progressing toward immortality.[188] When Greek philosophy and culture came along, the direction of architecture changed from upward and vertical to downward and horizontal. All of this suggested the Greek belief in democracy, human equality, and earth-bound gods.[189]

However, with the rise of the Roman Catholic Church, the practice of producing pointed tops to crown buildings re-emerged. Toward the end of the Byzantine period, Catholic Popes drew inspiration from the obelisks of ancient Egypt.[190] As religious architecture entered the Romanesque period, points began to appear on the surfaces and corners of every cathedral built in the Roman Empire. This trend reached its pinnacle during the era of Gothic architecture with Abbot Suger's construction of the cathedral at St. Denis.

Unlike Greek architecture, the characteristic line of Gothic architecture was vertical which suggested striving upwards. By this time, all throughout Italy, towers began to appear near the entrances of church buildings. The towers housed bells to call the people to worship.[191] These towers represented contact between heaven and earth.[192]

As the years passed, Gothic architects (enamored with verticality) sought to add a tall spire to every tower.[193] Spires (also called steeples)[194] were a symbol of man's aspiration to be united with His Creator.[195] In the centuries that followed, the towers grew taller and skinnier. They eventually became a visual focal point for the architecture. They also reduced in number, from the double-

---

[188] Zahi Havass, *The Pyramids of Ancient Egypt* (Pittsburgh: Carnegie Museum of Natural History, 1990), p. 1; Ernest H. Short, *A History of Religious Architecture* (New York: The MacMillan Company, 1936), p. 13.

[189] *A History of Religious Architecture*, p. 167.

[190] *The House of God*, p. 160.

[191] Charles Wicks, *Illustrations of Spires and Towers of the Medieval Churches of England* (New York: Hessling & Spielmeyer, 1900), p. 18.

[192] Paul and Teresa Clowney, *Exploring Churches* (Grand Rapids: Eerdmans Publishing Company, 1982), p. 13.

[193] *The Age of Faith*, p. 865.

[194] The British/Anglican term for steeple is "spire."

[195] *Exploring Churches*, p. 13.

towered "westwork" to the singular spire that so characterized the churches of Normandy and Britain.

In the year 1666, something happened that changed the course of tower architecture. A fire swept across the city of London damaging most of its 97 church edifices.[196] Sir Christopher Wren (1632-1723) was then commissioned to redesign all the churches of London. Using his own stylistic innovations in modifying the Gothic spires of France and Germany, Wren created the modern steeple.[197]

In summary, the modern steeple is a medieval invention finding its roots in the Gothic spires and towers.[198] It was improved and popularized by Sir Christopher Wren's building program in London following the Great Fire of 1666. From that point on, the steeple became a dominant feature of Anglo-Saxon architecture.

When the Puritans emerged, they made their church buildings far simpler than their Catholic and Anglican predecessors. But they kept the steeple and brought it into the new world of the Americas.[199] Thus most American churches sport a steeple—a structure that is rooted in the primitive architecture and philosophy of the Babylonians and Egyptians!

The message of the steeple is one that contradicts the message of the NT. Christians do not have to reach into the heavens to find God. He is here! With the coming of Emmanuel, God is with us.[200] And with His resurrection, we have an indwelling Lord. The steeple defies these realities.

---

[196] Gerald Cobb, *London City Churches* (London: Batsford, 1977), p. 15ff.

[197] Viktor Furst, *The Architecture of Sir Christopher Wren* (London: Lund Humphries, 1956), p. 16. Because the churches of London were so tightly sandwiched between other buildings, little room was left for emphasis on anything other than the spire itself. Consequently, Wren established the trend of building churches with relatively plain sides featuring a disproportionately tall and ornate spire on one end (Paul Jeffery, *The City Churches of Sir Christopher Wren,* London: The Hambledon Press, 1996, p.88).

[198] *The House of God*, p. 251.

[199] Peter Williams, *Houses of God* (Chicago: University of Illinois Press, 1997), pp. 7-9; Colin Cunningham, *Stones of Witness* (Gloucestershire: Sutton Publishing, 1999), p. 60.

[200] Matt. 1:23.

The Pulpit

The earliest sermons were delivered from the bishop's chair, or *cathedra,* which was positioned behind the altar.[201] Later the *ambo,*[202] a raised desk on the side of the chancel from which Bible lessons were read, became the place where sermons were delivered.[203] The *ambo* was taken from the Jewish synagogue.[204] However, it has earlier roots in the reading desks and platforms of Greco-Roman antiquity. John Chrysostom (347-407) was noted for making the *ambo* a place for preaching.[205]

As early as A.D. 250, the *ambo* was replaced by the pulpit. Cyprian (200-258) speaks of placing the leader of the church into public office upon the *pulpitum.*[206] Our word "pulpit" is derived from the Latin word *pulpitum* which means "a stage!"[207] The *pulpitum,* or pulpit, was propped up in the highest elevated place in the congregation.[208]

In time, the phrase "to ascend the platform" (*ad pulpitum venire*) became part of the religious vocabulary of the clergy.[209] By A.D. 252, Cyprian alludes to the raised platform which segregated the clergy from the laity as "*the sacred and venerated congestum of the clergy!*"[210]

By the end of the Middle Ages the pulpit became common in parish churches.[211] With the Reformation, it became the central

---

[201] Arthur Pierce Middleton, *New Wine in Old Wineskins* (Connecticut: Morehouse-Barlow Publishing, 1988), p. 76.

[202] The *ambo* is the Latin term for pulpit. It is derived from *ambon* which means "crest of a hill." Most *ambos* were elevated and reached by steps (*Encyclopedia of Early Christianity,* p. 29; Peter F. Anson, *Churches: Their Plans and Furnishings,* Milwaukee: Bruce Publishing Co., 1948, p. 154.

[203] *New Wine in Old Wineskins,* p. 76.

[204] *The Early Christians,* p. 172. *Encyclopedia of Early Christianity,* p. 29. The predecessor of the *ambo* is the "migdal" of the synagogue. "Migdal" means "tower" in Hebrew.

[205] *Encyclopedia of Early Christianity,* p. 29.

[206] Latin for "pulpit." *Building God's House in the Roman World,* p. 124.

[207] Christian Smith, *Going to the Root* (Scottdale: Herald Press, 1992), p. 83.

[208] *Building God's House in the Roman World,* p. 124.

[209] Ibid.

[210] Ibid.

[211] *New Wine in Old Wineskins,* p. 76.

piece of furniture in the church building.[212] The pulpit symbolized the replacement of the centrality of ritualistic action (the Mass) with clerical verbal instruction (the sermon).[213]

In Lutheran churches, the pulpit was moved to the front of the altar.[214] In Reformed churches the pulpit dominated until the altar finally disappeared and was replaced by the "communion table."[215] Today it is unthinkable to have a Protestant church service without the presence of the "sacred desk!"

The pulpit is the centerpiece of the Protestant church. So much so that a well-known pastor who spoke during a conference sponsored by the Billy Graham Evangelistic Association claimed: *"If the church is alive, it's because the pulpit is alive—if the church is dead, it's because the pulpit is dead."*[216]

The pulpit is harmful for it elevates the clergy to a position of prominence. True to its meaning, it puts the preacher at center "stage"—separating and placing him high above God's people.

The Pew and Balcony

Now enter the pew, the great inhibitor of face-to-face fellowship. The pew—the great symbol of lethargy and passivity in the modern church.[217] The pew—that which has made corporate worship a spectator sport.

The word "pew" is derived from the Latin *podium*. It means a seat raised up above floor-level or a "balcony."[218] Pews were unknown to the church building for the first thousand years of Christian history. In the early basilicas, the congregation stood

---

[212] *Exploring Churches*, p. 26.

[213] *Christian Worship and Its Cultural Setting*, p. 45.

[214] Owen Chadwick, *The Reformation* (Penguin Books, 1968), p. 422. In the 16th century, the pulpit was combined with the reading desk (or lectern) to make a single structure—the "two decker." The reading desk was the lower level part of the pulpit (*New Wine in Old Wineskins*, p. 77).

[215] *Christian Worship and Its Cultural Setting*, p. 45.

[216] "All Eyes to the Front: A Look at Pulpits Past and Present," *Your Church*, January/February 2002, p. 44.

[217] James F. White, *The Worldliness of Worship* (New York: Oxford University Press, 1967), p. 43.

[218] *The Oxford Dictionary of the Christian Church*, Third Edition, p. 1271; *Going to the Root*, p. 81.

throughout the entire service.[219] (It is this way today among many Eastern Orthodox.)[220]

By the 13th century, backless benches were gradually introduced into English parish buildings.[221] These benches were made of stone and placed against the walls. They were then moved into the body of the building (the area called the nave).[222] At first, the benches were arranged in a semi-circle around the pulpit. Later they were fixed to the floor.[223]

The modern "pew" was introduced in the 14th century.[224] But it only became common in the 15th century.[225] At that time, wooden benches supplanted the stone seats.[226] By the 18th century, box pews became popular.[227]

Box pews have a comical history. They were furnished with cushioned seats, carpets, and other accessories. They were sold to families and considered private property.[228] Box pew owners set out to make them as comfortable as possible.

Some decorated them with curtains, cushions, padded arm-chairs, fireplaces, and special compartments for pet dogs! It was not uncommon for owners to keep their pews sealed with lock and key![229] After much criticism from the clergy, these embellished pews were replaced with open seats.[230]

Because box pews often had high sides, the pulpits had to be

---

[219] *The Secular Use of Church Buildings*, p. 138. Occasionally a few wooden or stone benches were provided for the aged and sick.

[220] *New Wine in Old Wineskins*, p. 73.

[221] Ibid., p. 74. By the end of the Middle Ages, these pews were elaborately decorated with pictures of saints and fanciful animals (*To Preach or Not to Preach?*, p. 31; J.G. Davies, *The Westminster Dictionary of Worship,* Philadelphia: The Westminster Press, 1972, p. 312).

[222] Doug Adams, *Meeting House to Camp Meeting* (Austin: The Sharing Company, 1981), p. 14.

[223] *Exploring Churches*, p. 28.

[224] *Christian Liturgy*, p. 215.

[225] *Exploring Churches*, p. 28.

[226] *The Secular Use of Church Buildings*, p. 138.

[227] *Protestant Worship and Church Architecture*, p. 101.

[228] *Exploring Churches*, p. 28.

[229] *The Secular Use of Church Buildings*, p. 139; *Exploring Churches*, p. 28.

[230] *The Secular Use of Church Buildings*, p. 139. Some clergymen attacked the abuse of pew decorum. One preacher is noted for giving a sermon lamenting the pew saying that the congregation "wants nothing but beds to hear the Word of God on . . . "

elevated so as to be seen by the people. Thus the "wineglass" pulpit was born during colonial times.[231] The wineglass pulpit caused the pastor to be "high and lifted up" as in Isaiah's vision of the temple. 18th century family box pews were replaced with slip pews so that all the people faced the newly erected high platform where the pastor conducted the service.[232]

So what is the pew? The meaning of the word tells it all. It is a lowered "balcony"—a detached seating from which to watch performances on a stage (the pulpit). It immobilizes the congregation of the saints and renders them mute spectators. It hinders face-to-face fellowship and interaction.

Galleries (or church balconies) were invented by the Germans in the 16th century.[233] They were popularized by the Puritans in the 18th century.[234] Since then balconies have become the trademark of the Protestant church building.[235] Their purpose is to bring the congregation closer to the pulpit.[236] Again, hearing the preacher has always been the main consideration in Protestant church design.[237]

Modern Church Architecture

Over the last 200 years, the two dominating architectural patterns employed by Protestant churches are the divided chancel form (used in liturgical churches) and the concert stage form (used in evangelical churches).[238] The chancel is the area where the clergy (and sometimes the choir) conduct the service.[239] In the chancel-style church, there still exists a rail or screen that separates the clergy from the laity.

The concert-style church building was profoundly influenced by

---

[231] *New Wine in Old Wineskins*, p. 74.
[232] *Meeting House to Camp Meeting*, p. 14.
[233] *Protestant Worship and Church Architecture*, p. 85.
[234] Ibid., p. 107.
[235] Ibid., p. 85.
[236] Ibid., p. 107.
[237] *Exploring Churches*, p. 74.
[238] *Protestant Worship and Church Architecture*, p. 118.
[239] *Exploring Churches*, p. 17.

19th-century revivalism.[240] It is essentially an auditorium. The concert-style building is structured so as to emphasize the dramatic performance of the preacher and the choir.[241] Its structure implicitly suggests that the choir (or worship team) performs for the congregation to stimulate its worship or entertain them.[242] It also calls excessive attention to the preacher whether he is standing or sitting.

In the concert-style building, a small communion table usually appears on the floor below the pulpit. The communion table is typically decorated with brass candlesticks, a cross, and flowers.[243] Two candles on the communion table have become the sign of orthodoxy in most Protestant churches today.[244] As with so many parts of the church service, the presence of candles was borrowed from the ceremonial court of the Roman Empire.[245]

Yet despite these variations, all Protestant architecture produces the same sterile effects that were present in the Constantinian basilicas. They continue to maintain the unbiblical cleavage between clergy and laity, and they encourage the congregation to assume a spectator role.[246] The arrangement and mood of the building conditions the congregation toward passivity.[247] The pulpit platform acts like a stage, and the congregation occupies the theater.[248] In short, Christian architecture has been stalemated since it was born in the fourth century.

Exegeting the Building

At this point, you may be thinking to yourself, *"So what's the big deal? Who cares if the first-century Christians did not have*

---

[240] *Protestant Worship and Church Architecture*, p. 121ff.

[241] *From Temple to Meeting House*, pp. 237, 241.

[242] *Protestant Worship and Church Architecture*, p. 140.

[243] *Protestant Worship and Church Architecture*, p. 129. Some churches have built-in baptistries behind the pulpit and choir. In the Catholic tradition, candles were not commonly placed on the altar-table until the 11th century (*The Early Liturgy*, p. 133).

[244] *Protestant Worship and Church Architecture*, p. 134.

[245] Ibid., p. 133.

[246] Ibid., pp. 120, 141.

[247] Ibid., p. 125.

[248] Ibid., p. 129.

buildings? Or if church buildings were built on pagan beliefs and practices. Or if medieval Catholics based their architecture on pagan philosophy. What has that got to do with us today?"

In *Rethinking the Wineskin*, I explain that the social location of the church meeting expresses and influences the character of the church.[249] If you assume that where the church gathers is simply a matter of convenience, you are tragically mistaken. You are overlooking a basic reality of humanity. Every building we encounter elicits a response from us. By its interior and exterior, it explicitly shows us what the church is and how it functions.

To put it in the words of Henri Lefebvre, *"Space is never empty; it always embodies a meaning."*[250] This principle is incarnated in the architectural motto "form follows function." The form of the building reflects its particular function.[251]

The social setting of a church's meeting-place is a good index of that church's understanding of God's purpose for His Body. A church's location teaches us how to meet. It teaches us what is important and what is not. And it teaches us what is acceptable to say to each other and what is not.

We learn these lessons from the setting in which we gather—whether it be a church edifice or a private home. These lessons are by no means "neutral." Go into any given church building and exegete the architecture. Ask yourself what is higher and what is lower. Ask yourself what is at the front and what is at the back. Ask yourself in what ways it might be possible to "adjust" what goes on at the spur of the moment. Ask yourself

---

[249] *Rethinking the Wineskin*, Chapter 3. As J.G. Davies says, "The question of church building is inseparable from the question of the church and of its function in the modern world" (*The Secular Use of Church Buildings*, p.208).

[250] Leonard Sweet, "Church Architecture for the 21st Century," *Your Church Magazine*, March/April 1999, p. 10. In this article, Sweet tries to envision post-modern church buildings which break out of the old mold of architecture which promotes passivity. Ironically, however, Sweet himself is unwittingly held captive to the old paradigm of church buildings as being sacred spaces. He writes, "Of course, you are not just putting up a building when you build a church; you are constructing sacred space." This sort of paganistic thinking runs deep!

[251] *Christian Liturgy*, p. 212. The auditorium-styled church building turns the congregation into a passive audience while the Gothic-style scatters it through a long, narrow nave or into nooks and crannies (p. 604).

how easy or hard it would be for a church member to speak where he is seated so that all may see and hear him.

If you look at the church building setting and ask yourself these questions (and others like them), you will understand why the modern church has the character it does. If you ask the same set of questions about a living room, you will get a very different set of answers. You will understand why being church in a house setting (as were the early Christians) has the character it does.

The church's social location is a crucial player in church life. It cannot be assumed as simply "an accidental truth of history."[252] Social locations can teach good and godly people very bad lessons and choke their lives together. Calling attention to the importance of the social location of the church (house or church edifice) helps us to understand the tremendous power of our social environment.

To put a finer point on it, the church building is based on the benighted idea that worship is a qualitatively different kind of thing from everyday life. People vary, of course, on how profoundly they emphasize this disjunction. Some groups have gone out of their way to emphasize it by insisting that worship could only occur in specific kinds of spaces designed to make you feel differently than you feel in everyday life.

The disjunction between worship and everyday life characterizes Western Christianity. Worship is seen as something detached from the whole fabric of life and packaged for group consumption. Centuries of Gothic architecture have taught us badly about what worship really is. Few people can walk into a powerful cathedral without experiencing the power of the space.

The lighting is indirect and subdued. The ceilings are obscenely high. The colors are earthy and rich. Sound travels in a specific way. All these things work together to give us a sense of awe and wonder. They are designed to manipulate the senses and create a "worshipful atmosphere."[253]

Some traditions add smells to the mix. But the effect is always the same: Our senses interact with our space to bring us to a

---

[252] A quote from Gotthold Lessing (*Lessing's Theological Writings*).
[253] *Protestant Worship and Church Architecture*, p. 5.

particular state of the soul. A state of awe, mystery, and transcendence that equals an escape from normal life.[254]

We Protestants have thrown out some of these elements and replaced them with a specific use of music to achieve the same end. Consequently, in Protestant circles "good" worship leaders are those who can use music to evoke what other traditions use space to evoke. That which they evoke is a soulish sense of worshipfulness.[255] But this is disjointed from every day life. Not to mention that it is not real. Jonathan Edwards rightfully pointed out that emotions are transient and cannot be used to measure one's relationship with God.[256]

This disjunction between secular and spiritual is highlighted by the fact that the typical church building requires you to "process" in by walking up stairs or moving through a narthex. The reason for this is that you are going from everyday life to another life. Thus a transition is required. All of this flunks the Monday test. No matter how good Sunday was, Monday morning still comes to test our worship.[257]

Watch a choir robe up before the church service. They smile, laugh, and even joke. But once the service starts, they become different people. You will not catch them smiling or laughing. This false separation of secular and sacred . . . this "stained-glass mystique" of Sunday morning church flies in the face of truth and reality.

In addition, the church building is not a friendly place. It is cold, uncomfortable, and impersonal.[258] It is not designed for intimacy nor fellowship. In most church buildings, the seating consists of wooden pews bolted to the floor. The pews (or chairs) are arranged in rows, all facing toward the pulpit. The pulpit sits on an elevated platform where the clergy sits (remnants of the Roman basilica).

---

[254] *The Worldliness of Worship*, pp. 79-83.

[255] Plato was fearful of exposing the youth to certain types of music because it might excite the wrong emotions (*The Republic*, 3:398).

[256] *Protestant Worship and Church Architecture*, p. 19.

[257] These insights owe much to my friend Hal Miller.

[258] R. Sommer speaks of a "sociofugal space" as a place where people tend to avoid personal contact with one another. The modern church building fits Sommer's description rather nicely ("Sociofugal Space," *American Journal of Sociology*, 72, 1967, p. 655).

Again, the architecture of the Protestant church building points all of its arrows in the direction of the person who delivers the sermon. The building is suited for a pulpit domination. And it equally puts constraints on the functioning of the congregation.[259]

This arrangement makes it nearly impossible for one worshipper to look into the face of another. Instead, it creates a sit-and-soak form of worship that turns functioning Christians into "pew potatoes!" To state it differently, the very architecture prevents fellowship except between God and His people via the pastor! And yet despite these facts, we Christians still believe the building is sacred.

Granted, some of you may sternly object to the idea that the church building is sacred. But (for most of you) your actions betray you. Listen to yourself speak of the church building. You still call it "church" and sometimes refer to it as "God's house." The general consensus among Christians of all denominations is that *"a church is essentially a place set apart for worship."*[260] This has been true for the last 1700 years. Constantine is still living and breathing in the minds of most Christians today.

The Obscenely High Cost of Overhead

Most Christians mistakenly view the church building as a necessary part of worship. Therefore, the financial question of building and maintenance becomes a non-issue.

The church edifice demands a vast wasteland of money. In the United States alone, real estate owned by institutional churches today amounts to over 230 billion dollars.[261] Church building debt, service, and maintenance consumes about 18% of the 11 billion dollars that are tithed to churches annually.[262] Point: Modern Christians are wasting an astronomical amount of money on unnecessary edifices!

There is no good reason to possess a church building. In fact, all the traditional reasons put forth for "needing" a building collapse

---

[259] *To Preach or Not to Preach?*, p. 30.
[260] *The Secular Use of Church Buildings*, p. 206.
[261] *Going to the Root*, p. 95.
[262] Ibid.

under careful scrutiny.[263] We so easily forget that the early Christians turned the world upside down without them.[264] They grew rapidly for 300 years without the help (or hindrance) of church buildings.

In the business world, overhead kills. Overhead is what gets added onto the "real" work a business does for its clients. Overhead pays for the building, the pencils, and the accounting staff. Overhead kills because it prices out the business of the market without adding to the "real" value the workers deliver to their customers.

Those who opt to meet in homes rather than church edifices have cut out two very fat overhead accounts: Salaried pastors and church buildings. Contrast this with the overhead of a house church. Rather than paid staff and building "overhead" siphoning off 50-85% of the house church's monetary giving, its overhead amounts to a small percent of their budget. A house church can use more than 95% of its shared money for delivering real services like ministry, mission, and outreach to the world.[265]

Church buildings (as well as salaried pastors) represent very large on-going expenses rather than just one-time outlays. These budget-busters take their cut out of a church's monetary giving not just today, but next month, next year, and so on. By removing those two overhead accounts from a church's financial world, the church will manage to reduce its overhead to a few hundred dollars a year. The rest of the church's shared finances can be used to deliver the church's mission (another subject altogether).

Can We Defy This Tradition?

The church building is a hindrance not a help. It rips at the heart of the Christian faith—a faith that was born in living rooms. Every

---

[263] Howard Snyder demolishes most common arguments for "needing" church buildings in his book *Radical Renewal: The Problem of Wineskins Today* (Houston: Touch Publications, 1996), pp. 62-74.

[264] Acts 17:6.

[265] For a discussion on why the early Christians met in homes and how large congregations can move into house churches, see *Rethinking the Wineskin* Chapter 3.

Sunday morning, you sit in a building which has pagan origins and is built upon pagan philosophy.

There does not exist a shred of Biblical support for the church building. Yet you, dear Christian, continue to pay good money to sanctify your brick and stone. By doing so, you have supported an artificial setting where you are lulled into passivity and prevented from being natural or intimate.[266] (Even if you are having sweet fellowship in the parking lot, it is squelched once you hit the front door and enter the foyer.)

We are completely unaware of what we lost as Christians when we created the church building. We have become victims of our past. Tradition has shot us down.

We have been fathered by Constantine who gave us the prestigious status of owning a building. We have been blinded by the Romans and Greeks who forced upon us their hierarchically structured basilicas. We have been taken by the Goths who imposed upon us their Platonic architecture. We have been hijacked by the Egyptians and Babylonians who gave us our sacred steeples. And we have been swindled by the Athenians who imposed on us their Doric columns.[267]

We somehow have been taught to feel holier when we are in "the house of God." We have inherited a pathological dependency upon an edifice to carry out our worship to God. But the reality is that there is nothing more stagnating, artificial, impersonal or stuffy than a clinical church building! In that building, you are nothing more than a statistic—a name on an index card to be filed in the pastor's secretary's office. There is nothing warm or personal about it.

At bottom, the church building has taught us badly about what church is and what it does. The building is an architectural denial of the priesthood of all believers. It is a contradiction of the very

---

[266] One English Catholic writer put it this way, "If there is one simple method of saving the church's mission it is probably the decision to abandon church buildings for they are basically unnatural places . . . and they do not correspond to anything which is normal in everyday life" (*From Temple to Meeting Place*, p. 323).

[267] Richard Bushman, *The Refinement of America* (New York : Alfred Knopf, 1992,) p. 338. Between 1820 and 1840, American churches began to appear with Doric columns reminiscent of Greek classicism and archways reminiscent of ancient Rome (*Houses of God*, p. 12).

nature of the *ekklesia*—which is a countercultural community. The church building impedes our understanding and experience that the church is Christ's functioning Body that lives and breathes under His direct Headship.

The emergence of the church building is nothing more than Judaism and paganism breaking forth in a new guise. The implicit hierarchical distinctions present in its architecture would be rejected by most Protestants if they were put into words. But for centuries we have unconsciously accepted them. Why? Because of the blinding power of tradition.

It is high time we Christians wake up to the fact that we are not being Biblical or spiritual by accepting and supporting church buildings. John Newton rightly said, *"Let not him who worships under a steeple condemn him who worships under a chimney."* I wish to add a question to that quote: What Biblical or historical authority does any Christian have to gather under a steeple in the first place?

That the Christians in the apostolic age erected special houses of worship is out of the question . . . As the Savior of the world was born in a stable, and ascended to heaven from a mountain, so his apostles and their successors down to the third century, preached in the streets, the markets, on mountains, in ships, sepulchers, caves, and deserts, and in the homes of their converts. But how many thousands of costly churches and chapels have since been built and are constantly built in all parts of the world to the honor of the crucified Redeemer, who in the days of his humiliation had no place of his own to rest his head!

 -Philip Schaff

CHAPTER 4

THE PASTOR: THIEF OF EVERY-MEMBER FUNCTIONING

It is a universal tendency in the Christian religion, as in many other religions, to give a theological interpretation to institutions which have developed gradually through a period of time for the sake of practical usefulness, and then read that interpretation back into the earliest periods and infancy of these institutions, attaching them to an age when in fact nobody imagined that they had such a meaning.
-Richard Hanson

The Pastor.[1] He is the fundamental figure of the Protestant faith. He is the chief, cook, and bottle-washer of today's Christianity. So prevailing is the Pastor in the minds of most Christians that he is better known, more highly praised, and more heavily relied upon than Jesus Christ Himself!

Remove the Pastor and modern Christianity collapses. Remove the Pastor and virtually every Protestant church would be thrown into a panic. Remove the Pastor and Protestantism as we know it dies. The Pastor is the dominating focal point, mainstay, and centerpiece of the modern church. He is the embodiment of Protestant Christianity.

But here is the profound irony. There is not a single verse in the entire NT that supports the existence of the modern day Pastor! He simply did not exist in the early church.

(Note that I am using the term "Pastor" throughout this chapter

---

[1] I am capitalizing the word "Pastor" in this chapter to draw attention to the office rather than to the person that fills it.

to depict the modern pastoral *office* and *role*. I am not speaking of the specific *individuals* who fill this role. By and large, those who serve in the office of Pastor are wonderful people. They are honorable, decent, and often gifted Christians who love God and have a zeal to serve His people. But it is the *role* they are fulfilling that both Scripture and church history are opposed to as this chapter will show.)[2]

The Pastor is in the Bible . . . Right?

The word "Pastors" does appear in the NT:

And he gave some as apostles, and some as prophets, and some as evangelists, and some as PASTORS and teachers (Ephesians 4:11, NASB).

The following observations are to be made about this text.

- This is the only verse in the NT where the word "Pastor" is used.[3] One solitary verse is a mighty scanty piece of evidence on which to hang the entire Protestant faith! In this regard, there is more Biblical authority for snake handling than there is for the modern Pastor. (Mark 16:18 and Acts 28:3-6 both mention handling snakes. So snake handling wins out two verses to one verse.)[4]

- The word is used in the *plural*. It is "Pastors." This is significant. For whoever these "Pastors" are, they are plural in the church, not singular. Consequently, there is no Biblical support for the practice of *Sola Pastora* (single Pastor).

---

[2] Most men and women who become Pastors have never considered the roots of this office. And they were never offered any other alternative way by which to serve God. This, indeed, is a terrible tragedy. (See the *Calf-Path* poem on page 31.) Nevertheless, though their office is without Scriptural merit, Pastors often do help people. But they help people *despite* their office, not because of it.

[3] A derivative from of the word *poimen* is used in Acts 20:28 and 1 Peter 5:2-3.

[4] There is just as much Biblical support for the Pastor as there is for baptisms for the dead. Both are mentioned only once in the entire Bible! (1 Cor. 15:29).

- The Greek word translated "Pastors" is *poimen*. It means shepherds. ("Pastor" is the Latin word for shepherd.) "Pastor," then, is a metaphor to describe a particular function in the church. It is not an office or a title.[5] A first-century shepherd had nothing to do with the specialized and professional sense it has come to have in modern Christianity. Therefore, Ephesians 4:11 does not envision a pastoral office, but merely one of many functions in the church. Shepherds are those who naturally provide nurture and care for God's sheep. It is a profound error, therefore, to confuse shepherds with an office or title as is commonly conceived today.[6]

- At best, this text is oblique. It offers absolutely no definition or description of who Pastors are. It simply mentions them. Regrettably, we have filled this word with our own Western concept of what a Pastor is. We have read the modern idea of the modern Pastor back into the NT. Never in the imagination of a hallucinating man would any first-century Christian conceive of the modern pastoral office! Catholics have made the same error with the word "priest." You can find the word "priest" used in the NT to refer to a Christian three times.[7] Yet a priest in the first-century church was a far cry from the man who dresses in black and wears a backwards collar!

Richard Hanson makes this point plain when he says, *"For us the words bishops, presbyters, and deacons are stored with the associations of nearly two thousand years. For the people who first*

---

[5] The NT never uses the secular Greek words for civil and religious authorities to depict ministers in the church. Further, even though most NT authors were steeped in the Jewish priestly system of the Old Testament, they never use *hiereus* (priest) to refer to Christian ministry. Ordination to office presupposes a static and definable church leadership role that did not exist in the apostolic churches. Marjorie Warkentin, *Ordination: A Biblical-Historical View* (Grand Rapids: Eerdmans, 1982), pp. 160-161, 166; *Who is Your Covering?* Chapters 1-3.

[6] Tragically, some men would give their teeth just to be called "Pastor" or "Reverend." The words of Job come to mind: "Let me not, I pray you, accept any man's person, neither let me give flattering titles unto man" (Job 32:21).

[7] Revelation 1:6; 5:10; 20:6. Every believer is a priest according to the NT. R. Paul Stevens, *The Other Six Days: Vocation, Work, and Ministry in Biblical Perspective* (Grand Rapids: Eerdmans, 1999), pp. 173-181.

used them the titles of these offices can have meant little more than inspectors, older men and helpers . . . it was when unsuitable theological significance began to be attached to them that the distortion of the concept of Christian ministry began. "[8]

In my books *Rethinking the Wineskin* and *Who is Your Covering?*, I show that first-century shepherds were the local elders (presbyters)[9] and overseers of the church.[10] And their function was completely at odds with the modern pastoral role.[11]

Where Did He Come From?

If the modern Pastor was absent from the early church, where did he come from? And how did he rise to such a prominent position in the Christian faith? It is a painful tale, the roots of which are tangled and complex. Those roots reach as far back as the fall of man.

With the fall came an implicit desire in man to have a physical leader to bring him to God. For this reason, human societies throughout history have consistently created a special spiritual caste of religious icons. The medicine man, the shaman, the rhapsodist, the miracle worker, the witch-doctor, the soothsayer, the wise-man, and the priest have all been with us since Adam's blunder.[12]

Fallen man has always had the desire to erect a special priestly caste who is uniquely endowed to beseech the gods on his behalf.[13] This quest is in our bloodstream. It lives in the marrow of our bones. As fallen creatures, we seek a person who is endowed with

---

[8] Richard Hanson, *Christian Priesthood Examined* (Guildford and London: Lutterworth Press, 1979), pp. 34-35.

[9] This word is the spelling into English letters of the Greek word for "elder" (*presbuteros*).

[10] The terms "overseers" and "servants" were later ecclesiasticized into the words "bishops" and "deacons" (M. Smith, *From Christ to Constantine*, Downer's Grove: InterVarsity Press, 1971, p. 32).

[11] *Rethinking the Wineskin*, Chapters 5-6; *Who is Your Covering?*, Chapters 1-2.

[12] "Christianity . . . learnt from the example of pagan religions that most men find it difficult to understand or approach God without the aid of a man who in some sense stands for God, represents Him, and feels called to devote himself to this representative ministry" (*Christian Priesthood Examined*, p. 100).

[13] A distinguishing feature of every religion is a separate human priesthood.

special spiritual powers. And that person is always marked by special training, special garb, a special vocabulary, and a special way of life.[14]

We can see this instinct rear its ugly head in the history of ancient Israel. It made its first appearance during the time of Moses. Two servants of the Lord, Eldad and Medad, received God's Spirit and began to prophesy. In hasty response, a young zealot urged Moses to "restrain them!"[15] Moses reproved the young suppressor saying that *all* of God's people may prophesy. Moses had set himself against a clerical spirit that had tried to control God's people.

We see it again when Moses ascended Mount Horeb. The people wanted Moses to be a physical mediator between them and God. For they feared a personal relationship with the Almighty.[16]

This fallen instinct made another appearance during the time of Samuel. God wanted His people to live under His direct Headship. But Israel clamored for a human king instead.[17]

The seeds of the modern Pastor can even be detected in the NT era. Diotrephes, who "loved to the have the preeminence" in the church, illegitimately took control of its affairs.[18] In addition, some scholars have suggested that the doctrine of the Nicolaitans that Jesus condemns in Revelation 2:6 is a reference to the rise of an early clergy.[19]

Alongside of man's fallen quest for a human spiritual mediator is his obsession with the hierarchical form of leadership. All ancient cultures were hierarchical in their social structures to one degree or another. Regrettably, the post-apostolic Christians

---

[14] Walter Klassen, "New Presbyter is Old Priest Writ Large," *Concern 17*, 1969, p. 5. See also W. Klassen, J.L. Burkholder, and John Yoder, *The Relation of Elders to the Priesthood of Believers* (Washington: Sojourner's Book Service, 1969).

[15] Numbers 11:26-28.

[16] Exodus 20:19.

[17] 1 Samuel 8:19.

[18] 3 John 9-10.

[19] F.W. Grant, *Nicolaitanism or the Rise and Growth of Clerisy* (Bedford: MWTB), pp. 3-6. The Greek word *nicolaitane* means "conquering the people." *Nikos* mean "to conquer over" and *laos* means "the people." Grant believes that Nicolaitans are those who make "laity" out of God's people by raising up "clergy" to lord it over them. See also Alexander Hay, *What Is Wrong in the Church?*, p. 54.

adopted and adapted these structures into their church life as we shall see.

The Birth of One-Bishop-Rule

Up until the second century, the church had no official leadership. In this regard, the first-century churches were an oddity indeed. They were religious groups without priest, temple, or sacrifice.[20] The Christians themselves led the church under Christ's direct Headship.

Among the flock were the elders (shepherds or overseers). These men all stood on an equal footing. There was no hierarchy among them.[21] Also present were extra-local workers who planted churches. These were called "sent-ones" or apostles. But they did not take up residency in the churches for which they cared. Nor did they control them.[22] The vocabulary of NT leadership allows no pyramidal structures. It is rather a language of horizontal relationships that includes exemplary action.[23]

This was all true until Ignatius of Antioch (35-107) stepped on the stage. Ignatius was the first figure in church history to take the initial step down the slippery slope toward a single leader in the church. We can trace the origin of the modern Pastor and church hierarchy to him.

---

[20] James D.G. Dunn, *New Testament Theology in Dialogue* (Philadelphia: Westminster Press, 1987), pp. 123, 127-129.

[21] In the writings of the early church fathers, the words "shepherd," "overseers," and "elder" are always used interchangeably, as is the case in the NT. F.F. Bruce states, "That the language of the New Testament does not allow us to press a distinction between the Greek word translated "bishop" (*episkopos*) and that translated "elder" (*presbyteros*) need not be argued at length. Paul could address the assembled *elders* of the church of Ephesus as those whom the Holy Spirit had made *bishops*. Later, in the Pastoral Epistles (those to Timothy and Titus), the two terms still appear to be used interchangeably" (*The Spreading Flame*, Grand Rapids: Eerdmans, 1958, p. 65). In fact, bishops, elders, and shepherds (always in the plural) continue to be regarded as identical in the writings of 1 Clement, the *Didache*, and *Hermas*. They were seen as identical up until the beginning of the second century. See also James Mackinnon, *Calvin and the Reformation* (New York: Russell and Russell, 1962), pp. 80-81; Everett Ferguson, *Early Christians Speak: Faith and Life in the First Three Centuries* (Abilene: A.C.U. Press, Third Edition, 1999), pp. 169-173.

[22] See Chapter 5 of *Who is Your Covering?* for details.

[23] 1 Cor. 11:1; 2 Thess. 3:9; 1 Tim. 4:12; 1 Pet. 5:3.

Ignatius elevated one of the elders above all the others. The elevated elder was now called "the bishop." All the responsibilities that belonged to the college of elders were exercised by the bishop.[24]

In A.D. 107, Ignatius wrote a series of letters when on his way to be martyred in Rome. Six out of seven of these letters strike the same chord. They are filled with an exaggerated exaltation of the authority and importance of the bishop's office.[25]

According to Ignatius, the bishop has ultimate power and should be obeyed absolutely. Consider the following excerpts from his letters: *"All of you follow the bishop as Jesus Christ follows the Father ... No one is to do any church business without the bishop ... Wherever the bishop appears, there let the people be ... You yourselves must never act independently of your bishop and clergy. You should look on your bishop as a type of the Father ... Whatever he approves, that is pleasing to God ... "*[26]

For Ignatius, the bishop stood in the place of God while the presbyters stood in the place of the twelve apostles.[27] It fell to the bishop alone to celebrate the Lord's Supper, conduct baptisms, give counsel, discipline church members, approve marriages, and preach sermons.[28]

The elders sat with the bishop at the Lord's Supper. But it was the bishop who presided over it. He took charge of leading public prayers and ministry.[29] Only in the most extreme cases could a so-called "layman" take the Lord's Supper without the bishop

---

[24] *Early Christians Speak*, p. 173.

[25] *The Spreading Flame*, pp. 66-67.

[26] These quotes appear in Ignatius' letters to the churches in Asia Minor. *Early Christian Writings: The Apostolic Fathers* (New York: Dorset Press, 1968), pp. 75-123.

[27] Edwin Hatch, *The Organization of the Early Christian Churches* (London: Longmans, Green, and Co., 1895), p. 185. p. 106; *Early Christian Writings: The Apostolic Fathers*, p. 88. Hatch's book shows that the gradual evolution of the organization of the church and various elements of that organization were borrowed from Greco-Roman society.

[28] Robert M. Grant, *The Apostolic Fathers: A New Translation and Commentary, 6 Volumes* (New York: Thomas Nelson and Sons, 1964), Vol. 1, pp. 58, 171.

[29] R. Alastair Campbell, *The Elders: Seniority Within Earliest Christianity* (Clark T & T, 1994) p. 229.

present.[30] For the bishop, said Ignatius, must "preside" over the elements and distribute them.

To Ignatius' mind, the bishop was the remedy for dispelling false doctrine and establishing church unity.[31] Ignatius believed that if the church would survive the onslaught of heresy, it had to develop a rigid power structure patterned after the centralized political structure of Rome.[32] Single-bishop-rule would rescue the church from heresy and internal strife.[33]

Historically this is known as the "monoepiscopate" or "the monarchical episcopacy." It is the type of organization where the bishop is distinguished from the elders (the presbytery) and ranks above them.

At the time of Ignatius, the one-bishop-rule had not caught on in other regions.[34] But by the mid-second century, this model was firmly established in most churches.[35] By the end of the third century, it prevailed everywhere.[36]

The bishop eventually became the main administrator and distributor of the church's wealth.[37] He was the man responsible for teaching the faith and knowing what Christianity was all about.[38] The congregation, once active, was now rendered deaf and mute. The saints merely watched the bishop perform.

---

[30] *The Organization of the Early Christian Churches*, p. 124.

[31] Ibid., p. 100.

[32] Kenneth Strand, "The Rise of the Monarchical Episcopate," in *Three Essays on Church History* (Ann Arbor: Braun-Brumfield, 1967); *Ordination: A Biblical-Historical View*, p. 175.

[33] *Christian Priesthood Examined*, p. 69; *Early Christian Writings: The Apostolic Fathers*, pp. 63-72.

[34] *The Spreading Flame*, pp. 66-69; H. Richard Niebuhr and Daniel D. Williams, ed. *The Ministry in Historical Perspectives* (San Francisco: Harper and Row Publishers, 1956), pp. 23-25. When Ignatius wrote his letters, the one-bishop-rule was being practiced in such Asian cities as Ephesus, Philadelphia, Magnesia, and Smyrna. But it had not yet reached Greece or the West, such as Rome. It appears that the one-bishop-rule moved in a westward direction from Syria across the Empire.

[35] *Christian Priesthood Examined*, p. 67; *The Spreading Flame*, p. 69. J.B. Lightfoot's *The Christian Ministry* is the most satisfactory explanation of the historical evidence of how the bishop gradually developed out of the presbytery.

[36] *The Ministry in Historical Perspectives*, p. 25.

[37] S.L. Greenslade, *Shepherding the Flock*, p. 8.

[38] *Christian Priesthood Examined*, p. 68.

In effect, the bishop became *the* solo Pastor of the church[39]—the professional in common worship.[40] He was seen as the spokesperson and head of the congregation. The one through whose hands ran all the threads of control. All of these roles made the bishop the forerunner of the modern Pastor.

From Presbyter to Priest

By the mid-third century, the authority of the bishop had hardened into a fixed office.[41] Then Cyprian of Carthage (200-258) appeared, furthering the damage.

Cyprian was a former pagan orator and teacher of rhetoric.[42] When he became a Christian, he began to write prolifically. But some of Cyprian's pagan ideas were never abandoned.

Due to Cyprian's influence, the door was open to resurrect the Old Testament economy of priests, temples, altars, and sacrifices.[43] Bishops began to be called "priests,"[44] a custom that became common by the third century.[45] They were also called "Pastors" on

---

[39] Edwin Hatch, *The Growth of Church Institutions* (Hodder and Stoughton, 1895), p. 35.

[40] James F. White, *Protestant Worship and Church Architecture* (New York: Oxford University Press, 1964), pp. 65-66.

[41] *The Early Christian Church*, p. 92. For a brief synopsis of how the clergy developed, see *The Other Six Days*, pp. 39-48.

[42] *St. Cyprian of Carthage* (http://www.comeandseeicons.com/phm12.htm).

[43] James Hastings Nichols, *Corporate Worship in the Reformed Tradition* (Philadelphia: The Westminster Press, 1968), p. 25.

[44] *Early Christians Speak*, p. 168. Cyprian normally called the bishop *sacerdos*, which is Latin for "priest." Sacerdotal language taken from the Old Testament to define church offices quickly caught on (*Ordination: A Biblical-Historical View*, p. 177; *From Christ to Constantine*, p. 136). J. B. Lightfoot wrote that the "sacerdotal view of the ministry is one of the most striking and important phenomena in the history of the church" (J.B. Lightfoot, *Saint Paul's Epistle to the Philippians*, London: Macmillian & Co, 1888, p. 144).

[45] *Christian Priesthood Examined*, pp. 35, 95. There is no evidence that anyone thought of Christian ministers as priests until the year A.D. 200. Tertullian is the first to apply the term "priest" to bishops and presbyters. Throughout his writings, he calls the bishop and the presbyters *sacerdos* (priests) and he calls the bishop *sacerdos summus* (high priest). He does so without any explanation, indicating that his readers were familiar with these titles (p. 38). See also Hans Von Campenhausen, *Tradition and Life in the Church* (Philadelphia: Fortress Press, 1968), p. 220. Cyprian is also credited for saying that the bishop is the equivalent of the Old Testament high priest

occasion.[46] In the third century, every church had its own bishop.[47] And bishops and presbyters together started to be called "the clergy."[48]

The origin of the unbiblical doctrine of "covering" can be laid at the feet of Cyprian also.[49] Cyprian taught that the bishop has no superior but God. He was accountable to God alone. Anyone who separates himself from the bishop separates himself from God.[50] Cyprian also taught that a portion of the Lord's flock was assigned to each individual shepherd (bishop).[51]

After the Council of Nicea (325), bishops began to delegate the responsibility of the Lord's Supper to the presbyters.[52] Presbyters were little more than deputies of the bishop, exercising his authority in his churches.

Because the presbyters were the ones administering the Lord's Supper, they began to be called "priests."[53] More startling, the bishop came to be regarded as "the high priest" who could forgive

---

(*From Christ to Constantine*, p. 136). The historian Eusebius regularly calls clergy "priests" in his voluminous writings (*Christian Priesthood Examined*, p. 61).

[46] "Thus it was the bishop, as chief Pastor of the local church, who came to represent the fullness of the ministry. He was prophet, teacher, chief celebrant at the liturgical assembly, and chairman of the board of overseers of the Christian 'synagogue'" (*The Ministry in Historical Perspectives*, p. 28). Gregory the Great's work *The Book of Pastoral Rule* written in A.D. 591 is a discussion on the duties of the bishop's office. To Gregory, the bishop is a Pastor, and preaching is one of his most important duties. Gregory's book is a Christian classic and is still used to train Pastors in Protestant seminaries today. See also Philip Culbertson and Arthur Bradford Shippee, *The Pastor: Readings from the Patristic Period* (Minneapolis: Fortress Press, 1990).

[47] Note that the bishops at this time were essentially heads over local churches. They were not diocesan superintendents as they are today in Roman Catholicism. For a discussion of this development see *Early Christians Speak*, pp. 13-14.

[48] *The Ministry in Historical Perspectives*, p. 28.

[49] For a thorough discussion of this doctrine and its refutation, see my book *Who is Your Covering?*.

[50] *The Other Six Days*, pp. 41-42.

[51] *The Organization of the Early Christian Churches*, p. 171.

[52] *The Ministry in Historical Perspectives*, pp. 28-29.

[53] *The Elders*, p. 231; *The Ministry in Historical Perspectives*, p. 29.

sins![54] All of these trends obscured the NT reality that all believers are priests unto God.

By the fourth century, this graded hierarchy dominated the Christian faith.[55] The clergy caste was now cemented. At the head of the church stood the bishop. Under him was the college of presbyters. Under them stood the deacons.[56] And under all of them crawled the poor, miserable "laymen." One-bishop-rule became the accepted form of church government throughout the Roman Empire. (During this time, certain churches began to exercise authority over other churches—thus broadening the hierarchical structure.)[57]

By the end of the fourth century, the bishops walked with the great. They were given tremendous privileges. They got involved in politics which separated them further from the presbyters.[58] In his attempts to strengthen the bishop's office, Cyprian argued for an unbroken succession of bishops that traced back to Peter.[59] This idea is known as "apostolic succession."[60]

---

[54] J.G. Davies, *The Early Christian Church: A History of Its First Five Centuries* (Grand Rapids: Baker Books, 1965), p. 131; *The Apostolic Tradition of Hippolytus*, trans. Burton S. Easton (Cambridge: Cambridge University Press, 1934). Hippolytus distinguishes sharply between the powers of the bishop and the presbyters. His writings give the bishop the power to forgive sins and to allot penance (*Christian Priesthood Examined*, pp. 39-40). Presbyters and deacons could only baptize with the bishop's authority (*The Elders*, p. 233).

[55] *The Early Christian Church*, p. 187. In A.D. 318, Constantine recognized the jurisdiction of the bishop. In A.D. 333, the bishops were placed on an equal footing with Roman magistrates (p. 188).

[56] Hans Lietzmann, *A History of the Early Church, Volume II* (New York: The World Publishing Company, 1953), p. 247.

[57] According to the canons of the Council of Nicea, Alexandria, Rome, and Antioch had special authority over the regions around them (*From Christ to Constantine*, p. 95).

[58] *Christian Priesthood Examined*, p. 72. Hanson explains how the fall of the Roman Empire in the fifth century strengthened the bishop's office (pp. 72-77).

[59] Ann Fremantle, ed., *A Treasury of Early Christianity* (Viking Press, 1953), p. 301.

[60] Apostolic succession first appears in the writings of Clement of Rome and Irenaeus. It also appears in Hippolytus. But Cyprian turned it into a coherent doctrine (Robert M. Grant, *Early Christianity and Society*, San Francisco: Harper and Row Publishers, 1977, p. 38; N. Sykes, *Old Priest and New Presbyter*, Cambridge, 1956, p. 240).

Throughout his writings, Cyprian employs the official language of the Old Testament priesthood to justify this practice.[61] Like Tertullian (160-225) and Hippolytus (170-236) before him, Cyprian used the term *sacerdotes* to describe the presbyters and bishops.[62] But he went a step further.

It is upon Cyprian's lap that we can lay the non-NT concept of sacerdotalism—the belief that there exists a Divinely appointed person to meditate between God and the people. Cyprian argued that because the Christian clergy are priests who offer the holy sacrifice (the Eucharist) they are sacrosanct (holy) themselves![63]

We can also credit Cyprian with the notion that when the priest offers the Eucharist, he is actually offering up the death of Christ on behalf of the congregation.[64] To Cyprian's mind, the body and blood of Christ are once again sacrificed through the Eucharist.[65] Consequently, it is in Cyprian that we find the seeds of the medieval Catholic Mass.[66] This idea widened the wedge between clergy and laity. It also created an unhealthy dependence of the laity upon the clergy.

[61] G.S.M. Walker, *The Churchmanship of Cyprian*, (London: Lutterworth Press, 1968), p. 38. Many of the church fathers treated the Old Testament Scriptures as containing a normative ordering of the church. The use of Old Testament priest terminology for church office-bearers became common as early as the second century (*Ordination: A Biblical-Historical View*, pp. 50, 161; *Christian Priesthood Examined*, pp. 46, 51).

[62] *Christian Priesthood Examined*, p. 59; *Ordination: A Biblical-Historical View*, p. 39.

[63] *Christian Priesthood Examined*, p. 54.

[64] Ibid., p. 58. In both the *Didache* and 1 Clement, the Eucharist is referred to as a "sacrifice" and an "offering" performed by the bishops (*Tradition and Life in the Church*, p. 220).

[65] The word "sacrifice" as used in a liturgical sense first appears in the *Didache* (*Tradition and Life in the Church*, p. 220).

[66] The idea that the priest offers the sacrifice of Christ through the Eucharist is sacerdotalism. On this score, Richard Hanson poignantly remarks, "This sacerdotal concept of priesthood appears to obscure, if not actually abolish, the doctrine of the priesthood of all believers. It drains believers' priesthood all away into the priesthood of the clergy" (*Christian Priesthood Examined*, p. 98).

The Role of the Priest

Up until the Middle Ages, the presbyters (now commonly called "priests") played second fiddle to the bishop. But during the Middle Ages there was a shift. The presbyters began to represent the priesthood while the bishops were occupied with political duties.[67] The parish (local) priests became more central to the life of the church than the bishop.[68] It was the priest who now stood in God's place and controlled the sacraments.

As Latin became the common language in the mid-fourth century, the priest would invoke the words *hoc est corpus meum*. These Latin words mean "This is my body."

With these words, the priest became the overseer of the supercilious hokum that began to mark the Catholic Mass. Ambrose of Milan (339-397) can be credited for the idea that the mere utterance of *hoc est corpus meum* magically converted bread and wine into the Lord's physical body and blood.[69] (The stage magic phrase "hocus pocus" comes from *hoc est corpus meum*.) According to Ambrose, the priest was endowed with special powers to call God down out of heaven into bread!

Because of his sacramental function, the word *presbyteros* came to mean *sacerdos* (priest). Consequently, when the Latin word "presbyter" was taken into English, it had the meaning of "priest" rather than "elder."[70] Thus in the Roman Catholic church, "priest" was the widely used term to refer to the local presbyter.

---

[67] Ibid., p. 79.

[68] In the third century, each priest chose a bishop to oversee and coordinate his functioning. In the fourth century, things got more complex. Bishops needed supervision. Hence was born archbishops and metropolitans who governed the churches of a province (Will Durant, *The Age of Faith*, New York: Simon & Schuster, 1950, pp. 45, 756-760).

[69] *Concerning the Mysteries*, 9:52,54. In the Eastern churches a prayer is offered for the Spirit to do the magic. In the western churches, the prayer was left out, for the words themselves did the trick (Gregory Dix, *The Shape of the Liturgy*, London: Dacre Press, 1964, p. 240-241, 275; Josef A. Jungmann, *The Mass of the Roman Rite*, New York: Benziger, 1951-55, Volume 1, p. 52).

[70] *The Elders*, pp. 234-235. The word "priest" is etymologically a contraction of "presbyter." By the close of the Old English period, the English term "priest" had become the current word for "presbyter" and "sacerdos" (*The Oxford Dictionary of the Christian Church*, Third Edition, p. 1325).

The Influence of Greco-Roman Culture

The Greco-Roman culture that surrounded the early Christians reinforced the graded hierarchy that was slowly infiltrating the church. Greco-Roman culture was hierarchical by nature. This influence seeped into the church when new converts brought their cultural baggage into the believing community.[71]

Human hierarchy and "official" ministry institutionalized the church of Jesus Christ. By the fourth century, these elements hardened the arteries of the once living, breathing *ekklesia* of God—within which ministry was functional, Spirit-led, organic, and shared by all believers.

But how and why did this happen?

We may trace it to the time of the death of the itinerant apostolic workers (church planters). In the late first and early second centuries, local presbyters began to emerge as the resident "successors" to the unique leadership role played by the apostolic workers.[72] This gave rise to a single leading figure in each church.[73] Without the influence of the extra-local workers who had been mentored by the NT apostles, the church began to drift toward the organizational patterns of her surrounding culture.[74]

Prominent teachers in the church who had adopted pagan thinking also had a great influence. Following on the heels of Ignatius of Antioch, Cyprian made the case that the organization of the church should be modeled after the Roman Empire. As a result, imperialism and an impregnable hierarchy made inroads into the Christian faith.[75]

As we have already seen, the role of the bishop began to change from being the head of a local church to becoming the representative of everybody in a given area.[76] Bishops ruled over the

---

[71] *The Organization of the Early Christian Churches*, pp. 30-31.

[72] *Early Christians Speak*, p. 172.

[73] Ibid., p. 172.

[74] David Norrington gives an indepth discussion of how hierarchical structures and ecclesiastical specialists began to emerge in the church (*To Preach or Not to Preach?*, pp. 24-25).

[75] *Early Christianity and Society*, p. 43.

[76] *Christian Priesthood Examined*, p. 71.

churches just like Roman governors ruled over their provinces.[77] Eventually, the bishop of Rome was given the most authority of all and finally evolved into the "Pope."[78]

Thus between the years A.D. 100 and A.D. 300, church leadership came to be patterned after the leadership of the Roman government.[79] And the hierarchy of the Old Testament was used to justify it.[80] The one-bishop-rule had swallowed up the priesthood of all believers.

Ignatius effectively made the bishop the local authority. Cyprian made him a representative of all the churches by his doctrine of apostolic succession.[81]

---

[77] Robert F. Evans, *One and Holy: The Church in Latin and Patristic Thought* (London: Camelot Press, 1972), p. 48.

[78] Before Constantine, the Roman bishop exercised no jurisdiction outside of Rome. While he was honored, he did not have that kind of ecclesiastical authority (*Church History in Plain Language,* p. 151). The word "pope" comes from the title "papa," a term used to express the fatherly care of any bishop. It was not until the sixth century that the term began to be used exclusively for the bishop of Rome. Here is a brief sketch of the origin of the Roman Catholic Pope: At the end of the second century, Roman bishops were given great honor. Stephen I (d. 257) was the first to use the Petrine text (Matthew 16:18) to support the preeminence of the Roman bishop. But this was not universally held. The emergence of the modern Pope can be traced to Leo the Great (440-461). Leo was the first to make a theological and Biblical claim for the primacy of the Roman bishop. Under him, the primacy of Rome was finally established. With the coming of Gregory the Great (540-604), the "papal chair" was extended and enhanced. (Incidentally, Gregory became by far the largest landowner in Italy, setting a precedent for rich and powerful Popes to follow.) By the mid-third century, the Roman church had 30,000 members, 150 clergyman, and 1500 widows and poor people (Justo L. Gonzalez, *The Story of Christianity: Volume 1,* p. 242; Philip Schaff, *History of the Christian Church: Volume 4,* pp. 212, 218-219; Bruce Shelley, *Church History in Plain Language,* Waco: Word Books, 1982, pp. 150-151; *The Early Christian Church,* pp. 135-136, 250; *The Age of Faith,* p. 521; *Christian Priesthood Examined,* p. 76ff.). Gregory is also the first to use the term "servant of the servants of God" (Philip Schaff, *History of the Christian Church: Volume 3,* Michigan: Eerdmans, 1910, p. 534; *Volume 4,* p. 329).

[79] *Early Christianity and Society,* p. 43; *The Early Christian Church,* pp. 188-189.

[80] *Ordination: A Biblical-Historical View,* pp. 35, 48. Church officers were regarded as the successors of the Levites (p. 168).

[81] *A Treasury of Early Christianity,* p. 301.

Constantine and Roman Hierarchy

Keep in mind that the social world into which Christianity spread was governed by a single ruler—the Emperor. Soon after Constantine took the throne in the early fourth century, the church became a full-fledged, top-down, hierarchically organized society.[82]

Edwin Hatch writes, *"For the most part the Christian churches associated themselves together upon the lines of the Roman Empire*[83] *... The development of the organization of the Christian churches was gradual [and] the elements of which that organization were composed were already existing in human society."*[84]

We can trace the hierarchical leadership structure as early as ancient Egypt, Babylon, and Persia.[85] It was later carried over into the Greek and Roman culture where it was perfected.

Historian D.C. Trueman writes, *"The Persians made two outstanding contributions to the ancient world: The organization of their empire and their religion. Both of these contributions have had considerable influence on our western world. The system of imperial administration was inherited by Alexander the Great, adopted by the Roman Empire, and eventually bequeathed to modern Europe."*[86]

Will Durant makes a similar point saying that Christianity *"grew by the absorption of pagan faith and ritual; it became a triumphant church by inheriting the organizing patterns and genius of Rome ... As Judea had given Christianity ethics, and*

---

[82] *Early Christianity and Society*, pp. 11-12. "The organization of the church adapted itself to the political and geographical divisions of the Empire" (*History of the Christian Church: Volume 3*, p. 7).

[83] This not only applied to the graded hierarchy it adopted into its leadership structure, but also to the way the church divided itself up into gradations of dioceses, provinces, and municipalities all controlled by a top-down leadership system (*The Organization of the Early Christian Churches*, p. 185). As Shelley put it, "As the church grew, it adopted, quite naturally, the structure of the Empire" (Bruce Shelley, *Church History in Plain Language*, Waco: Word Books, 1982, p 152).

[84] *The Organization of the Early Christian Churches*, p. 213.

[85] Will Durant, *Caesar to Christ* (New York: Simon & Schuster, 1950), pp. 670-671.

[86] D.C. Trueman, *The Pageant of the Past: The Origins of Civilization* (Toronto: Ryerson, 1965), p. 105.

Greece had given it theology, so now Rome gave it organization; all these, with a dozen absorbed and rival faiths, entered into the Christian synthesis.[87]

By the fourth century, the church followed in the same steps of the Roman Empire. Emperor Constantine organized the church into dioceses along the pattern of the Roman regional districts.[88] (The word "diocese" was a secular term that referred to the larger administrative units of the Roman Empire.)[89] Later, Pope Gregory shaped the ministry of the entire church after Roman Law.[90]

Again Durant laments, *"When Christianity conquered Rome the ecclesiastical structure of the pagan church, the title and vestments of the pontifex maximus . . . and the pageantry of immemorial ceremony, passed like maternal blood into the new religion, and captive Rome captured her conqueror."*[91]

All of this was at gross odds with God's way for His church. When Jesus entered the drama of human history, He obliterated both the religious professional icon as well as the hierarchical form of leadership.[92] As an extension of Christ's nature and mission, the early church was the first "lay-led" movement in history. But with the death of the apostles and the men they trained, things began to change.[93]

Since that time, the church of Jesus Christ has sought its pattern for church organization from the societies in which it has been placed. This despite our Lord's warning that He would be initiating a new society with a unique character.[94] In striking contrast to the Old Testament provisions made at Mt. Sinai, neither Jesus nor Paul imposed any fixed organizational patterns for the New Israel.

---

[87] *Caesar to Christ*, pp. 575, 618. Durant writes, "The Roman Church followed in the footsteps of the Roman State" (p. 618).
[88] *The Other Six Days*, p. 44; *The Pageant of the Past*, p. 311; Robin Lane Fox, *Pagans and Christians* (San Francisco: Harper, 1986), p. 573).
[89] *The Oxford Dictionary of the Christian Church*, Third Edition, p. 482.
[90] *The Other Six Days*, p. 44.
[91] *Caesar and Christ*, pp. 671-672.
[92] Matt. 20:25-28; 23:8-12; Luke 22:25-27. In *Who is Your Covering?*, I explore the significance of these passages in detail.
[93] Paul trained a number of men to take his place. Among them were Timothy, Titus, Gaius, Trophimus, Tychichus, etc. See Gene Edwards' *Overlooked Christianity* (Sargent: Seedsowers, 1997) for details.
[94] Matthew 23:8-11; Mark 10:42ff.

Constantine and the Glorification of the Clergy

From A.D. 313-325, Christianity was no longer a struggling religion trying to survive the Roman government. It was basking in the sun of imperialism, loaded with money and status.[95] To be a Christian under Constantine's reign was no longer a handicap. It was an advantage. It was fashionable to become a part of the Emperor's religion. And to be among the clergy was to receive the greatest of advantages.[96]

Constantine exalted the clergy. In A.D. 313, he gave the Christian clergy exemption from paying taxes—something that pagan priests had traditionally enjoyed.[97] He also made them exempt from mandatory public office and other civic duties.[98] They were freed from being tried by secular courts and from serving in the army.[99] (Bishops could be tried only by a bishop's court, not by ordinary law courts.)[100]

In all these things the clergy was given special class status. Constantine was the first to use the words "clerical" and "clerics" to depict a higher social class.[101] He also felt that the Christian clergy deserved the same privileges as governmental officials. So bishops sat in judgment like secular judges.[102]

Clergymen received the same honors as the highest officials of the Roman Empire and even the Emperor himself.[103] The brute fact

---

[95] *Christian Priesthood Examined*, p. 62.

[96] At this time, the term "clergy" broadened to include all officials in the church (*The Ministry in Historical Perspectives*, p. 29). See also Norman Towar Boggs, *The Christian Saga* (New York: Macmillan Company, 1931), pp. 206-207.

[97] *Christian Priesthood Examined*, p. 62; *Caesar and Christ*, pp. 656-657, 668.

[98] Monsignor Louis Duchesne, *Early History of the Christian Church: From Its Foundation to the End of the Fifth Century* (London: John Murray, 1912), p. 50; Paul Johnson, *A History of Christianity* (New Your: Simon & Schuster, 1976), p. 77; Robin Lane Fox, *Pagans and Christians* (New York: Alfred Knopf, 1987), p. 667.

[99] Such exemptions had been granted to such professions as physicians and professors. Dave Andrews, *Christian Anarchy* (Lion Publications, 1999), p. 26.

[100] Father Michael Collins and Matthew A. Price, *The Story of Christianity* (DK Publishing, 1999), p.74.

[101] *A History of Christianity*, p. 77. A century later, Julian the Apostate was using these same terms (clerical, clerics) in a negative sense.

[102] *Pagans and Christians*, p. 667.

[103] Josef A. Jungmann, S.J., *The Early Liturgy: To the Time of Gregory the Great* (Notre Dame: Notre Dame Press, 1959), pp. 130-131.

is that Constantine gave the bishops of Rome more power than he gave Roman governors![104] He also ordered that the clergy receive fixed annual allowances (ministerial pay)!

The net result of this was alarming: The clergy had the prestige of church office-bearers, the privileges of a favored class, and the power of a wealthy elite.[105] They had become an isolated class with a separate civil status and way of life. (This included clergy celibacy.)[106]

They even dressed and groomed differently from the common people.[107] Bishops and priests shaved their heads. This practice, known as the *tonsure*, comes from the old Roman ceremony of adoption. All those who had shaved heads were known as "clerks" or "clergy."[108] They also began wearing the clothes of Roman officials.[109]

It should come as no surprise that so many people in Constantine's day experienced a sudden "call to the ministry."[110] To their minds, being a church officer had become more of a career than a calling.[111]

---

[104] *Caesar and Christ*, pp. 618-619.

[105] *The Organization of the Early Christian Churches*, pp. 153-155.

[106] Ibid., p. 163. In the first three centuries of Christianity, priests were not required to be celibate. In the West, the Spanish Council of Elivra held in A.D. 306 was the first to require clergy to be celibate. This was reasserted by Pope Siricius in A.D. 386. Any priest who married or continued to live with his wife was defrocked. In the East, priests and deacons could marry before ordination, but not after. Bishops had to be celibate. Gregory the Great did a great deal to promote clerical celibacy, which many were not following. Clerical celibacy only widened the gulf between clergy and the so-called "ordinary" people of God (*The Oxford Dictionary of the Christian Church*, Third Edition, p. 310; *History of the Christian Church, Volume 1*, pp. 441-446; *The Story of Christianity: Volume 1* (Gonzalez), p. 246; *The Age of Faith*, p. 45).

[107] The bishop's dress was that of the ancient robe of a Roman magistrate. Clergy were not to let their hair grow long like the pagan philosophers (*The Organization of the Early Christian Churches*, pp. 164-165).

[108] *The Story of Christianity*, p. 74.

[109] See Chapter 5.

[110] *Christian Priesthood Examined*, p. 62

[111] *The Ministry in Historical Perspectives*, p. 29.

A False Dichotomy

Under Constantine, Christianity was both recognized and honored by the State. This blurred the line between the church and the world. The Christian faith was no longer a minority religion. Instead, it was protected by Emperors. As a consequence, church membership grew rapidly. Truck loads of new converts were made who were barely converted. They brought into the church a wide variety of pagan ideas. In the words of Will Durant, *"While Christianity converted the world; the world converted Christianity, and displayed the natural paganism of mankind."*[112]

As we have already seen, the practices of the mystery religions began to be employed into the church's worship.[113] And the pagan notion of the dichotomy between the sacred and profane found its way into the Christian mindset.[114] It can be rightfully said that the clergy/laity class distinction grew out of this very dichotomy. The Christian life was now being divided into two parts: Secular and spiritual—sacred and profane.

But by the fourth century, this false idea was universally embraced by Christians. And it led to the profoundly mistaken idea that there are sacred professions (a call to the "ministry") and ordinary professions (a call to a worldly vocation).[115] Historian Philip Schaff rightly describes these factors as creating "the secularization of the church" where the "pure stream of Christianity" had become polluted.[116] Take note that this mistaken dichotomy still lives in the minds of most believers today. But the

---

[112] *Caesar and Christ*, p. 657.

[113] See Chapter 1.

[114] Frank C. Senn, *Christian Worship and Its Cultural Setting* (Philadelphia: Fortress Press, 1983), pp. 40-41.

[115] Everything ought to be done for God's glory, for He has sanctified the mundane (1 Cor. 10:31). The false dichotomy between the sacred and profane has been forever abolished in Christ. Such thinking belongs to both paganism and ancient Judaism. For the Christian, "Nothing is unclean in itself," and "What God has cleansed do not make common" (Acts 10:15; Rom. 14:14). For an indepth discussion on the fallacy of the sacred/profane disjunction, see J.G. Davies, *The Secular Use of Church Buildings* (New York: The Seabury Press, 1968), pp. 222-237.

[116] *The History of Christianity: Volume 3*, pp. 125-126.

concept is pagan, not Christian. It ruptures the NT reality that everyday life is sanctified by God.[117]

Clement of Rome (died in 100) was the first Christian writer to make a distinction in *status* between Christian leaders and non-leaders. He is the first to use the word "laity" in contrast to ministers.[118] Clement argued that the Old Testament order of priests should find fulfillment in the Christian church.[119]

Tertullian is the first writer to use the word "clergy" to refer to a separate class of Christians.[120] Both Tertullian and Clement of Alexandria (150-215) popularized the word "clergy" in their writings.[121]

By the third century, the clergy/laity gap widened to the point of no return.[122] Clergymen were the trained leaders of the church—the guardians of orthodoxy—the rulers and teachers of the people. They possessed gifts and graces not available to lesser mortals.

The laity were the second-class, untrained Christians. The great theologian Karl Barth rightly said, *"The term 'laity' is one of the worst in the vocabulary of religion and ought to be banished from the Christian conversation."*[123]

The terms "clergy" and "laity" do not appear in the NT.[124] Neither does the concept that there are those who do ministry (clergy) and those to whom ministry is done (laity). Thus what we have in Tertullian and the two Clements is a clear break from the

---

[117] *New Testament Theology in Dialogue*, p. 127.
[118] 1 Clement 40:5. See also *Early Christians Speak*, p. 168; R. Paul Stevens, *The Abolition of the Laity* (Carlisle: Paternoster Press, 1999), p. 5.
[119] *Ordination: A Biblical-Historical View*, p. 38.
[120] *On Monogamy, 12.*
[121] *The Abolition of the Laity*, p. 28.
[122] *To Preach or Not to Preach?*, p. 25.
[123] *The Abolition of the Laity*, p. 24.
[124] The term "laity" is derived from the Greek word *laos* which means the people of God (see 1 Pet. 2:9-10). The term "clergy" is derived from the Greek word *kleros* which means a lot, a share, or an inheritance. The NT never uses the word *kleros* for leaders. It rather uses it for the whole people of God. For it is God's people that are God's inheritance (see Col. 1:12; Eph. 1:11; Gal. 3:29; 1 Pet. 5:3). In this connection, it is ironic that Peter in 1 Peter 5:3 exhorts the elders of the church to not lord over the *kleros* ("clergy")! Again, *kleros* and *laos* both refer to the whole of God's flock.

first-century Christian mindset where all believers shared the same status.

The distinction between clergy and laity—pulpiteer and pew-sitter—belongs to the other side of the cross. With the New Covenant in Christ, clergy and laity are abolished. There is only the people of God.

Along with these mindset changes came a new vocabulary. Christians began to adopt the vocabulary of the pagan cults. The title *pontifex* (pontiff, a pagan title) became a common term for Christian clergy in the fourth century. So did "Master of Ceremonies," and "Grand Master of the Lodge."[125] All of this reinforced the mystique of the clergy as the custodians of the mysteries of God.[126]

By the fifth century, the thought of the priesthood of all believers had completely disappeared from the Christian horizon. Access to God was now controlled by the clergy caste. Clerical celibacy began to be enforced. Infrequent communion became a regular habit of the so-called laity. The church building was now veiled with incense and smoke. Clergy prayers were said in secret. And the small but profoundly significant screen that separated clergy from laity was introduced.

In a word, by the end of the fourth century on into the fifth, the clergy had become a sacerdotal caste—a spiritually elite group of "holy men."[127] This leads us to the thorny subject of ordination.

The Fallacy of Ordination

In the fourth century, theology and ministry were the domain of the priests. Work and war were the domain of the laity.[128] What

---

[125] *Christian Priesthood Examined*, p. 64. Terms like *coryphaeus* (Master of Ceremonies) and *hierophant* (Grand Master of the Lodge) were freely borrowed from pagan cults and used for the Christian clergy. Tertullian was the first to use the term "supreme pontiff" (bishop of bishops) to refer to the bishop of Rome in his work *On Chastity* written at about A.D. 218. Tertullian, however, uses the term sarcastically (*The Spreading Flame*, p. 322).

[126] *Christian Priesthood Examined*, p. 64.

[127] Ibid., pp. 65-66; *Tradition and Life in the Church*, pp. 222-223.

[128] *Ordination: A Biblical-Historical View*, p. 40.

was the rite of passage into the sacred realm of the priest? *Ordination.*[129]

Before we examine the historical roots of ordination, let us look at how leadership was recognized in the early church. The apostolic workers (church planters) of the first century would revisit a church after a period of time. In some of those churches, the workers would publicly acknowledge elders. In every case, the elders were already "in place" before they were publicly endorsed.[130]

Elders naturally emerged in a church through the process of time. They were not appointed to an external office.[131] Instead, they were recognized by virtue of their seniority and contribution to the church. According to the NT, recognition of certain gifted members is something that is instinctive and organic.[132] There is an internal principle within every believer of recognizing the various ministries in the church.

Strikingly, there are only three passages in the NT that tell us that elders were publicly recognized. Elders were acknowledged in the churches in Galatia. Paul told Timothy to acknowledge elders in Ephesus. He also told Titus to recognize them in the churches in Crete.

The words "ordain" (KJV) in these passages do not mean to place into office.[133] They rather carry the idea of endorsing, affirming, and showing forth what has already been happening.[134] They also carry the thought of blessing.[135] Public recognition of

---

[129] Ibid., p. 167.

[130] See *Rethinking the Wineskin*, Chapter 5; *Who is Your Covering*, Chapter 2.

[131] According to Bible commentator Alfred Plummer, the Greek words translated "ordain" in the NT do not have special ecclesiastical meanings. None of them implies the rite of ordination or a special ceremony ("The Pastoral Epistles," in *The Expositor's Bible*, ed. W. Robertson Nicoll, New York: Armstrong, 1903, Vol. 23, pp. 219-221). See also *Who is Your Covering?* Chapters 1-3.

[132] Acts 16:2; 1 Thess. 1:5; 5:12; 1 Cor. 16:18; 2 Cor. 8:22; Php. 2:22; 1 Tim. 3:10.

[133] *Ordination: A Biblical-Historical View*, p. 4. Translators of the KJV have used *ordain* for 21 different Hebrew and Greek words. 17th-century ecclesiastical misunderstanding influenced this poor word choice.

[134] The Greek word *cheirotoneo* in Acts 14:23 literally means "to stretch forth the hand" as in voting. Hence, it is likely that the apostles laid hands on those whom the majority of the church deemed were already functioning as overseers among them.

[135] *The Elders*, pp. 169-170.

elders and other ministries was typically accompanied by the laying on of hands by apostolic workers. (In the case of workers being sent out, this was done by the church or the elders.)[136]

In the first century, the laying on of hands merely meant the endorsement or affirmation of a function, not the installment into an office or the giving of special status. Regrettably, it came to mean the latter in the late second and early third centuries.[137]

During the third century, "ordination" took on an entirely different meaning. It was a formalized Christian rite.[138] By the fourth century, the ceremony of ordination was embellished by symbolic garments and solemn ritual.[139] Ordination produced an ecclesiastical caste that usurped the believing priesthood.

From where do you suppose the Christians got their pattern of ordination? They patterned their ordination ceremony after the Roman custom of appointing men to civil office.[140] The entire process down to the very words came straight from the Roman civic world![141]

By the fourth century, the terms used for appointment to Roman office and for Christian ordination became synonymous.[142] When Constantine made Christianity the religion of choice, church leadership structures were now buttressed by political sanction.

---

[136] Acts 13:2; 1 Tim. 4:14. Paul, an older worker, also laid hands on Timothy, a younger worker (2 Tim. 1:6).

[137] *Ordination: A Biblical-Historical View*, pp. 104, 111, 127, 130. Warkentin does a thorough study on the NT meaning of the "laying on of hands" in Chapters 9-11 of her book. Her conclusion: "The laying on of hands has nothing to do with routine installation into office in the church, whether as elder, deacon, pastor, or missionary" (p. 156).

[138] The earliest record of the ordination rite is found in the *Apostolic Traditions* of Hippolytus (200-220). By the fourth century, references abound to it (*Ordination: A Biblical-Historical View*, pp. 25, 41).

[139] *Ordination: A Biblical-Historical View*, p. 104.

[140] *The Organization of the Early Christian Churches*, pp. 129-133.

[141] Ibid. This same tendency was picked up by Judaism as early as the first century. Jewish scribes who were proficient in the interpretation of the Torah and the oral traditions ordained men for office in the Sanhedrin. These men were viewed as mediators of the will of God to all of Israel. The "ordained" of the Sanhedrin became so powerful that by the early second century the Romans put to death anyone who performed Jewish ordination! (*Ordination: A Biblical-Historical View*, pp. 16, 21-23, 25).

[142] Ibid., p. 35. This is evident from the *Apostolic Constitutions* (A.D. 350-375).

The forms of the Old Testament priesthood were combined with Greek hierarchy.[143] Sadly, the church was secure in this new form—just as it is today.

Augustine (293-373) lowered the bar more by teaching that ordination confers a "definite irremovable imprint" on the priest that empowers him to fulfill his priestly functions![144] For Augustine, ordination was a permanent possession that could not be revoked.[145]

Christian ordination, then, came to be understood as that which constitutes the essential difference between clergy and laity. By it, the clergy was empowered to administer the sacraments. It was believed that the priest, who performs the Divine service, should be the most perfect and holy of all Christians.[146]

Gregory of Nazianzus (329-389) and Chrysostom (347-407) raised the standard so high for priests that danger loomed for them if they failed to live up to the holiness of their service.[147] According to Chrysostom, the priest is like an angel. He is not made of the same frail stuff as the rest of men![148]

How was the priest to live in such a state of pure holiness? How was he to be worthy to serve in "the choir of angels"? The answer was ordination. By ordination, the stream of Divine graces flowed into the priest, making him a fit vessel for God's use. This idea, also known as "sacerdotal endowment," first appears in Gregory of Nyssa (330-395).

Gregory argued that ordination makes the priest, "invisibly but actually a different, better man," raising him high above the laity.[149] *"The same power of the word,"* says Gregory, *"makes the priest venerable and honorable, separated . . . While but yesterday he was one of the mass, one of the people, he is suddenly rendered*

---

143 Ibid., p. 45.
144 *Tradition and Life in the Church*, p. 224.
145 *Ministry in Historical Perspectives*, p. 75.
146 *Tradition and Life in the Church*, p. 227.
147 Ibid., p. 228.
148 *Ministry in Historical Perspectives*, p. 71.
149 *Tradition and Life in the Church*, p. 229.

a guide, a president, a teacher of righteousness, an instructor in hidden mysteries . . . "[150]

Listen to the words of one fourth century document: *"The bishop, he is the minister of the Word, the keeper of knowledge, the mediator between God and you in several parts of your Divine worship . . . He is your ruler and governor . . . He is next after God your earthly god, who has a right to be honored by you.* "[151]

Through ordination, the priest (or bishop) was granted special Divine powers to offer the sacrifice of the Mass. Ordination also made him a completely separate and holy class of man![152] Priests came to be identified as the "vicars of God on the earth." They became part of a special order of men. An order set apart from the so-called "lay members" of the church.

To show this difference, both the priest's life-style and dress were different from that of laymen.[153] Regrettably, this concept of ordination has never left the Christian faith. It is alive and well in modern Christianity. In fact, if you are wondering why and how the modern Pastor got to be so exalted as the "holy man of God," these are his roots.

Eduard Schweizer, in his classic work *Church Order in the New Testament,* argues that Paul knew nothing about an ordination that confers ministerial or clerical powers to a Christian.[154] First-century shepherds (elders, overseers) did not receive anything that resembles modern ordination. They were not set *above* the rest of the flock. They were those who served *among* them.[155]

First-century elders were merely endorsed publicly by outside workers as being those who cared for the church. Such acknow-

---

[150] *Ministry in Historical Perspectives,* p. 75. Ordination was believed to confer upon the recipient a *character indelibilis.* That is, something sacred had entered into him (*Ordination: A Biblical-Historical View,* p. 42; *History of the Christian Church: Volume 3,* p. 489).
[151] *The Apostolic Constitutions* II.4.26.
[152] Kevin Giles, *Patterns of Ministry Among the First Christians* (Melbourne: Collins Dove, 1991), p. 195.
[153] David D. Hall, *The Faithful Shepherd* (Chapel Hill: The University of North Carolina Press, 1972), p. 6.
[154] Eduard Schweizer, *Church Order in the New Testament* (Chatham: W. & J. Mackay, 1961), p. 207.
[155] Acts 20:28, NASB; 1 Peter 5:2-3.

ledgment was simply the recognition of a function. It did not confer special powers. Nor was it a permanent possession as Augustine believed.

The modern practice of ordination creates a special caste of Christian. Whether it be the priest in Catholicism or the Pastor in Protestantism, the result is the same: The most important ministry is closeted among a few "special" believers.

Such an idea is as damaging as it is nonscriptural. The NT nowhere limits preaching, baptizing, or distributing the Lord's Supper to the "ordained."[156] Eminent scholar James D.G. Dunn put it best when he said that the clergy-laity tradition has done more to undermine NT authority than most heresies![157]

Since church office could only be held through the rite of ordination, the power to ordain became the crucial issue in holding religious authority. The Biblical context was lost. And proof-texting methods were used to justify the clergy/laity hierarchy.[158] The ordinary believer, generally uneducated and ignorant, was at the mercy of a professional clergy![159]

The Reformation

The Reformers of the 16th century brought the Catholic priesthood sharply into question. They attacked the idea that the priest had special powers to convert wine into blood. They rejected apostolic succession. They encouraged the clergy to marry. They revised the liturgy to give the congregation more participation. They also abolished the office of the bishop and reduced the priest back to a presbyter.[160]

Unfortunately, however, the Reformers carried the Roman Catholic clergy/laity distinction straight into the Protestant

---

[156] *New Testament Theology in Dialogue*, p. 138ff.

[157] Ibid., pp. 126-129.

[158] *Ordination: A Biblical-Historical View*, p. 45.

[159] *Ordination: A Biblical-Historical View*, p. 51; *The Organization of the Early Christian Churches*, pp. 126-131. Ordination grew into an instrument to consolidate clerical power. Through it, the clergy could lord over God's people as well as secular authorities. The net effect is that modern ordination sets up artificial barriers between Christians and hinders mutual ministry.

[160] *Christian Priesthood Examined*, p. 82.

movement. They also kept the Catholic idea of ordination.[161] Although they abolished the office of the bishop, they resurrected the one-bishop-rule, clothing it in new garb.

The rallying cry of the Reformation was the restoration of the priesthood of all believers. However, this restoration was only partial. Luther (1483-1546), Calvin (1509-1564), and Zwingli (1484-1531) affirmed the believing priesthood with respect to one's *individual* relationship to God. They rightly taught that every Christian has direct access to God without the need of a human mediator. This was a wonderful restoration. But it was one-sided.

What the Reformers failed to do was to recover the *corporate* dimension of the believing priesthood. They restored the doctrine of the believing priesthood *soteriologically*—i.e., as it related to salvation. But they failed to restore it *ecclesiologically*—i.e., as it related to the church.[162]

In other words, the Reformers only recovered the priesthood of the *believer* (singular). They reminded us that every Christian has individual and immediate access to God. As wonderful as that is, they did not recover the priesthood of *all* believers (collective plural). This is the blessed truth that every Christian is part of a clan that shares God's Word one with another. (It was the Anabaptists who recovered this practice. Regrettably, this recovery was one of the reasons why Protestant and Catholic swords were red with Anabaptist blood.)[163]

While the Reformers opposed the Pope and his religious hierarchy, they still held to the narrow view of ministry which they inherited. They believed that "ministry" was an institution that was

---

[161] While Luther rejected the idea that ordination changes the ordained person's character, he nevertheless held to its importance. To Luther's mind, ordination is a rite of the church. And a special ceremony was necessary for the carrying out of pastoral duties (*Christian Liturgy*, p. 297).

[162] "The priesthood of all believers refers not only to each person's relation to God and to one's priesthood to neighbor, as in Luther; it refers also to the equality of all people in the Christian community with respect to formal function" (John Dillenberger, *Protestant Christianity: Interpreted Throughout Its Development*, p. 61).

[163] *The Faithful Shepherd*, p. 8. For a compelling treatment of the Anabaptist story, see Peter Hoover's *The Secret of the Strength: What Would the Anabaptists Tell This Generation?* (Shippensburg: Benchmark Press, 1998).

closeted among the few who were "called" and "ordained."[164] Thus the Reformers still affirmed the clergy-laity split. Only in their rhetoric did they state that all believers were priests and ministers. In their practice they denied it. So after the smoke cleared from the Reformation, we ended up with the same thing that the Catholics gave us—a selective priesthood!

Luther held to the idea that those who preach needed to be specially trained.[165] Like the Catholics, the Reformers held that only the "ordained minister" could preach, baptize, and administer the Lord's Supper.[166] As a result, ordination gave the minister a special aura of Divine favor that could not be questioned.

Tragically, Luther and the other Reformers violently denounced the Anabaptists for practicing every-member functioning in the church.[167] The Anabaptists believed it was every Christian's right to stand up and speak in a meeting. It was not the domain of the clergy. Luther was so opposed to this practice that he said it came from "the pit of hell" and those who were guilty of it should be put to death![168] (Behold your heritage dear Protestant Christian!)

In short, the Reformers retained the idea that ordination was the key to having power in the church. It was the ordained minister's duty to convey God's revelation to His people.[169] And he was paid for this role.

Like the Catholic priest, the Reformed minister was viewed by the church as the "man of God"—the paid mediator between God

---

[164] J.L. Ainslie, *The Doctrines of Ministerial Order in the Reformed Churches of the 16th and 17th Centuries* (Edinburgh, 1940), pp. 2,5.

[165] *Ordination: A Biblical-Historical View*, pp. 57-58.

[166] Ibid., pp. 61-62.

[167] The Anabaptists both believed and practiced Paul's injunction in 1 Corinthians 14:26, 30-31 that every believer has the right to function at any time in a church meeting. In Luther's day, this practice was known as the *Sitzrecht*—"the sitter's right" (*The Secret of the Strength*, pp. 58-59).

[168] Luther announced that "the *Sitzrecht* was from the pit of hell" and was a "perversion of public order . . . undermining respect for authority." Within 20 years, over 116 laws were passed in German lands throughout Europe making this "Anabaptist heresy" a capital offense (*The Secret of the Strength*, p. 59, 198). Further, Luther felt that if the whole church publicly administered the Lord's Supper it would be a "deplorable confusion." To Luther's mind, one person must take on this task—the Pastor (Paul Althaus, *The Theology of Martin Luther*, Philadelphia: Fortress Press, 1966, p. 323).

[169] *Ordination: A Biblical-Historical View*, p. 105.

and His people.[170] Not a mediator to forgive sins, but a mediator to communicate the Divine will.[171] So in Protestantism an old problem took on a new form. The jargon changed, but the poison remained.

From Priest to Pastor

John Calvin did not like the word "priest" to refer to ministers.[172] He preferred the term "Pastor."[173] In Calvin's mind, "Pastor" was the highest word one could use for ministry. He liked it because the Bible referred to Jesus Christ, "the great Shepherd of the sheep" (Heb. 13:20).[174] Ironically, Calvin believed that he was restoring the NT bishop (*episkopos*) in the person of the Pastor![175]

Luther also did not like the word "priest" to define the new Protestant ministers. He wrote, *"We neither can nor ought to give the name priest to those who are in charge of the Word and sacrament among the people. The reason they have been called priests is either because of the custom of the heathen people or as a vestige of the Jewish nation. The result is injurious to the church."*[176] So he too adopted the terms "preacher," "minister," and "Pastor" to refer to this new office.

---

[170] Ibid., p. 105. Protestants today speak of "the ministry" as a mediatorial body set within the larger Body of Christ rather than a function shared by all.

[171] Just as the Roman Catholic clergy was seen as the gatekeeper of salvation, the Protestant clergy was viewed as the trustee of Divine revelation. According to the *Augsburg Confession* of 1530, the highest office in the church was the preaching office. In ancient Judaism, the rabbi interpreted the Torah for the people. In the Protestant church, the minister is regarded as the custodian of God's mysteries (*Ordination: A Biblical-Historical View*, p. 168).

[172] John Calvin, *Institutes of the Christian Religion* (Westminster Press, 1960), Bk. 4, Ch. 8, No. 14.

[173] "Pastor" is from the Latin which was used to translate "shepherd." William Tyndale preferred the term "Pastor" in his Bible translation. Tyndale debated Sir Thomas More over the issue of "Pastor" vs. "priest." Tyndale, a Protestant, took the position that "Pastor" was exegetically correct (see *The Parker Society Series on the English Reformers* for this exchange).

[174] *The Faithful Shepherd*, p. 16.

[175] *Old Priest and New Presbyter*, p. 111.

[176] *Luther's Works*, 40, 35.

Zwingli and Martin Bucer (1491-1551) also favored the word "Pastor." They wrote popular treatises on it.[177] As a result, the term began to permeate the churches of the Reformation.[178] However, given their obsession with preaching, the Reformers' favorite term for the minister was "preacher."[179] And this was what the common people generally called them.[180]

It was not until the 18th century that the term "Pastor" came into common use, eclipsing "preacher" and "minister."[181] This influence came from the Lutheran Pietists.[182] Since then the term has become widespread in mainstream Christianity.[183]

---

[177] One of the most influential books during the Reformation was Bucer's *The Pastorale*. In the same spirit, Zwingli published a tract entitled *The Pastor*.

[178] Calvin's church order of Pastors with governing elders in Geneva became the most influential model during the Reformation. It became the pattern of the Protestant churches in France, Holland, Hungary, Scotland, as well as among the English Puritans and their descendants (*Ministry in Historical Perspectives*, p. 131, 115-117.). Calvin also gave rise to the idea that the Pastor and teacher were the only two "ordinary" officers in Ephesians 4:11-12 that continue perpetually in the church (*The Faithful Shepherd*, p. 28). During the 17th century, the Puritans used the term "Pastor" in some of their published works. 17th-century Anglican and Puritan works on pastoral care referred to parish (local) clergy as "parsons" (George Herbert's *The Country Parson*) and "Pastors" (Richard Baxter's *The Reformed Pastor*).

[179] *Ministry in Historical Perspectives*, p. 116. "The German Reformers also adhered to the medieval usage and called the preacher *Pfarrer*, i.e. parson (derived from *parochia*—parish and *parochus*—parson). While Lutheran preachers are called "Pastors" in the United States, they are still called *Pfarrer* (head of the parish) in Germany. Given the gradual transition from Catholic priest to Protestant Pastor, it was not uncommon for people to still call their new Protestant preachers by the old Catholic titles like "priest."

[180] *The Ministry in Historical Perspectives*, p. 116.

[181] The word "Pastor" has always appeared in theological literature dating as far back as the Patristic period. The word choice was dependent on the function you wished to highlight: A Pastor guided in moral and spiritual ways. The priest officiated the sacraments. Even so, the term "Pastor" was not on the lips of the common believer until after the Reformation.

[182] *The Ministry in Historical Perspectives*, p. 116.

[183] Ibid. The word "priest" belongs to the Catholic/Anglican tradition, the word "minister" belongs to the Reformed tradition, and the word "Pastor" belongs to the Lutheran and evangelical tradition (p. viii). The Reformers did speak of their minister as "Pastor," but they mostly called him "preacher." The word "Pastor" later evolved to become the predominant term in Christianity for this office. This was due to the mainstreaming of these groups which sought distance from "high church" vocabulary. The term "minister" was introduced gradually into the English-speaking world by the Nonconformists and Dissenters. They wished to distinguish the Protestant "ministry" from the Anglican clergy (*The Ministry in Historical Perspectives*, p. 116).

Even so, the Reformers elevated the Pastor to be the functioning head of the church. According to Calvin, *"The pastoral office is necessary to preserve the church on earth in a greater way than the sun, food, and drink are necessary to nourish and sustain the present life."*[184]

The Reformers believed that the Pastor possessed Divine power and authority. He did not speak in his own name, but in the name of God. Calvin further reinforced the primacy of the Pastor by treating acts of contempt or ridicule toward the minister as serious public offenses.[185]

This should come as no surprise when you realize what Calvin took as his model for ministry. He did not take the church of the apostolic age. Instead, he took as his pattern the one-bishop-rule of the second century![186] This was true for the other Reformers as well.[187]

The irony here is that John Calvin bemoaned the Roman Catholic church because it built its practices on "human inventions" rather than on the Bible.[188] But Calvin did the same thing! In this regard, Protestants are just as guilty as are Catholics. Both denominations base their practices on human tradition.

Calvin taught that the preaching of the Word of God and the proper administration of the sacraments are the marks of a true church.[189] To his mind, preaching, baptism, and the Eucharist were

---

[184] *Institutes*, IV: 3:2, p. 1055.

[185] *The Ministry in Historical Perspectives*, p. 138.

[186] "For his (Calvin's) model of the ministry goes back to the church of the early second century rather than to that of the strictly apostolic age. In the apostolic age the local Christian community was under the charge not of a single pastor, but of a number of functionaries known interchangeably, as he notes, as presbyters (elders) and bishops. It was only in the second century that the single bishop or pastor of the Christian community came into existence, as in the Epistles of Ignatius . . . It was at this stage of the development of the ministerial office in the early second-century church that Calvin took as his model" (*Calvin and the Reformation*, pp. 81-82).

[187] James H. Nichols writes, "The Reformers also generally accepted the second-century system of an institutionalized ministry of pastors or bishops to lead the laity in worship . . . They did not attempt to return to the age of the apostles . . . " (*Corporate Worship in the Reformed Tradition*, p. 21).

[188] *Ministry in Historical Perspectives*, p. 111.

[189] *Institutes*, IV:1:9, p. 1023.

to be carried out by the Pastor and not the congregation.[190] For all the Reformers, the primary function of a minister is preaching.[191]

Like Calvin, Luther also made the Pastor a separate and exalted office. While he argued that the keys of the kingdom belonged to all believers, Luther confined their use to those who held offices in the church.[192] *"We are all priests,"* said Luther, *"insofar as we are Christians, but those whom we call priests are ministers selected from our midst to act in our name, and their priesthood is our ministry."*[193]

Sadly, Luther believed that all are *in* the priesthood, but not all can *exercise* the priesthood.[194] This is sacerdotalism, pure and simple. Luther broke from the Catholic camp in that he rejected a sacrificing priesthood. But in its place, he believed that the ministry of God's Word belonged to a special order.[195]

The following are characteristic statements made by Luther in his exaltation of the Pastor: *"God speaks through the preacher . . . A Christian preacher is a minister of God who is set apart, yea, he is an angel of God, a very bishop sent by God, a savior of many*

---

[190] John H. Yoder, "The Fullness of Christ," *Concern 17,* 1969, p. 71.

[191] *The Ministry in Historical Perspectives,* p. 131. The preeminent place of preaching is best reflected in Luther's *German Mass*: Three services on Sunday. In the early morning at five or six o'clock, a sermon was given on the Epistle of the day. At the main service at eight or nine o'clock, the minister preached on the Gospel of the day. The sermon at the Vesper service in the afternoon was based on the Old Testament. The rest of the days of the week were devoted to preaching as well (p. 131). Luther was abrasive, powerful, and dramatic. He communicated his own person in his sermons without superimposing himself on the message. He was a voracious preacher, delivering an estimated 4,000 sermons (*Christian History,* Volume XII, No. 3, Issue 39, p. 27). His messages were awe-inspiring, poetic, and creative. Zwingli preached directly and naturally, yet he was too intellectual. Calvin was consistent in his exhaustive expounding of passages, but he was always impersonal. Bucer was long-winded and had a penchant for rambling (p. 133). Even so, early Protestant preaching was very doctrinaire, being obsessed with "correct and pure doctrine." For this reason, Reformation preachers were primarily Bible teachers (p. 135).

[192] *The Faithful Shepherd,* p. 8.

[193] *The Ministry in Historical Perspectives,* p. 112. The Reformers substituted the word "minister" for "priest." Ilion T. Jones, *A Historical Approach to Evangelical Worship* (New York: Abingdon Press, 1954), p. 141.

[194] "This notion became the common property of the Reformation" (*Ministry in Historical Perspectives,* p. 113).

[195] B.A. Gerrish, "Priesthood and Ministry in the Theology of Luther," *Church History,* XXXIV (1965), pp. 404-422.

people, a king and prince in the Kingdom of Christ . . . There is nothing more precious or nobler in the earth and in this life than a true, faithful parson or preacher."[196]

Said Luther, *"We should not permit our pastor to speak Christ's words by himself as though he were speaking them for his own person; rather, he is the mouth of all of us and we all speak them with him in our hearts . . . It is a wonderful thing that the mouth of every pastor is the mouth of Christ, therefore you ought to listen to the pastor not as a man, but as God.*"[197] You can hear the echoes of Ignatius ringing through the words of Luther.

These ideas corrupted Luther's view of the church. He felt it was nothing more than a preaching station. *"The Christian congregation,"* said Luther, *"never should assemble unless God's Word is preached and prayer is made, no matter for how brief a time this may be.*"[198] Luther believed that the church is simply a gathering of people who listen to preaching. For this reason, he called the church building a *Mundhaus,* which means a mouth or speech-house![199] He also made this statement: *"The ears are the only organs of a Christian.*"[200]

Dear Protestant Christian, behold your roots!

The Cure of Souls

Both Calvin and Luther shared the view that the two key functions of the Pastor were the proclamation of the Word (preaching) and the celebration of the Eucharist (communion). But Calvin added a third element. He emphasized that the Pastor had a duty to provide care and healing to the congregation.[201] This is known as the "cure of souls."

---

[196] *The Ministry in Historical Perspectives*, pp. 114-115.
[197] *The Theology of Martin Luther*, p. 326.
[198] "Concerning the Ordering of Divine Worship in the Congregation," *Works of Martin Luther* (Philadelphia: Muhlenberg Press, 1932), VI, p. 60.
[199] *The Ministry in Historical Perspectives*, p. 114.
[200] *Luther's Works*, Vol. 29, p. 224.
[201] John T. McNeill, *A History of the Cure of Souls* (New York: Harper and Row, 1951).

The "cure of souls" goes back to the fourth and fifth centuries.[202] We find it in the teaching of Gregory of Nazianzus. Gregory called the bishop a "Pastor"—a physician of souls who diagnoses his patient's maladies and prescribes either medicine or the knife.[203]

Luther's early followers also practiced the care of souls.[204] But in Calvin's Geneva, it was raised to an art form. Each Pastor and one elder were required to visit the homes of their congregants. Regular visits to the sick and those in prison were also observed.[205]

For Calvin and Bucer, the Pastor was not merely a preacher and a dispenser of the sacraments. He was the "cure of souls" or the "curate." His task was to bring healing, cure, and compassion to God's hurting people.[206]

This idea lives in the Protestant world today. It is readily seen in the modern concepts of "pastoral care," "pastoral counseling," and "Christian psychobabble." In the modern church, the burden of such care falls on the shoulders of one man—the Pastor. (In the first century, it fell on the shoulders of the entire church and to a group of seasoned men called "elders.")[207]

The Primacy of the Pastor

In short, the Protestant Reformation struck a blow to Roman Catholic sacerdotalism. But it was not a fatal blow. The Reformers still retained the one-bishop-rule. It merely underwent a semantic

---

[202] Gregory of Nazianzus, Chrysostom, Augustine, and Gregory the Great wrote a good deal on the "cure of souls" (*A History of the Cure of Souls*, p. 100). In A.D. 591, Gregory wrote a treatise for Pastors called *The Book of Pastoral Rule*. This work is still used in seminaries today. And it owes a great deal to Gregory of Nazianzus (p. 109). Gregory the Great was more of a Pastor to the Western church than any of the other Popes.

[203] *A History of the Cure of Souls*, p. 108. Gregory Nazianzus articulated these things in his Second Oration penned in A.D. 362.

[204] *A History of the Cure of Souls*, p. 177.

[205] *The Ministry in Historical Perspectives*, p. 136. In 1550, an order was issued that ministers should visit each home at least once a year.

[206] Bucer wrote the most outstanding of all the books on the "cure of souls" entitled *True Cure of Souls* in 1538. This book came out in German and Latin versions (*A History of the Cure of Souls*, p. 177).

[207] See *Rethinking the Wineskin*, Chapters 5-6 and *Who is Your Covering?* Chapter 1.

change. The Pastor now played the role of the bishop. He came to be regarded as the local head of a church—the leading elder.[208] As one writer put it, *"In Protestantism, the preachers tend to be the spokesmen and representatives of the church and the church is often the preacher's church. This is a great danger and threat to the Christian religion, not unrelated to clericalism."*[209]

The reforms made by the Reformers were not radical enough to turn the tide that began with Ignatius and Cyprian. The Reformation embraced the Catholic hierarchical structure with unthinking acceptance. It also maintained the unscriptural distinction between the ordained and unordained.

In its rhetoric the Reformers decried the clergy-laity split. But in their practice they fully retained it. As Kevin Giles says, *"Differences between Catholic and Protestant clergy were blurred in practice and theology. In both kinds of churches, the clergy were a class apart; in both, their special status was based on Divine initiatives (mediated in different ways); and in both, certain duties were reserved to them."*[210]

The long-standing, post-Biblical tradition of the one-bishop-rule (now embodied in the Pastor) prevails in the Protestant church today. Because the clergy/laity faultline is etched in stone, there exists tremendous psychological pressures that make so-called "lay" people feel that ministry is the responsibility of the Pastor. "It is his job. He is the expert," is the thinking.

---

[208] Many Reformed churches distinguish between "teaching" elders and "ruling" elders. Teaching elders occupy the traditional position of bishop or minister, while ruling elders handle administration and discipline. This form of church polity was brought to New England from Europe (David Hall, *The Faithful Shepherd*, Chapel Hill: University of North Carolina Press, 1972, p. 95). Eventually, due to the unpopularity of the office, the ruling elders were dropped and the teaching elder remained. This was also true in the Baptist churches of the 18th and 19th centuries. Often these churches lacked the financial resources to support one "minister." In this way, by the end of the 19th century, the evangelical churches adopted the "single Pastor" tradition (Mark Dever, *A Display of God's Glory*, Washington D.C.: Center for Church Reform, 2001, p. 20; R.E.H. Uprichard, Irish Biblical Studies Journal, June 18, 1996, pp. 149, 154). So the single Pastor in evangelical churches evolved from a plurality of elders in the Reformed tradition.

[209] *The Ministry in Historical Perspectives*, p. 114. The so-called "lay-preacher" emerged out of the evangelical revivals of the 18th century (p. 206).

[210] *Patterns of Ministry Among the First Christians*, pp. 195-196.

The NT word for minister is *diakonos.* It means "servant." But this word has been prostituted because men have professionalized the ministry. We have taken the word "minister' and equated it with the Pastor with no Scriptural justification whatsoever. In like manner, we have mistakenly equated preaching and ministry with the pulpit sermon. Again, without Biblical justification.

Following the trend of Calvin and Luther, Puritan writers John Owen (1616-1683) and Thomas Goodwin (1600-1680) elevated the Pastorate as a permanent fixture in God's house.[211] Owen and Goodwin led the Puritans to focus all authority into the pastoral role.[212] To their minds, the Pastor is given "the power of the keys." He alone is ordained to preach,[213] administer the sacraments,[214] read Scripture publicly,[215] and be trained in the original Biblical languages, as well as logic and philosophy.

Both the Reformers and the Puritans held the idea that God's ministers must be competent professionals. Therefore, Pastors had to have extensive academic training to fulfill their office.[216]

All of these features explain how and why the Pastor is now treated as an elite class . . . a special Christian . . . someone to be revered (hence the title "Reverend"). The Pastor and his pulpit are central to Protestant worship.[217]

How the Pastor Destroys Body Life

Now that we have unearthed the roots of the modern Pastor, let us shift our attention to the practical effects a Pastor has on the people of God.

---

[211] John Owen, *True Nature of a Gospel Church* (Abridged Edition), pp. 41, 99.

[212] Ibid., p. 55

[213] *The Doctrines of Ministerial Order in the Reformed Churches of the 16th and 17th Centuries*, pp. 37, 49, 59, 61-69.

[214] *True Nature of a Gospel Church*, p. 68; *The Doctrines of Ministerial Order in the Reformed Churches of the 16th and 17th Centuries*, pp. 56, 63, 65; Thomas Goodwin, *Works*, Vol. 11, p. 309.

[215] *Baptist Reformation Review: Vol. 10, No. 2, 1981*, pp. 21-22.

[216] *The Faithful Shepherd*, pp. 28-29.

[217] *The Doctrines of Ministerial Order in the Reformed Churches of the 16th and 17th Centuries*, p. 51.

The unscriptural clergy/laity distinction has done untold harm to the Body of Christ. It has ruptured the believing community into first and second-class Christians. The clergy/laity dichotomy perpetuates an awful falsehood. Namely, that some Christians are more privileged than others to serve the Lord.

Our ignorance of church history has allowed us to be robbed blind. The one-man ministry is entirely foreign to the NT, yet we embrace it while it suffocates our functioning. We are living stones, not dead ones. However, the pastoral office has transformed us into stones that do not breathe.

Permit me to get personal. The pastoral office has stolen your right to function as a member of Christ's Body! It has shut your mouth and strapped you to a pew. It has distorted the reality of the Body, making the Pastor a giant mouth and transforming you into a tiny ear.[218] It has rendered you a mute spectator who is proficient at taking sermon notes and passing an offering plate!

But that is not all. The modern pastoral office has overthrown the main thrust of the letter to the Hebrews—the ending of the old priesthood. It has made ineffectual the teaching of 1 Corinthians 12-14, that every member has both the right and the privilege to minister in a church meeting. It has voided the message of 1 Peter 2 that every brother and sister is a functioning priest.

Being a functioning priest does not mean that you may only perform pinched forms of ministry like singing songs in your pew, raising your hands during worship, flipping transparencies, or teaching a Sunday school class. That is not the NT idea of ministry. These are mere aids for the Pastor's ministry! As one scholar put it, *"Much Protestant worship, up to the present day, has also been infected by an overwhelming tendency to regard worship as the work of the Pastor (and perhaps the choir) with the majority of the laity having very little to do but sing a few hymns and listen in a prayerful and attentive way."*[219]

We treat the Pastor as if he were the professional expert. We expect doctors and lawyers to serve us, not to train us to serve

---

[218] To put this tragedy in the form of a Biblical question, "And if they were all one member, where would the Body be?" (1 Cor. 12:19).

[219] J.G. Davies, *The New Westminster Dictionary of Liturgy and Worship*, 1st American Edition (Philadelphia: Westminster Press), p. 292.

others. And why? Because they are the experts. They are trained professionals. Unfortunately, we look upon the Pastor in the same way. All of this does violence to the fact that every believer is a priest. Not only before God, but to one another.

But there is something more. The modern Pastorate rivals the functional Headship of Christ in His church. It illegitimately holds the unique place of centrality and headship among God's people. A place that is only reserved for one Person—the Lord Jesus. Jesus Christ is the *only* Head over a church and the final word to it.[220] By his office, the Pastor displaces and supplants Christ's Headship by setting himself up as the church's human head.

For this reason, nothing so hinders the fulfillment of God's eternal purpose as does the modern pastoral role. Why? Because that purpose is centered on making Christ's Headship visibly manifested in the church through the free, open, every-member functioning of the Body. As long as the pastoral office is present, you will never witness such a thing.

How the Pastor Destroys Himself

The modern Pastor not only does damage to God's people, he does damage to himself. The pastoral office has a way of chewing up all who come within its pale. Depression, burn-out, stress, and emotional breakdown are terribly high among Pastors. At the time of this writing, there are reportedly more than 500,000 Pastors serving churches in the U.S.[221] Of this mass number, consider the following statistics that lay bare the lethal danger of the pastoral office:

---

[220] In this regard (and contrary to popular opinion), the Pastor is *not* "the cerebellum, the center for communicating messages, coordinating functions, and conducting responses between the Head and the Body." He is not called to give "authoritative communication of the truth from the Head to the Body." And he is not the "accurate communicator of the needs from the Body to the Head." The Pastor is described with these inflated terms in the David L. McKenna's "The Ministry's Gordian Knot," *Leadership*, Winter, 1980, pp. 50-51.

[221] This figure comes from the Barna Research Group (*East Hillsborough Christian Voice*, February 2002, p. 3). Half of these churches have fewer than 100 active members ("Flocks in Need of Shepherds", *The Washington Times,* July 2, 2001).

- 94% feel pressured to have an ideal family.
- 90% work more than 46 hours a week.
- 81% say they have insufficient time with their spouses.
- 80% believe that pastoral ministry affects their family negatively.
- 70% do not have someone they consider a close friend.
- 70% have lower self-esteem than when they entered the ministry.
- 50% feel unable to meet the needs of the job.[222]
- 80% are discouraged or deal with depression.
- 40%+ report that they are suffering from burnout, frantic schedules, and unrealistic expectations.[223]
- 33% consider pastoral ministry an outright hazard to the family.[224]
- 33% have seriously considered leaving their position in the past year.[225]
- 40% of pastoral resignations are due to burnout.[226]

Most Pastors are expected to juggle 16 major tasks at once.[227] And most crumble under the pressure. For this reason, 1,600 ministers in all denominations across the U.S. are fired or forced to resign each month.[228] Over the past 20 years, the average length

---

[222] 1991 Survey of Pastors (Fuller Institute of Church Growth) quoted by London and Wiseman, *Pastors at Risk*, Victor Books, 1993; "Is the Pastor's Family Safe at Home?," *Leadership*, Fall 1992; *Physician Magazine*, September/October 1999, p. 22.

[223] Compilation of surveys from *Focus on the Family Pastors Gatherings*.

[224] Fuller Institute of Church Growth (Pasadena: Fuller Theological Seminary, 1991).

[225] "Flocks in Need of Shepherds," *The Washington Times*, July 2, 2001.

[226] *Vantage Point*, Denver Seminary, June 1998, p. 2.

[227] *East Hillsborough Christian Voice*, February 2002, p. 3.

[228] Ibid. From July 2nd to July 6th, 2001, *The Christian Citizen* (November 2000) reported that 1400 Pastors leave the pastorate each month. In the same vein, *The Washington Times* ran a series of five articles on the "clergy crisis" that is sweeping America (by Larry Witham). It stated the following: Very few of the clergy in this country are young. Only 8% are 35 or younger. Of the 70,000 students enrolled in the nation's 237 accredited theological seminaries, only a third want to lead a church as a Pastor. The pastorate draws more older candidates. Usually those who arrive after dead-end jobs or divorces. In like manner, a clergy shortage has hit most mainline Protestant churches in Canada. "While it may be personally enriching to minister to a flock, it's also daunting—for not a lot of money—to meet expectations

of a pastorate has declined from seven years to just over two years![229]

Unfortunately, few Pastors have connected the dots to discover that it is their office that causes this underlying turbulence.[230] Simply put: Jesus Christ never intended any person to sport all the hats the Pastor is expected to wear! He never intended any man to bear such a load.

The demands of the pastorate are crushing. So much so they will drain any mortal dry. Imagine for a moment that you were working for a company that paid you on the basis of how good you made your people feel? What if your pay depended on how entertaining you were, how friendly you were, how popular your wife and children were, how well-dressed you were, and how perfect was your behavior?

Can you imagine the unmitigated stress this would cause you? Can you see how such pressure would force you into playing to a pretentious role—all to keep your power, your prestige, and your job security? (For this reason, most Pastors are impervious to receiving any kind of help.)

The pastoral profession dictates standards of conduct like any other profession, whether it be teacher, doctor, or lawyer. The profession dictates how Pastors are to dress, speak, and act. This is one of the major reasons why many Pastors live very artificial lives.

In this regard, the pastoral role fosters dishonesty. Congregants expect their Pastor to always be cheerful, available at a moment's call, never resentful, never bitter, have perfectly disciplined

---

as a theologian, counselor, public speaker, administrator and community organizer all in one" (*Christian Century*, October 10, 2001, p. 13).

[229] *Vantage Point*, Denver Seminary, June 1998, p. 2.

[230] Marketing for *The Zondervan 2002 Pastor's Annual*, a famous book distributor used this ironic promotion: "Man works from sun to sun, but a Pastor's work is never done. That's because he must wear so many different hats: preacher, teacher, counselor, administrator, worship leader, and oftentimes fixer of the furniture too! For Pastors who'd like a hand with some of these hats, we here at Christianbook.com have just the resource for you." By the same token, a web-page designed to encourage wounded and burned-out clergy flies under the name www.woundedshepherds.com. These resources are like applying bandaids over cancer. They treat the symptom and ignore the root problem: The pastoral office.

families, and to be completely spiritual at all times.[231] Pastors play to this role like actors in a Greek drama. This accounts for the strange voice change when most Pastors pray. It accounts for the pious way they fold their hands. The unique way they say *"the Lord"* (typically pronounced *"the Lawd"*). And the special way they dress.[232]

All of these things are largely smoke and moon beams—utterly void of spiritual reality. Most Pastors cannot stay in their office without being corrupted on some level. The power-politics endemic to the office is a huge problem that isolates many of them and poisons their relationship with others.

In an insightful article to Pastors entitled *Preventing Clergy Burnout*, the author suggests something startling. His advice to Pastors gives us a clear peek into the power-politics that goes with the pastorate.[233] He implores Pastors to *"Fellowship with clergy of other denominations. These persons cannot harm you ecclesiastically, because they are not of your official circle. There is no political string they can pull to undo you."*[234]

Professional loneliness is another virus that runs high among Pastors. The lone-ranger plague drives some ministers into other careers. It drives others into crueler fates.[235]

All of these pathologies find their root in the history of the pastorate. It is "lonely at the top" because God never intended for anyone to be at the top—except His Son! In effect, the modern Pastor tries to shoulder the 58 NT "one another" exhortations all

---

[231] *East Hillsborough Christian Voice*, February 2002, p. 3.

[232] I realize that not all Pastors play to this role. But the few who manage to resist this incredible pressure are exotically rare. They are dramatic exceptions to an all-too tragic norm.

[233] Alarmingly, 23% of Protestant clergy have been fired at least once, and 41% of congregations have fired at least two Pastors (Survey done by *Leadership* printed in G. Lloyd Rediger's *Clergy Killers: Guidance for Pastors and Congregations Under Attack* (Philadelphia: Westminster/John Knox, 1997).

[234] J. Grant Swank, "Preventing Clergy Burnout," *Ministry*, November 1998, p. 20.

[235] Larry Yeagley, "The Lonely Pastor," *Ministry*, September 2001, p. 28; Michael L. Hill and Sharon P. Hill, *The Healing of a Warrior: A Protocol for the Prevention and Restoration of Ministers Engaging in Destructive Behavior* (Cyberbook, 2000).

by himself.[236] It is no wonder that most of them get crushed under the weight.[237]

Conclusion

The modern Pastor is the most unquestioned element in modern Christianity. Yet he does not have a strand of Scripture to support his existence nor a fig leaf to cover it!

Rather, the modern Pastor was born out of the single-bishop-rule first spawned by Ignatius and Cyprian. The bishop evolved into the local presbyter. In the Middle Ages, the presbyter grew into the Catholic priest. During the Reformation, he was transformed into the "Preacher," "the Minister," and finally "the Pastor"—the man upon whom all of Protestantism hangs. To juice it all down to one sentence: The Protestant Pastor is nothing more than a slightly reformed Catholic priest!

Catholic priests had seven duties at the time of the Reformation: Preaching, the sacraments, prayers for the flock, a godly life, discipline, church rites, supporting the poor, and visiting the sick.[238] The Protestant Pastor takes upon himself all of these responsibilities—plus he sometimes blesses civic events.

The famed poet John Milton put it best when he said: *"New presbyter is but old priest writ large!"*[239] This being interpreted means: The modern Pastor is but an old priest written in larger letters!

---

[236] For a list of the "one another" exhortations, see *Who is Your Covering?*, Chapter 1.

[237] *Searching Together*, Volume 23:4, Winter 1995 discusses this issue at length.

[238] Johann Gerhard in *Church Ministry* by Eugene F.A. King (St. Louis: Concordia Publishing House, 1993), p. 181.

[239] From Milton's 1653 poem *On the New Forces of Conscience.*

I majored in Bible in college. I went to the seminary and I majored in the only thing they teach there: the professional ministry. When I graduated, I realized that I could speak Latin, Greek, and Hebrew, and the only thing on earth I was qualified for was to be Pope. But someone else had the job.

-Anonymous Pastor

CHAPTER 5

SUNDAY MORNING COSTUMES: COVERING UP THE PROBLEM

Beware of those who go about in long robes.
-Jesus Christ

E very Sunday morning, over 300 million Protestants put on their best clothes to attend Sunday morning church.[1] But no one seems to question why. Thousands of pastors wear special garb that separates them from their congregants. And no one seems to care.

In this chapter, we will explore the origin of "dressing up" for church. We will also trace the roots of the "clergy costume."

Dressing Up for Church

The practice of "dressing up" for church is a relatively recent phenomenon. It began in the late-18th century with the Industrial Revolution, and it became widespread in the mid-19th century. Before this time, "dressing up" for social events was only known among the very wealthy. The reason was simple. Only the well-to-do aristocrats of society could afford nice clothing! Common folks only had two sets of clothes: Work clothes for laboring in the field and less tattered clothing for going into town.[2]

---

[1] Denominations like the Vineyard are the exception. Such neo-denominations espouse a casual form of worship that typically includes coffee and donuts before the service. Shorts and T-shirts are common apparel in a Vineyard church service. Of the 347,000 Protestant churches in the United States and the 22,200 churches in Canada comprising 230 denominations, most congregants "dress up" for Sunday morning church (this figure comes from "Religious Market" magazine—american-churchlists@infoUSA.com). If we add the number of non-Protestant Christians that "dress up" for church, the number is astronomical.

[2] Max Barsis, *The Common Man Through the Centuries* (New York: Unger, 1973).

"Dressing up" for any occasion was only an option for the wealthiest nobility.[3] In medieval Europe up until the 18th century, dress was a clear marker of one's social class. In some places like England, poor people were actually forbidden to wear the clothing of the "better" people.[4]

This changed with the invention of mass textile manufacturing and the development of urban society.[5] Fine clothes became more affordable to the common people. The middle class was born and those within it were able to emulate the envied aristocracy. For the first time, the middle class could distinguish themselves from the peasants.[6] To demonstrate their newly improved status, they could now "dress up" for social events just like the well-to-do.[7]

Some Christian groups in the late 18th and early 19th centuries resisted this cultural trend. John Wesley wrote against wearing expensive or flashy clothing.[8] The early Methodists resisted the idea of "dressing up" for church so much that they turned away anyone who wore expensive clothing to their meetings.[9] The early

---

[3] Leigh Eric Schmidt, "A Church Going People is a Dress-Loving People," *Church History* (58), pp. 38-39.

[4] Ibid.

[5] James Hargreaves invented the "spinning jenny" in 1764 creating finer more colorful clothing that was affordable to the masses (Elizabeth Ewing, *Everyday Dress 1650-1900*, London: Bratsford, 1984, pp. 56-57).

[6] Richard Bushman, *The Refinement of America* (New York: Knopf, 1992), p. 313.

[7] Henry Warner Bowden and P.C. Kemeny, ed., *American Church History: A Reader* (Nashville, Abingdon Press, 1971), pp. 87-89. Dress and hierarchy were closely connected in colonial America. A pamphlet published anonymously in Philadelphia in 1722 entitled *The Miraculous Power of Clothes, and Dignity of the Taylors: Being an Essay on the Words, Clothes Make Men* suggested the following: Social status, station, and power were displayed, expressed, and sustained through dress. The connection between dress and hierarchy in colonial society invested clothes with symbolic power. This mindset eventually seeped into the Christian church.

[8] Rupert Davies, *A History of the Methodist Church in Great Britain* (London: Epworth, 1965), p. 193; *Journals of Wesley*, Nehemiah Curnock, ed. (London: Epworth Press, 1965), p. 193. Wesley's teaching on clothing has been called "a gospel of plainness." His main message was that Christians ought to dress plainly, neatly, and simply. Wesley spoke on this subject so often that he is credited for coining the phrase: "Cleanliness is next to godliness." However, he borrowed it from a rabbi (Phinehas Ben-Yair, *Song of Songs*, Midrash Rabbah, I.1:9).

[9] *A History of the Methodist Church in Great Britain*, p. 197.

Baptists also condemned fine clothing, teaching that it separated the rich from the poor.[10]

Nevertheless, despite these protests, mainstream Christians began wearing fine clothes whenever they could. The growing middle class prospered, creating bigger homes, larger church buildings, and fancier clothing.[11] As the Victorian enculturation of the middle class grew, fancier church buildings began to draw more influential people in society.[12] This caused the more common congregations (Methodists, Baptists, etc.) to work harder to try to keep up with the improvements of their own buildings.[13]

This all came to a head when in 1843, Horace Bushnell, an influential Congregational minister in Connecticut, published an essay called *Taste and Fashion*. In it, Bushnell argued that sophistication and refinement were attributes of God and that Christians should emulate them.[14] Thus was born the idea of "dressing up" for church to honor God! Church members now worshipped in elaborately decorated buildings sporting their formal clothes to honor God.[15]

Following hard on the heels of Bushnell, a North Carolina Presbyterian named William Henry Foote wrote in 1846 that *"a church-going people are a dress loving people."*[16] This statement simply expressed the formal dress ritual that mainstream Christians had adopted when going to church. The trend was so powerful that by the 1850s, even the "formal-dress-resistant" Methodists got

---

[10] "A Church Going People is a Dress-Loving People," p. 40.

[11] *The Refinement of America*, pp. 335, 352.

[12] Ibid., p. 350. Denominations with a greater number of wealthy members (Episcopal, Unitarian, etc.) began selling pews to wealthy families to fund elaborate church building programs. "On top of pew costs, worshippers had to wear clothes in keeping with the splendor of the building, and the style of the congregation became an insurmountable barrier for many. A century earlier a common farmer could dress up for church by putting on a blue check shirt. In the genteel atmosphere of the new beautiful churches, more was required."

[13] Ibid., pp. 335, 342, 346.

[14] Ibid., pp. 328, 331.

[15] Ibid., p. 350.

[16] "A Church Going People is a Dress-Loving People," p. 36.

absorbed by it. And they too began wearing their "Sunday best" for church.[17]

Accordingly, like virtually every other accepted church practice, dressing up for church is the result of the Christian being influenced by his surrounding culture. Today, you dear Christian, "suit up" for Sunday morning church without ever asking why. But now you know the story behind this mindless custom.

It is purely the result of 19th-century middle class efforts to become like their wealthy aristocrat contemporaries, showing off their improved status by their clothing. (This effort was also helped along by Victorian notions of respectability.) Put another way, wearing your "Sunday best" is simply a product of secular culture. It has nothing to do with the Bible, Jesus Christ, or the Holy Spirit!

So What Is Wrong With It?

So what is the big deal about "dressing up" for church? I agree that it is hardly a burning issue. In fact, I care little about what a person wears when attending a church meeting. It is what "dressing up" for church represents that is the burning issue.

First, it reflects the false cleavage between the secular and the sacred. To think that God cares one wit if you wear dressy threads on Sunday to "meet Him" is a violation of the New Covenant. We have access to God's presence at all times and in all circumstances. Does He really expect His people to dress up for a beauty pageant on Sunday morning?

Second, wearing attractive, flashy clothes on Sunday morning screams out a false message: That church is the place where Christians hide their real selves and "dress them up" to look nice and pretty.[18] Think about it. Wearing your "Sunday best" for

---

[17] *The Refinement of America*, p. 319. "The early Methodists knew fashionable dress was the enemy, and now the enemy was winning." Schmidt writes, "People were concerned on the Sabbath . . . to dress themselves in their best clothes; Sunday best was already proverbial. Even pietists and evangelicals who insisted on plain dress nonetheless made sure that their bodies were gravely and decently clothed" ("A Church Going People is a Dress-Loving People," p. 45).

[18] God looks at the heart; He is not impressed with the garb we wear (1 Sam. 16:7; Luke 11:39; 1 Pet. 3:3-5). Our worship is in the spirit, not in physical outward forms (John 4:20-24).

church is little more than impression management. It gives the house of God all the elements of a stage show: Costumes, makeup, props, lighting, ushers, special music, Master of Ceremonies, performance, and the featured program.[19]

"Dressing up" for church violates the reality that the church is made up of real people with messy problems. Real people who may have gotten into a major-league bickering match with their spouses just before they drove into the parking lot and put on a colossal smile to cover it up!

Wearing our "Sunday best" conceals a basic underlying problem. It fosters the inflated illusion that we are somehow "good" because we are dressing up for God. It is a study in pretense that is dehumanizing and constitutes a false witness to the world.

Face it. As fallen humans, we are seldom willing to appear to be what we really are. We almost always rely on our performance or dress to give people a certain impression of what we want them to believe we are. All of this differs markedly from the simplicity that marked the early church.

Third, "dressing up" for church smacks against the primitive simplicity that was the sustaining hallmark of the early church. The first-century Christians did not "dress up" to attend church meetings. They met in the simplicity of living rooms. They did not dress to exhibit their social class. In fact, the early Christians made concrete efforts to show their absolute disdain for social class distinctions.[20]

In the church, all social distinctions are erased. The early Christians knew well that they were a new species on this planet. For this reason, James levels a rebuke to those believers who were

---

[19] Christian Smith, "Our Dressed Up Selves," *Voices in the Wilderness* (Sept/Oct. 1987), p. 2.

[20] In his book *Ante Pacem: Archaeological Evidence of Church Life Before Constantine* (Mercer University Press/Seedsowers, 1985), Graydon Snyder states that there are about 30 extant letters written by Christians before Constantine. These letters lean toward only one name, which indicates that the Christians did not use the full names of their brethren. The reason: So their social ranks would be hidden from one another! (Private Emails from Graydon Snyder, 10/12/2001 and 10/14/2001.)

treating the rich saints better than the poor saints. He boldly reproves the rich for dressing differently from the poor![21]

And yet, many Christians are under the false delusion that it is "irreverent" to dress in informal clothing when attending Sunday morning church service. It is not dissimilar to how the Scribes and the Pharisees accused the Lord and His disciples of being "irreverent" for not following the tradition of the elders.[22]

In short, to say that the Lord expects His people to dress in fine clothing when the church gathers is to add to the Scriptures and speak where God has not spoken.[23] Such a practice is human tradition at its best.

The Garb of the Clergy

Let us now shift gears and look at the development of the clergy costume. Christian clergy did not dress differently from the common people until the coming of Constantine.[24]

Contrary to popular opinion, the clergy costume (including the "ecclesiastical vestments" of the high church tradition) did not originate with the priestly dress of the Old Testament. It rather has its origin in the secular dress of the Greco-Roman world.[25]

Clement of Alexandria (150-215) argued that the clergy should wear better garments than the laity. (By this time the church liturgy

---

[21] Jam. 2:1-5. This passage also indicates that a person wearing fashionable clothing to the church meeting was the exception, not the standard.

[22] Mark 7:1-13.

[23] Deu. 4:2; Prov. 30:6; Rev. 22:18.

[24] "Vestments," *The Catholic Encyclopedia 1913 On-Line Edition* (www.new-advent.org/cathen); "Sacred Rights Ceremonies: The Concept and Forms of Ritual: Christianity," *Encyclopedia Britannica* (On-line edition, 1994-1998). Shortly before Constantine, clergymen wore a cloak of fine material when administering the Eucharist.

[25] "Vestments," *The Catholic Encyclopedia.* Under "Origin" the entry reads: "The Christian vestments did not originate in the priestly dress of the Old Testament, they have, rather, developed from the secular dress of the Graeco-Roman world." See also Janet Mayo, *A History of Ecclesiastical Dress* (New York: Holmes & Meier Publishers, 1984), pp. 11-12. Mayo writes, "A consideration of ecclesiastical vestments will reveal that they had their origins in secular Roman dress. The view that vestments were of Levitical origin and came from Jewish priestly garments is a later idea . . ." For a rare history of the religious costume, see Amelia Mott Gummere, *The Quaker: A Study in Costume* (New York, 1901).

was regarded as a formal event.) Clement said that the minister's clothes should be "simple" and "white."[26]

White was the color of the clergy for centuries. This custom appears to have been borrowed from the pagan philosopher Plato who wrote that *"white was the color of the gods."* In this regard, both Clement and Tertullian (160-225) felt that dyed colors were displeasing to the Lord.[27]

With the coming of Constantine, distinctions between bishop, priest, and deacon began to take root.[28] When Constantine moved his court to Byzantium and renamed it Constantinople in A.D. 330, the official Roman dress was gradually adopted by the priests and deacons.[29] The clergy were now identified by wearing the garb of secular officials.[30]

After the Germanic conquests of the Roman Empire from the fourth century onward, fashions in secular dress changed. The flowing garments of the Romans gave way to the short tunics of the Goths. But the clergy, wishing to remain distinct from the laity, continued to wear the old-fashioned and archaic Roman costumes![31]

The clergy wore these outdated garments during the church service following the model of the secular court ritual.[32] When laymen adopted the new style of dress, the clergy believed that such dress was "worldly" and "barbarian." They retained what they

---

[26] "On Clothes" in *The Instructor*, Ante-Nicene Fathers, Vol. 2, p. 284.

[27] "On Clothes" in *The Instructor*, Bk 2. Ch. 11; *A History of Ecclesiastical Dress*, p. 15.

[28] *A History of Ecclesiastical Dress*, pp. 14-15.

[29] Ibid., pp. 14-15; Kenneth Scott Latourette, *A History of Christianity* (New York: Harper and Brothers, 1953), p 211. *The Westminster Dictionary of Church History* (Philadelphia: The Westminster Press, 1971), p. 284.

[30] "The bishop's dress was the ancient robe of a Roman magistrate." Edwin Hatch, *The Organization of the Early Christian Churches* (London: Longman's, Green, and Co., 1895), p. 164. The bishop's dress indicated a specific caste structure. It included a white fringed saddlecloth or *mappula*, and flat black slippers, *campagi*, and *undones* or white stockings. This was the dress of the Roman magistrates. (Paul Johnson, *A History of Christianity*, New York: Simon & Schuster, 1976, p. 133).

[31] Frank Senn, *Christian Worship and Its Cultural Setting* (Philadelphia: Fortress Press, 1983), p. 41; "Sacred Rights Ceremonies: The Concept and Forms of Ritual": Christianity," *Encyclopedia Britannica* (On-line edition, 1994-1998).

[32] Private Email from Eugene TeSelle, Professor of Church History and Theology, Vanderbilt University, 1/18/2000.

considered to be "civilized" dress. And this is what became the clerical costume.[33] This practice was supported by the theologians of the day. For example, Jerome (347-420) remarked that the clergy should never enter into the sanctuary wearing everyday garments.[34]

From the fifth century onward, bishops wore purple.[35] In the sixth and seventh centuries, clergy garb became more elaborate and costly.[36] By the Middle Ages, their clothing acquired mystical and symbolic meanings.[37] Special vestments were spawned around the sixth and seventh centuries. And there grew up the custom of keeping a special set of garments in the vestry to put over one's street clothes.[38]

During the seventh and eighth centuries, the vestments were accepted as sacred objects inherited from the robes of Levitical priests in the Old Testament.[39] (This was a rationalization to justify

---

[33] *A History of Ecclesiastical Dress*, p. 15; Ilion T. Jones, *A Historical Approach to Evangelical Worship* (New York: Abingdon Press, 1954), p. 117.

[34] Jerome said that God is honored if the bishop wears a white tunic more handsome than usual. Private Email from Frank Senn 7/18/2000. See also Jerome, "Against Jovinianus" Book 2.34 (*Nicene and Post-Nicene Fathers,* Series II, Vol. VI) and "Lives of Illustrious Men," Chapter 2 (*Nicene/Post-Nicene Fathers,* Series II, Vol. III).

[35] Father Michael Collins and Matthew A. Price, *The Story of Christianity* (DK Publishing, 1999), pp. 25, 65.

[36] *A Historical Approach to Evangelical Worship*, pp. 116-117. Mayo's *A History of Ecclesiastical Dress* goes into great detail on the development of each piece of the clerical vestments through each stage of history in each tradition. No distinctive head-dress was worn for the first thousand years, and the girdle was not known until the eighth century (*A Concise Cyclopedia of Religious Knowledge*, New York: Charles L. Webster & Company, 1890, p. 943.)

[37] *A History of Ecclesiastical Dress*, p. 27; Isidore of Pelusium (d. around 440) was the first to ascribe symbolic interpretations to parts of the vestments. The entire priestly garb was given symbolic meanings around the eighth century in the West and the ninth century in the East ("Vestments," *The Catholic Encyclopedia*). The Medievals had a love affair with symbolism. So they could not resist giving all the vestments religious "spiritual" meanings. These meanings are still alive today in liturgical churches.

[38] *Christian Worship and Its Cultural Setting*, p. 41. The vestry, or sacristy, was a special room in the church building where the clerical vestments and other sacred vessels were kept.

[39] *A History of Ecclesiastical Dress*, p. 27.

the practice.) By the 12th century, the clergy began wearing everyday street clothes that distinguished them from the people.[40]

What the Reformation Changed

During the Reformation, the break with tradition and clerical vestments was slow and gradual.[41] In the place of the clergy vestments, the Reformers adopted the scholar's black gown.[42] It was also known as the "philosopher's cloak" as it had been worn by philosophers in the fourth and fifth centuries.[43] So prevalent was the new clerical garb that the black gown of the secular scholar became *the* garment of the Protestant pastor.[44]

The Lutheran pastor wore his long black gown in the streets. He also wore a round "ruff" around his neck that grew larger with time. It grew so large that by the 17th century the ruff was called "the millstone ruff."[45] (The ruff is still worn in some Lutheran churches today.)

Interestingly, however, the Reformers still retained the clerical vestments. The Protestant pastor wore them when he administered the Lord's Supper.[46] This is still the case today in most Protestant denominations. The pastor will put his clerical robes on when he

---

[40] *The Story of Christianity*, pp. 25, 65.

[41] *A History of Ecclesiastical Dress*, p. 64. Zwingli and Luther quickly discarded the garments of the Catholic priest. David D. Hall, *The Faithful Shepherd* (Chapel Hill: The University of North Carolina Press, 1972), p. 6.

[42] Zwingli was the first to introduce the scholar's gown in Zurich in the autumn of 1523. Luther began to wear it in the afternoon of October 9, 1524 (*The Ministry in Historical Perspectives*, p. 147). See also George Marsden, *The Soul of the American University: From Protestant Establishment and Established Nonbelief* (New York: Oxford University Press, 1994), p. 37.

[43] H.I. Marrou, *A History of Education in Antiquity* (New York: Sheed and Ward, 1956), p. 206. "The philosopher could be recognized by his cloak, which was short and dark and made of coarse cloth." See also M.A. Smith, *From Christ to Constantine* (Downer's Grove: InterVarsity Press, 1973), p. 105.

[44] H. Richard Niebuhr and Daniel D. Williams, *The Ministry in Historical Perspectives* (San Francisco: Harper and Row Publishers, 1956), p. 147. The black gown was "clerical streetwear" in the 16th century (*Christian Worship and Its Cultural Setting*), p. 42.

[45] Owen Chadwick, *The Reformation* (Penguin Books, 1968), pp. 422-423.

[46] *A History of Ecclesiastical Dress*, p. 66.

lifts the bread and the cup. At that moment, he shows himself for what he really is: *A Reformed Catholic priest!*

Even so, the garb of the Reformed pastor symbolized spiritual authority. To don the black gown was to show the minister's spiritual power.[47] This trend continued throughout the 17th and 18th centuries. Pastors always wore dark clothing, preferably black. (This was the traditional color for lawyers and doctors during the 16th century. It was the color of "professionals.")

Black soon became the color of every minister in every branch of the church.[48] The black scholar's gown eventually evolved into the "frock-coat" of the 1940s. The frock-coat was later replaced by the black or grey "lounge suit" of the 20th century.[49]

At the beginning of the 19th century, all clergymen wore white collars with a tie. In fact, it was considered highly improper for a clergyman to appear without a tie.[50] Low church clergy (Baptists, Pentecostals, etc.) wore the collar and necktie. High church clergy (Anglicans, Episcopalians, Lutherans, etc.) adopted the clerical collar—often dubbed the "dog collar."[51]

The origin of the clerical collar goes back to 1865. It was not a Catholic invention as is popularly believed. It was invented by the Anglicans.[52] Priests in the 18th and 19th centuries traditionally wore black cassocks (floor-length garments with collars that stood straight up) over white garments (sometimes called the alb).

In other words, they wore a black collar with white in the middle. The clerical collar was simply a removable version of this collar. It was invented so that priests, both Anglican and Catholic, could slip it over their street clothes and be recognized as "men of God" in any place!

---

[47] *American Church History: A Reader*, p. 89.

[48] *A History of Ecclesiastical Dress*, pp. 77-78.

[49] Ibid., p. 118.

[50] Ibid., p. 94.

[51] Ibid., pp. 94,118.

[52] *The Ministry in Historical Perspectives*, p. 164. According to *The London Times* (March 14, 2002), the clerical collar was invented by the Rev. Dr. Donald McLeod of Glasgow. A popular belief is that the clerical collar was invented by the Catholic Counter-Reformation to prevent priests from wearing large ruffs like Protestant pastors wore (*The Reformation*, p. 423). But it seems to have come into being well after this.

Today, it is the dark suit with a tie that is the clerical costume of most Protestant pastors. Many pastors would not be caught dead without it! It is often worn when the pastor appears at non-religious public events. Some Protestant pastors wear the clergy collar also—just in case people forget that he is "a man of God."

Are Clergy Costumes Harmful?

A costumed clergy is an affront to the spiritual principles that govern the house of God. It strikes at the heart of the church by separating God's people into two classes: "Professional" and "non-professional."

Like "dressing up" for church, the clerical costume—whether it be the elaborate vestments of the "high church" minister or the dark suit of the evangelical pastor—is rooted in worldly culture. The distinctive garb of the clergy goes back to the fourth century, when clergymen adopted the dress of Roman secular officials.

The Lord Jesus and His disciples knew nothing of wearing special clothing to impress God or to distinguish themselves from God's people.[53] Wearing special garb for religious purposes was rather a characteristic of the Scribes and Pharisees.[54] And neither Scribe nor Pharisee could escape the Lord's penetrating gaze when He said, *"Beware of the teachers of the Law. They like to walk around in flowing robes and love to be greeted in the marketplaces and have the most important seats in the synagogues and the places of honor at banquets."*[55]

---

[53] Luke 7:25; 2 Cor. 8:9. It appears that the nicest clothes that Jesus owned while on earth were given to him in mockery—Luke 23:11. Recall that the Son of God entered this earth, not in kingly garments, but wrapped in swaddling clothes (Luke 2:7). Note that John the Baptist is the most extreme case of those who did not seek to impress God by their clothing (Matt. 3:4).

[54] Matt. 23:5; Mark 12:38.

[55] Luke 20:46, NIV.

Beware lest any man spoil you through philosophy and vain deceit, after the tradition of men, after the rudiments of the world, and not after Christ.
   -Paul of Tarsus

CHAPTER 6

MINISTERS OF MUSIC:
SECOND-STRING CLERGY

*We cannot avoid bringing our culture to church with us;
it is part of our very being. But in the light of tradition we
need to sort out those cultural influences that contribute
to the integrity of Christian worship from those that
detract from it.*
-Frank C. Senn

Walk into any modern church and the liturgy will virtually always begin with singing hymns, choruses, or praise and worship songs. There is no exception.
In every case, there will be a person (or a team of people) that both leads and controls the singing. In more traditional churches, it will be the "choir director" or the "music minister."[1] It may even be the choir itself. In more contemporary churches, it will be the "worship leader" or the "praise and worship team."

Leading up to the sacred sermon, those who "lead worship" select the songs that are to be sung. They begin those songs. They decide how those songs are to be sung. And they decide when those songs are over. God's people in no way, shape, or form lead the singing. They are rather led by someone else who is often part of the clerical staff—or who receives similar honor.

This is in stark contrast to the first-century way. In the early church, worship and singing were in the hands of God's people.[2] The church herself led her own songs. Singing and leading songs was a corporate affair, not a professional event led by specialists.

---

[1] In some churches, this role is played by the ever-talented pastor.
[2] Eph. 5:19; Col. 3:16. Note the words "speaking to yourselves" and "one another" in these passages.

The Origins of the Choir

This all began to change with the advent of the Christian choir. The origin of the Christian choir dates back to the fourth century. Shortly after the Edict of Milan (A.D. 313), the persecution of Christians ceased. Under Constantine's reign, choirs were developed and trained to help celebrate the Eucharist. The practice was borrowed from Roman custom, which began its imperial ceremonies with processional music. Special schools were established and choir singers were given the status of a second-string clergy.[3]

The roots of the choir are found in the pagan Greek temples and Greek dramas.[4] Will Durant stated it beautifully: *"In the Middle Ages, as in ancient Greece, the main fountainhead of drama was in religious liturgy. The Mass itself was a dramatic spectacle; the sanctuary a sacred stage; the celebrants wore symbolic costumes; priest and acolytes engaged in dialogue; and the antiphonal responses of priest and choir, and of choir to choir, suggested precisely that same evolution of drama from dialogue that had generated the sacred Dionysian play."*[5]

With the advent of the choir in the Christian church, singing

---

[3] Edwin Liemohn, *The Organ and Choir in Protestant Worship* (Philadelphia: Fortress Press, 1968), p. 8.
[4] The Greeks had trained choirs to accompany their pagan worship (H.W. Parke, *The Oracles of Apollo in Asia Minor,* Croomhelm, 1995, pp. 102-103). Greek plays, both tragedy and comedy, were accompanied by orchestras (Marion Bauer & Ethel Peyser, *How Music Grew,* New York: G.P. Putnam's Sons, 1939, pp. 36, 45; Elizabeth Rogers, *Music Through the Ages,* New York: G.P. Putnam's Sons, 1967, p. 87; Carl Shaulk, *Key Words in Church Music,* St. Louis: Concordia Publishing House, 1978, p. 64; Johannes Quasten, *Music & Worship in Pagan and Christian Antiquity,* Washington D.C.: National Association of Pastoral Musicians, 1983, p. 76; Alfred Sendrey, *Music in the Social and Religious Life of Antiquity,* Rutherford: Fairleigh Dickinson University Press, pp. 327, 412). There were typically between 15 and 24 people in the Greek choirs (Claude Calame, *Choruses of Young Women in Ancient Greece,* Lanham: Rowman & Littlefield, 2001, p. 21). Some have tried to argue that the Christians borrowed choirs and chanting from the Jewish synagogue. But this is highly unlikely as the third and fourth-century Christians borrowed little to nothing from the Jews. Instead, they drew heavily from their surrounding Greco-Roman culture. Interestingly, Greek music had its genesis in the Orient and Asia Minor (*Music Through the Ages,* p. 95).
[5] Will Durant, *The Age of Faith* (New York: Simon & Schuster, 1950), p. 1027.

shifted from the hands of God's people to the clerical staff composed of trained singers.[6] This shift was partly due to the fact that heretical doctrines were spread through hymn singing. The clergy felt that if the singing of hymns was in their control, it would curb the spread of heresy.[7] But it was also rooted in the ever growing power of the clergy as the main performers in the Christian drama.[8]

By A.D. 367, congregational singing was altogether banned. It was replaced by the trained choirs.[9] Thus was born the trained professional singer in the church. Singing in Christian worship was now the domain of the clergy and choir.

Ambrose (339-397) is credited for creating the first post-apostolic Christian hymns.[10] These hymns were modeled on the old Greek modes and called by Greek names.[11] Ambrose also created a collection of liturgical chants which are still used today in some Catholic churches.[12] The liturgical chant is the direct descendent of

---

[6] *The Organ and Choir in Protestant Worship*, pp. 8-9. Up until the fourth century, congregational singing was a characteristic feature of Christian worship.

[7] *The Study of the History of Music*, pp. 16, 24.

[8] *How Music Grew*, pp. 71-72.

[9] *Music Through the Ages*, p. 108. The Council of Laodicea (A.D. 367) forbade all others to sing in church beside the canonical singers. This act was to ensure that the quality of singing could be more homogeneous and controllable by those directing the worship (J.G. Davies, *The New Westminster Dictionary of Liturgy and Worship: First American Edition*, Philadelphia: Westminster Press, 1986, p. 131; Arthur Mees, *Choirs and Choral Music*, New York: Greenwood Press, 1969, pp. 25-26).

[10] Ambrose's hymns were orthodox. The Arians used hymns plentifully to promote their heretical teachings about Jesus. (Arians believed that Jesus was a creature created by God.)

[11] *How Music Grew*, p.71. "The Greek musical system was the precursor of that of the early Christian church, and the line of descent is unbroken from Greece, through Rome, to the Middle Ages and modern times." Edward Dickinson, *The Study of the History of Music* (New York: Charles Schribner's Sons, 1905), p. 9. Actually, the earliest full text we have of a Christian hymn is dated around A.D. 200. Ambrose simply brought hymn writing to a common peak in the church. Christian music at this time drew from popular Greek idioms (Barry Leisch, *The New Worship: Straight Talk on Music and the Church*, Grand Rapids: Baker Book House, 1996, p. 35).

[12] *Music Through the Ages*, p. 106.

the pagan Roman chant, which goes back to the ancient Sumarian cities.[13]

Papal choirs began in the fifth century.[14] When Gregory the Great became Pope near the end of the sixth century, he reorganized the *Schola Cantorum* (school of singing) in Rome. (This school was founded by Pope Sylvester who died in A.D. 335.)[15]

With this school, Gregory established professional singers who trained Christian choirs all throughout the Roman Empire. The singers trained for nine years. They had to memorize every song they sang—including the famous "Gregorian chant."[16] Gregory wiped out the last vestiges of congregational singing, believing it was the exclusive right of trained singers. He believed that singing was a clerical function.

Trained choirs, trained singers, and the end of congregational singing all reflected the cultural mindset of the Greeks. Much like oratory (professional speaking), the Greek culture was built around an audience-performer dynamic. Tragically, this trait was carried over from the temples of Diana and the Greek dramas straight into the Christian church! The congregation of God's people became spectators not only in spoken ministry, but in singing as well![17] Regrettably, the spirit of Greek spectatorship still lives in the modern church.

Boys choirs also go back to the days of Constantine. Most of them were created from orphanages.[18] Boys choirs stayed with the

---

[13] *How Music Grew*, p. 70; *Music Through the Ages*, p. 61. "From words which have survived we know that each [Sumarian] temple practiced well-organized liturgies chanted in the techniques of solo and response (between priest and choir) and antiphony (choir to choir)." See also *The Study of the History of Music*, p. 25.

[14] *The Study of the History of Music*, p. 18.

[15] *Music Through the Ages*, p. 109; Andrew Wilson-Dickson, *The Story of Christian Music* (Oxford: Lion Publishing, 1992), p. 43; David Appleby, *History of Church Music* (Chicago: Moody Press, 1965), p. 28.

[16] *How Music Grew*, pp. 73-75; *Music Through the Ages*, p. 109. All singing at this time was without musical instruments.

[17] Edward Dickinson, *The Study of the History of Music* (New York: Charles Schribner's Sons, 1905), p. 14.

[18] "Choir," *The Catholic Encyclopedia, 1913 On-Line Edition* (www.newadvent.org/cathen/); *Key Words in Church Music*, pp. 64-65. "Choir," *Harper's Encyclopedia of Religious Education* (San Francisco: Harper & Row Publishers, 1971).

church for hundreds of years after their founding. The Vienna Boys Choir, for example, was founded in Vienna, Austria in 1498. The choir sang exclusively for the court, at Mass, and at private concerts and state events.[19] A little known fact is that Boys choirs came from the pagans.[20] The pagans believed that the voice of young boys possessed special features.[21]

Funeral Processions

During the days of Constantine, Roman betrothal practices and funeral processions were adapted and transformed into Christian "weddings" and "funerals."[22] Both were borrowed from pagan practice.[23] As one scholar put it, *"The pagan cult of the dead was too much a part of the past lives of many Christians, formerly pagans, for them simply to be able to replace pagan dirges and funeral music with Psalmody."*[24]

The so-called funeral dirge that is observed and accepted by Christians also came out of paganism.[25] It was brought into the Christian church in the early third century. Tertullian was opposed to Christian funeral procession simply because it had a pagan origin.[26]

Not only did the funeral procession emerge out of paganism. But so did the funeral oration. It was the common practice of pagans in the Roman Empire to hire one of the town's eloquent professors to speak at the funeral of a loved one. The speaker followed a little handbook for such occasions. He would work himself up to a passionate pitch and then say of the deceased, *"He*

---

[19] http://www.bach-cantatas.com/Bio/Wiener-Sangerknaben.htm. For a discussion on the pagan origin of women's choirs, see *Music & Worship in Pagan and Christian Antiquity*, pp. 77-86.

[20] *The Oracles of Apollo in Asia Minor,* pp. 102-103; *Music & Worship in Pagan and Christian Antiquity,* p. 87ff. "The pagans frequently used boys choirs in their worship, especially on festive occasions."

[21] Ibid., p. 87.

[22] Frank Senn, *Christian Worship and Its Cultural Setting* (Philadelphia: Fortress Press, 1983), p. 41.

[23] See Chapter 1.

[24] *Music & Worship in Pagan and Christian Antiquity,* pp. 86, 160ff.

[25] Ibid., p. 163.

[26] Ibid., pp. 164-165.

now lives among the gods, traversing the heavens and looking down on life below."[27] It was his job to comfort the loved ones of the deceased. This role is filled today by the modern pastor, even down to the very words of the oration!

The Contribution of the Reformation

The major musical contribution of the Reformers was the restoration of congregational singing and the use of instruments. John Huss (1372-1415) of Bohemia and his followers (called Hussites) were among the first to restore congregational singing in the church.[28]

Luther also encouraged congregational singing at certain parts of the service.[29] But congregational hymn singing did not reach its peak until the 18th century during the Wesleyan revival in England.[30]

In Reformation churches, the choir remained. It both supported and led congregational singing.[31] 150 years after the Reformation,

---

[27] Ramsay MacMullen, *Christianizing the Roman Empire: A.D. 100-400* (London: Yale University Press, 1984), pp. 11-13

[28] Ilion T. Jones, *A Historical Approach to Evangelical Worship* (New York: Abingdon Press, 1954), p. 257. The Hussites created the first Protestant hymn book in 1505 in Prague. See also John Mark Terry, *Evangelism: A Concise History* (Nashville: Broadman & Holman Publishers, 1994), p. 68.

[29] *A Historical Approach to Evangelical Worship*, p. 257. During Luther's day, some 60 hymnbooks were published. More specifically, Luther augmented congregational singing as part of the liturgy. He left a Latin Mass, which was sung by the choir in towns and universities, and a German Mass, which was sung by the congregation in villages and rural places. These two models were merged in Lutheran practice in the 16th-18th centuries. The Reformed were opposed to both choral music and congregational hymns. They approved only the singing of metrical (versified) Psalms and other Biblical canticles. From their perspective, choirs and hymns were Roman. So Lutheran use of them demonstrated a half-baked reform (private Email from Frank Senn, 11/18/2000).

[30] *A Historical Approach to Evangelical Worship*, p. 257. The hymns of Isaac Watts, John Wesley, and Charles Wesley were widely used. Hymn writing and singing swept all Free Churches on two continents during this time.

[31] *The Organ and Choir in Protestant Worship*, p. 15. James F. White remarks that "to this day there remains considerable confusion of exactly what the function of the choir is in Protestant worship, and there is no single good rationale for the existence of the choir in Protestantism" (John F. White, *Protestant Worship and Church Architecture*, New York: Oxford University Press, 1964, p. 186).

congregational singing became a generally accepted practice.[32] By the 18th century, the organ would take the place of the choir in leading Christian worship.[33]

Interestingly, there is no evidence of musical instruments in the Christian church service until the Middle Ages.[34] Before then, all singing during the service was unaccompanied by musical instruments.[35] The church fathers took a dim view of musical instruments, associating them with immorality and idolatry.[36] Calvin continued this practice. He felt that musical instruments were pagan. Consequently, for two centuries, Reformed churches sang Psalms without the use of instruments.[37]

The organ was the first instrument used by post-Constantinian Christians.[38] Organs were found in Christian churches as early as the sixth century. But they were not used during the Mass until the 12th century. By the 13th century, the organ became an integral part of the Mass.[39]

The organ was first used to give the tone to the priests and the choir.[40] During the Reformation, the organ became the standard instrument used in Protestant worship. While Calvinists (and

---

[32] *The Organ and Choir in Protestant Worship,* pp. 15-16.

[33] Ibid., p. 19. In the 17th century, the organ would play parts against the unison singing of the congregation, thus drowning out the people. Genevan churches tore out the organs from their church buildings because they did not want worship to be stolen from the people (*The Story of Christian Music,* pp. 62, 76-77). As with the steeple and other embellishments, evangelical churches eventually imported organs from the Anglicans during the 1800s to keep up with the competition. Richard Bushman, *The Refinement of America* (New York: Alfred Knopf, 1992), pp. 336-337.

[34] Everett Ferguson, *Early Christians Speak: Faith and Life in the First Three Centuries* (Abilene: A.C.U. Press, Third Edition, 1999), p. 157.

[35] Church fathers like Clement of Alexandria (of the third century), Ambrose, Augustine and Jerome (of the fourth and fifth centuries) all opposed using musical instruments in their worship. Like Calvin later on, they associated musical instruments with pagan ceremonies and Roman theatrical productions. Edwin Liemohn, *The Organ and Choir in Protestant Worship* (Philadelphia: Fortress Press, 1968), p. 2; *Music & Worship in Pagan and Christian Antiquity,* p. 64.

[36] *Early Christians Speak,* p. 157.

[37] *A Historical Approach to Evangelical Worship,* pp. 255-256. The Genevan *Psalter,* published in 1522, was the standard hymnbook for Reformed churches in Europe and the United States for over 200 years.

[38] Ibid., p. 256.

[39] *The Organ and Choir in Protestant Worship,* p. 4.

[40] Ibid., p. 3.

Puritans) removed, demolished and ruined church organs, Lutherans made full use of them.[41] The first organ to be purchased by an American church was in 1704.[42]

The first Protestant choirs began flourishing in the mid-18th century.[43] Special seats were assigned to choir members to show forth their special status.

At first, the function of the choir was to set the tune in leading congregational singing. But before long, the choir began to contribute special selections.[44] Thus was born "special music" by the choir as the congregation watched it perform.

By the end of the 19th century, the children's choir made its appearance in American churches.[45] By this time, it became customary for the choir in non-liturgical churches to play "special music." (This practice was eventually carried over to liturgical churches as well.)[46]

The location of the choir is worth noting. In the late-16th century, the choir moved from the chancel (clergy platform) to the rear gallery where a pipe organ was installed.[47] But during the Oxford Movement of the late-19th and early-20th centuries, the choir returned to the chancel. It was at this time that choir members began wearing ecclesiastical robes.[48] By the 1920s and 1930s, it was customary for American choirs to wear these special vestments to match the newly acquired neo-Gothic church

---

[41] Ibid., pp. 3, 32-33. Wesleyans forbade organs in 1796, preferring the bass viol as the only legal instrument in worship. But organs were installed 12 years later in Wesleyan churches (pp. 91-92). The Lutheran organ became an indispensable feature of Lutheran worship. Ironically, the Lutheran organ music tradition was founded by a Dutch Calvinist named Jan Pieterszoon Sweelinck in the early 17th century (*Christian Liturgy*, p. 534).

[42] The church was Trinity Church in New York. For a discussion on the first organs used in America, see *The Organ and Choir in Protestant Worship*, pp. 110-111.

[43] Ibid., p. 113; *Protestant Worship and Church Architecture*, p. 110.

[44] *Organ and Choir in Protestant Worship*, p. 115.

[45] Ibid., p. 125. The First Presbyterian Church in Flemington, New Jersey is credited with being the first to organize a children's choir.

[46] Ibid.

[47] *Christian Liturgy*, p. 490.

[48] *The Organ and Choir in Protestant Worship*, p. 127; *The Story of Christian Music*, p. 137.

buildings.[49] The choir was now standing with the clergy in front of the people parading around in archaic clerical clothes![50]

The Origin of the Worship Team

In many contemporary churches, whether charismatic or non-charismatic, the choir has been replaced by the recent phenomenon of the worship team.[51] In churches of this ilk the meeting place boasts few religious symbols (except for banners perhaps).

At the front of the stage is a simple podium, some plants, amplifiers, speakers, and lots of wires. The dress is usually casual. Folding chairs or theater seats typically replace pews. The standard worship team will include an amplified guitar, drums, keyboard, possibly a bass guitar, and some special vocalists. Words are usually projected onto a screen or a bare wall by an overhead (or video) projector. Someone "called of God" to the task will flip lyric transparencies or scuttle through powerpoint slides that have been pre-selected before the service. There is a glaring absence of songbooks or hymnals.

In such churches, worship means following the band's pre-scribed songs. The "praise and worship time" typically lasts 30 to 40 minutes. The first songs are usually upbeat praise choruses.[52] The worship team will then lead a lively, hand-clapping, body-swaying, hand-raising, (sometimes dancing) congregation into a potpourri of individualistic, gentle, worshipful singing. (The focus of all the songs is individual experience. First person pro-nouns—*"I, me, my"*—dominate virtually every song.)[53]

As the band leaves the stage, ushers pass the offering plates. This will usually be followed by the sermon where the pastor will

---

[49] *Christian Worship in Its Cultural Setting*, p. 49.

[50] A. Madeley Richardson, *Church Music* (London: Longmans, Green, & Co., 1910), p. 57.

[51] Denominations like the Vineyard, Calvary Chapel, and Hope Chapel hold the market share for these sorts of churches. However, many denominational and non-denominational churches have adopted the same style of worship.

[52] The recovery of singing choruses of Scripture was brought in by the Jesus movement of the 1970s (David Kopp, *Praying the Bible for Your Life*, Waterbrook, 1999, pp. 6-7).

[53] This maps perfectly with the baby boomers' self-focus.

dominate the rest of the service. In many churches, the pastor will call the worship team to return to the stage to play a few more worshipful songs as he winds up his sermon. "Ministry time" may ensue as the band plays on.

The song liturgy I have just described works like clockwork in most charismatic and non-denominational churches. But where did it come from?

The origin of the "worship team" traces back to the founding of Calvary Chapel in 1965. Chuck Smith, the founder of the denomination, started a ministry for hippies and surfers. Smith welcomed the newly converted hippies to retune their guitars and play their now redeemed music in church. He gave the counter-culture a stage for their music—allowing them to play Sunday night performances and concerts. The new musical forms began to be called "praise and worship."[54] As the Jesus movement began to flourish, Smith founded the record company *Maranatha Music* in 1973. Its goal was to distribute the songs of these young artists.[55]

The Vineyard, under the influence of musical genius John Wimber, followed suit with the worship team concept beginning in 1977. In that year, he founded the Anaheim Vineyard Christian Fellowship.[56] The Vineyard has probably shown more influence on the Christian family in establishing worship teams and worship music than Calvary Chapel. Vineyard music is regarded as more intimate and worshipful, while Calvary Chapel's music is known more for its upbeat, praise-oriented songs.[57]

American hymnody had been experiencing reform earlier than both Calvary Chapel and the Vineyard. Beginning in Dublane, Scotland in 1962, a group of dissatisfied British church musicians tried to revitalize traditional Christian songs.

---

[54] Michael S. Hamilton, "The Triumph of Praise Songs: How Guitars Beat Out the Organ in the Worship Wars," *Christianity Today,* 7/12/99.

[55] Donald E. Miller, *Reinventing American Protestantism* (Berkeley: University of Berkeley Press, 1997), pp. 65, 83.

[56] Wimber took over the Vineyard movement in 1982 from Ken Gulliksen.

[57] *Reinventing American Protestantism*, pp. 19, 46-52, 84.

They spawned a new type of music influenced by certain popular folk artists.[58] This reform set the stage for the revolutionary musical changes to take root in the Christian church by Calvary Chapel and the Vineyard.[59] In due time, the guitar replaced the organ as the central instrument that led worship in the Protestant church. Although patterned after the rock concert of secular culture, the worship team has become as common as the pulpit.

So What Is the Problem?

Perhaps you are wondering, *"What is wrong with having a choir leader, a worship leader, or a worship team to lead the church's singing?"* Nothing. Except that it robs God's people of a vital function: To select and lead their own singing in the meetings—to have Divine worship in their own hands—to allow Jesus Christ to lead the singing of His church rather than a human facilitator.

Listen to Paul's description of a church meeting: *"Every one of you brings a song . . ."*[60] *"Speaking to one another with psalms, hymns and spiritual songs."*[61] Song leaders, choirs, and worship teams make this impossible. They also put limits on the Headship of Christ—specifically His ministry of leading His brethren into singing praise songs to His Father. Of this ministry (which is little known today), the writer of Hebrews says, *"Both the one who makes men holy and those who are made holy are of the same*

---

[58] Led by Congregational minister Eric Routley, these artists spawned a new kind of Christian music influenced by Bob Dylan and Sydney Carter. This new style was spread to the US by George Shorney Jr. of Hope Publishing Company. The new Christian hymns were a reform, but not a revolution. The revolution came when rock 'n' roll was adapted into Christian music with the coming of the Jesus movement. With the emergence of Calvary Chapel and then the Vineyard, "baby boomer" music forms had now been incorporated into the Christian church ("The Triumph of Praise Songs").

[59] Since the advent of contemporary Christian music, the "worship wars" have begun, constituting a divisive force which has balkanized Christian churches into "old-styled-traditional-music-lovers" vs. "new-styled-contemporary-music-lovers." Not a few churches have been splintered right down the middle over what form of music is to be used during the church service. Contemporary vs. traditional music has become the root, stem, and branch of the new sectarian, Christian tribalism that plagues the modern church.

[60] 1 Cor. 14:26.

[61] Eph. 5:19, NIV.

family. So Jesus is not ashamed to call them brothers. He [Jesus] says, "I will declare your name to my brothers; in the presence of the congregation [ekklesia] I will sing your praises."[62]

When worship songs can only be sung by the talented, it becomes closer to entertainment than corporate worship.[63] And only those who "make the cut" are allowed to participate in the ministry of leading songs. A ministry that belongs in the hands of all of God's people.

I gather with churches where every member is free to start a song spontaneously. Imagine: Every brother and sister leading songs under the Headship of Christ! Even writing their own songs and bringing them to the meeting for all to learn. One after another. Without long pauses. Everyone participating in the singing. Average, ordinary, run-of-the-mill, garden-variety Christians. With no visible leader present. Such an experience is unknown in the institutional church. Yet it is available for all who wish to experience Christ's Headship in a meeting. Further, the singing in such churches is intensely corporate rather than individualistic and subjective.[64]

Let me warn you, however. Once you have tasted the experience of having worship and praise songs in your own hands, you will never wish to go back to standing in a pew and being led about by a choir director or a worship team. You will most likely be ruined for anything else.

As wonderful as the worship team is, there is something higher and infinitely richer. It is high time that the ministry of music and song be taken away from the second-string clergy and be given back to the people of God. Only then may the Lord's children fully understand the words of the Psalmist:

"By the rivers of Babylon, there we sat down, yea, we wept, when we remembered Zion. We hanged our harps upon the willows

---

[62] Hebrews 2:11-12, NIV.

[63] I have no problem at all with talented musicians performing for an audience to encourage, instruct, inspire, or even entertain them. However, that ought not to be confused with the ministry of praise and worship singing which belongs to the whole church.

[64] Eph. 5:19 and Col. 3:16 capture the flavor of the corporate nature of first-century Christian singing.

in the midst thereof. For there they that carried us away captive required of us a song; and they that wasted us required of us mirth, saying, 'Sing us one of the songs of Zion.' How shall we sing the Lord's song in a strange land? . . . When the Lord turned again the captivity of Zion, we were like them that dream. Then was our mouth filled with laughter, and our tongue with singing: then said they among the heathen, The Lord hath done great things for them. "[65]

---

[65] Psalm 137:1-4; 126:1-2.

The real trouble is not in fact that the church is too rich but that it has become heavily institutionalized, with a crushing investment in maintenance. It has the characteristics of the dinosaur and battleship. It is saddled with a plant and a programme beyond its means, so that it is absorbed in problems of supply and pre-occupied with survival. The inertia of the machine is such that the financial allocations, the legalities, the channels of organization, the attitudes of mind, are all set in the direction of continuing and enhancing the status quo. If one wants to pursue a course which cuts across these channels, then most of one's energies are exhausted before one ever reaches the enemy lines.

    -John A.T. Robinson

CHAPTER 7

TITHING AND CLERGY SALARIES: SORE SPOTS ON THE WALLET

Unlike so many, we do not peddle the Word of God for profit.

-Paul of Tarsus

*W*ill a man rob God? Yet you rob me. But you ask, 'How do we rob you?' In tithes and offerings. You are under a curse—the whole nation of you—because you are robbing me. Bring the whole tithe into the storehouse, that there may be food in my house. Test me in this, says the Lord Almighty, and see if I will not throw open the floodgates of heaven and pour out so much blessing that you will not have room enough for it.[1]

This passage from Malachi Chapter 3 seems to be many a pastor's favorite Bible text. Especially when church giving is at low tide. If you have spent any time in the modern church, you have heard this passage thundered from the pulpit on numerous occasions. I have had it pushed down my throat so many times I have lost count.

Consider some of the rhetoric that goes with it:

"God has commanded you to faithfully give your tithes. If you do not tithe, you are robbing God Almighty, and you put yourself under a curse."

"Let's repeat the 'Tither's Creed' together shall we? 'The tithe is the Lord's. In truth we learned it. In faith we believe it. In joy we give it. The tithe!'"

"Your tithes and offerings are necessary if God's work will go on!" ("God's work," of course, means salarying the pastoral staff and footing the monthly electric bill to keep the building afloat.)

---

[1] Malachi 3:8-10, NIV.

What is the result of this sort of pressure? God's people are guilted into giving one-tenth of their incomes every week. When they do, they feel they have made God happy. And they can expect Him to bless them financially. When they fail, they feel they are being disobedient, and a financial curse looms over them.

But let us take a few steps backward and ask the penetrating question: *"Does the Bible teach us to tithe? And . . . are we spiritually obligated to fund the pastor and his staff?"*

The answer to these two questions is shocking. (If you are a pastor, it is arresting. So you may want to take out your heart medicine now!)

Is Tithing Biblical?

Tithing *does* appear in the Bible. So yes, tithing is Biblical. But it is *not* Christian. The tithe belongs to ancient Israel. It was essentially their income tax. Never do you find first-century Christians tithing in the NT.

Most Christians do not have the foggiest idea about what the Bible teaches regarding the tithe. So let us look at it. The word "tithe" simply means the tenth part.[2] The Lord instituted three kinds of tithes for Israel as part of their taxation system. They are:

- A tithe of the produce of the land to support the Levites who had no inheritance in Canaan.[3]

- A tithe of the produce of the land to sponsor religious festivals in Jerusalem. If the produce was too burdensome for a family to carry to Jerusalem, they could convert it into money.[4]

---

[2] In the Old Testament, the Hebrew word for "tithe" is *maaser,* which means a tenth part. In the NT, the Greek word is *dekate,* which again means a tenth. The word is not taken from the religious world, but from the world of mathematics and finance.
[3] Lev. 27:30-33; Num. 18:21-31.
[4] Deu. 14:22-27. This is sometimes called "the festival tithe."

- A tithe of the produce of the land collected every third year for the local Levites, orphans, strangers, and widows.[5]

This was the Biblical tithe. Notice that God commanded Israel to give 23.3% of their income every year, as opposed to 10%.[6] These tithes consisted of the produce of the land—which is, the seed of the land, the fruit of the land, and the herd or the flock. It was the product of the land, not money.

A clear parallel can be seen between Israel's tithing system and the modern taxation system present in America. Israel was obligated to support their national workers (priests), their holidays (festivals), and their poor (strangers, widows, and orphans) by their annual tithes. Most modern tax systems serve the same purpose.

With the death of Jesus, all ceremonial, governmental, and religious codes that belonged to the Jews were nailed to His cross and buried . . . never to come out again to condemn us. For this reason, we never see Christians tithing in the NT. No more than we see them sacrificing goats and bulls to cover their sins!

Paul writes, *"And when you were dead in your transgressions and the uncircumcision of your flesh, He made you alive together with Him, having forgiven us all our transgressions, having canceled out the certificate of debt consisting of decrees against us and which was hostile to us; and He has taken it out of the way, having nailed it to the cross . . . Therefore let no one act as your judge in regard to food or drink or in respect to a festival or a new moon or a Sabbath day—things which are a mere shadow of what is to come; but the substance belongs to Christ."*[7]

Tithing belonged exclusively to Israel under the Law. When it comes to financial stewardship, we see the first-century saints giving cheerfully according to their ability—not dutifully out of a

---

[5] Deu. 14:28-29; 26:12-13. Jewish historian Josephus and other scholars believe this is a third tithe used in a different way from the second. Stuart Murray, *Beyond Tithing* (Carlisle: Paternoster Press, 2000), pp. 76, 90.

[6] 20% yearly and 10% every three years equals 23.3% per year. God commanded all three tithes (Neh. 12:44; Mal. 3:8-12; Heb. 7:5).

[7] Col. 2:13-17, NASB; see also Heb. 6-10.

command.[8] Giving in the early church was voluntary.[9] And those who benefited from it were the poor, orphans, widows, sick, prisoners, and strangers.[10]

I can hear someone making the following objection right now: *"But what about Abraham? He lived before the Law. And we see him tithing to the high priest Melchizedek.[11] Does this not overturn your argument that the tithe is part of the Mosaic Law?"*

No it does not. First, Abraham's tithe was completely voluntary. It was not compulsory. God did not command it as He did with the tithe for Israel.

Second, Abraham tithed out of the spoils that he acquired after a particular battle he fought. He did not tithe out of his own regular income or property. Abraham's act of tithing would be akin to you winning the lottery, a mega-jackpot, or receiving a work-bonus, then tithing it.

Third, and most important, this is the only time that Abraham tithed out of his 175 years of life on this earth. We have no evidence that he ever did such a thing again. Consequently, if you wish to use Abraham as a "proof text" to argue that Christians must tithe, then you are only obligated to tithe one time![12]

This brings us back to that oft-quoted text in Malachi 3. What was God saying there? First, this passage was directed to ancient Israel when they were under the Mosaic Law. God's people were holding back their tithes and offerings. Consider what would happen if a large portion of Americans refused to pay their income

---

[8] This is very clear from 2 Cor. 8:3-12; 9:5-13. Paul's word on giving is: Give as God has prospered you—according to your ability and means.

[9] *The Early Christians,* p. 86.

[10] *Christian History,* Issue 37, Vol. XII, No. 1, p. 15.

[11] Gen. 14:17-20.

[12] The same is true for Jacob. According to Genesis 28:20-22, Jacob vowed to tithe to the Lord. But like Abraham's tithe, Jacob's tithe was completely voluntary. And as far as we know, it was not a lifetime practice. If Jacob began tithing regularly (and this cannot be proven), he waited for 20 years to pass before he started! To quote Stuart Murray, "Tithing appears to be almost incidental to the stories (of Abraham and Jacob) and no theological significance is accorded to this practice by the author."

taxes. American law views this as robbery.[13] Those found guilty would be punished for stealing from the government.

In the same way, when Israel held back her taxes (tithes), she was stealing from God—the One who instituted the tithing system. The Lord then commanded His people to bring their tithes into the storehouse. The storehouse was located in the chambers of the temple. The chambers were set apart to hold the tithes (which was produce, not money) for the support of the Levites, the poor, the strangers, and the widows.[14]

Notice the context of Malachi 3:8-10. In verse 5, the Lord says that He will judge those who oppress the widow, the fatherless, and the stranger. He says, *"So I will come near to you for judgment. I will be quick to testify against sorcerers, adulterers and perjurers, against those who defraud laborers of their wages, who oppress the widows and the fatherless, and deprive aliens of justice, but do not fear me."*

The widows, fatherless, and strangers were the rightful recipients of the tithe. Because Israel was withholding her tithes, she was guilty of oppressing these three groups. Herein is the heart of God in Malachi 3:8-10: *Oppression to the poor.*

How many times have you heard preachers point this out when they harangued you with Malachi 3? Out of the scores of sermons I have heard on tithing, I never once heard a whisper about what the passage was actually talking about. That is, tithes were for the purpose of supporting the widows, the fatherless, the strangers, and the Levites (who owned nothing). This is what the Lord's word in Malachi 3 has in view.

The Origin of the Tithe and the Clergy Salary

Cyprian (200-258) is the first Christian writer to mention the practice of financially supporting the clergy. He argued that just as the Levites were supported by the tithe, so the Christian clergy

---

[13] I realize that some Christians believe that it is perfectly legal to refuse to pay income taxes. However, not a few of those people are in jail right now for acting on this belief!

[14] Neh. 12:44; 13:12-13; Deu. 14:28-29; 26:12.

should be supported by the tithe.[15] But this is misguided thinking. Today, the Levitical system has been abolished. We are all priests now. So if a priest demands a tithe, then all Christians should tithe to one another!

Cyprian's plea was exceedingly rare for his time. It was neither picked up nor echoed by the Christian populace until much later.[16] Other than Cyprian, no Christian writer before Constantine ever used Old Testament references to advocate tithing.[17] It was not until the fourth century, 300 years after Christ, that *some* Christian leaders began to advocate tithing as a Christian practice to support the clergy.[18] But it did not become widespread among Christians until the eighth century![19] According to one scholar, *"For the first seven hundred years they [tithes] are hardly ever mentioned."*[20]

Charting the history of Christian tithing is a fascinating exercise. Tithing evolved from the State to the church. Giving a tenth of one's produce was the customary rent-charge for lands that were leased in Western Europe. As the church increased its ownership of land across Europe, the 10% rent-charge was given to the church. This gave the 10% rent-charge a new meaning. It came to be identified with the Levitical tithe![21] Consequently, the Christian tithe as an institution was based on a fusion of Old Testament practice and pagan institution.[22]

---

[15] Cyprian, *Epistle 65.1*; *Beyond Tithing*, p. 104.

[16] *Beyond Tithing*, pp. 104-105; *Early Christians Speak*, p. 86.

[17] *Beyond Tithing*, p. 112. Chrysostom advocated tithing to the poor in some of his writings (pp. 112-117).

[18] Ibid., p. 107. *The Apostolic Constitutions* (c. 380) support tithing to fund the clergy by arguing from the Old Testament Levitical system (pp. 113-116). Augustine argued for tithing, but he did not present it as the norm. In fact, Augustine knew that he did not represent the historic position of the church in his support of tithing. Tithing was practiced by some pious Christians in the fifth century, but it was by no means a widespread practice (pp. 117-121).

[19] Edwin Hatch, *The Growth of Church Institutions* (Hodder and Stoughton, 1895), pp. 102-112.

[20] Ibid., p. 102.

[21] Ibid., p. 103. The pseudo-Isodorian Decretals prove that tithes evolved from rent payments for the use of church lands. The Council of Valence in 855 states that this "decree deals with the payment of tithes as rent, about which some of the lessees of church lands appear to have been slack, and then urges their general payment by all Christians" (pp. 104-105). See also *Beyond Tithing*, p. 138.

[22] *Beyond Tithing*, p. 137.

By the eighth century, the tithe became required by law in many areas of Western Europe.[23] By the end of the tenth century, the distinction of the tithe as a rent-charge and a moral requirement supported by the Old Testament had faded.[24] The tithe became mandatory throughout Christian Europe.[25]

To put it another way, before the eighth century the tithe was practiced as a voluntary offering.[26] But by the end of the tenth century, it had devolved into a legal requirement to fund the State church—demanded by the clergy and enforced by the secular authorities![27]

Thankfully, most modern churches have done away with the tithe as a legal requirement.[28] But the practice of tithing is as much alive today as it was when it was legally binding. Sure, you may not be physically punished if you fail to tithe. But if you are not a tither in most modern churches, you will be barred from a slew of ministry positions. And you will be forever guilted from the pulpit![29]

As far as clergy salaries go, ministers were unsalaried for the first three centuries. But when Constantine appeared, he instituted the practice of paying a fixed salary to the clergy from church

---

[23] Ibid., p.134. Charlemagne codified tithing and made it obligatory throughout his enlarged kingdom in 779 and 794 (p.139); *The Age of Faith*, p. 764.

[24] *Beyond Tithing*, p. 140.

[25] Ibid., p. 111.

[26] The exception to this was in Gaul during the sixth century. The Synod of Tours in 567 made tithing mandatory in the region. The Synod of Macon in 585 threatened those who refused to tithe with excommunication. For a short but detailed discussion on Christian giving in the patristic church, see Alan Kreider's *Worship and Evangelism in Pre-Christendom*, Alan/Gron Liturgical Study, 1995, pp. 34-35.

[27] *Beyond Tithing*, pp. 2, 140. Theologians and legislators worked out the details of the tithing system.

[28] Strikingly, the church of England did away with the tithe as a legal requirement as recent as the 1930s (*Beyond Tithing*, pp. 3-6).

[29] Please note that I am a firm believer in supporting the Lord's work financially and of liberal giving. Scripture enjoins both, and the kingdom of God desperately needs both. What I am attacking in this chapter is the tithe as a Christian law and what it is normally used for: Clergy salaries and church building overhead.

funds and municipal and imperial treasuries.[30] Thus was born the clergy salary, a harmful practice that has no root in the NT.[31]

The Root of All Evil

If a believer wishes to tithe out of personal decision or conviction, that is fine. Tithing becomes a problem when it is represented as God's command, binding upon every believer.

Mandatory tithing equals oppression to the poor.[32] Not a few poor Christians have been thrown headlong into further poverty because they have been told that if they do not tithe, they are robbing God.[33] When tithing is taught as God's command, Christians who can barely make ends meet are guilted into deeper poverty. In this way, tithing evacuates the gospel from being "good news to the poor."[34] Rather than good news, it becomes a heavy burden. Instead of liberty, it becomes oppression. We are so apt to forget that the original tithe that God established for Israel was to benefit the poor, not hurt them!

Conversely, modern tithing is good news to the rich. To a high-earner, 10% is but a paltry sum. Tithing, therefore, appeases the consciences of the rich, while it has no significant impact on their lifestyles. Not a few wealthy Christians are deluded into thinking they are "obeying God" because they throw a measly 10% of their income into the offering plate.

---

[30] C.B. Hassell, *History of the Church of God, from Creation to A.D. 1885* (Gilbert Beebe's Sons Publishers, 1886), pp. 374-392, 472; M.A. Smith, *From Christ to Constantine* (Downer's Grove: InterVarsity Press, 1973), p. 123. The Montanists of the second century were the first to pay its leaders, but this practice did not become widespread until Constantine came along (*From Christ to Constantine*, p. 193).

[31] For a response to those Biblical passages that some have used to defend clergy (pastor) salaries, see *Rethinking the Wineskin*, Chapter 5.

[32] Not to mention the overlooked complexities of tithing. Consider the following: Does one tithe on net or gross? How do tax exemptions apply? Murray details the ignored complexities of trying to import the Biblical system of tithing as practiced by ancient Israel to our culture today. In a system of jubilee years, Sabbaths, gleanings and firstfruits, tithing made sense and helped to distribute the nation's wealth. Today, it often leads to gross injustices (see *Beyond Tithing*, Chapter 2).

[33] According to Edwin Hatch, "No institution of the Middle Ages has given rise to more mistakes than the institution of tithes."

[34] Matt. 11:5; Luke 4:18; 7:22; 1 Cor. 1:26-29; Jam. 2:5-6.

But God has a very different view of giving. Recall the parable of the widow's mite: *"Jesus saw the rich putting their gifts into the temple treasury. He also saw a poor widow put in two very small copper coins. 'I tell you the truth,' He said, 'this poor widow has put in more than all the others. All these people gave their gifts out of their wealth; but she out of her poverty put in all she had to live on.'"*[35]

Sadly, tithing is often viewed as a litmus test for discipleship. If you are a good Christian, you will tithe (so it is thought). But this is a bogus application. Tithing is no sign of Christian devotion. If it were, all first-century Christians would be condemned as being undevoted!

The lingering root behind the sustained push for tithing in the modern church is the clergy salary. Not a few pastors feel that they must preach tithing to remind their congregation of its obligation to support them and their programs. And they will use the promise of financial blessing or the fear of a financial curse to ensure that the tithes keep rolling in.

In this way, modern tithing is the equivalent of a Christian lottery. Pay the tithe, and God will give you more money in return. Refuse to tithe, and God will punish you. Such thoughts rip at the heart of the good news of the gospel.

The same can be said about the clergy salary. It too has no NT merit. In fact, the clergy salary runs against the grain of the entire New Covenant.[36] Elders (shepherds) in the first century were never

---

[35] Luke 21:1-4, NIV.
[36] See Acts 20:17-38 (note that these are Paul's last words to the Ephesian elders, thinking he would never see them again—so they are significant); 1 Thess. 2:9; 1 Pet. 5:1-2.

salaried.[37] They were men with an earthly vocation.[38] They gave to the flock rather than took from it.[39]

Salarying pastors makes them paid professionals. It elevates them above the rest of God's people. It creates a clerical caste that turns the living Body of Christ into a business. Since the pastor and his staff are "paid" to do ministry—they are the paid professionals. The rest of the church lapses into a state of passive dependence.

If every Christian got in touch with the call that lies upon them to be functioning priests in the Lord's house (and they were permitted to exercise that call), the question would immediately arise: *"What on earth are we paying our pastor for!?"*

But in the presence of a passive priesthood, such questions never arise.[40] On the contrary, when the church functions as she should, a professional clergy becomes unnecessary. Suddenly, the thought that says, *"that is the job of the pastor"* looks heretical. Put simply, a professional clergy fosters the pacifying illusion that the Word of God is classified (and dangerous) material that only card-carrying experts can handle.[41]

But that is not all. Paying a pastor forces him to be a man-pleaser. It makes him the slave of men. His meal-ticket is attached

---

[37] *Rethinking the Wineskin*, Chapter 5. For scholarly support for this statement, see F.F. Bruce, *The New International Commentary on the New Testament* (Grand Rapids: Eerdmans, 1986), p. 418; Simon J. Kistemacher, *New Testament Commentary: Acts* (Grand Rapids: Baker Book House, 1990), pp. 737, 740; Rolland Allen, *Missionary Methods: St. Paul's or Ours?* (Grand Rapids: Eerdmans, 1962), p. 50; Watchman Nee, *The Normal Christian Church Life* (Anaheim, CA: Living Stream Ministry, 1980), pp. 62-63, 139-143; R.C.H. Lenski, *Commentary on Saint Paul's Epistles to Timothy* (Minneapolis: Augsburg Publishing House, 1937), p. 683; R.C.H. Lenski, *Commentary on Saint Paul's Epistle to the Galatians* (Minneapolis: Augsburg Publishing House, 1961), pp. 303-304.

[38] The entire brunt of NT references to elders makes this plain. In addition, 1 Tim. 3:7 says that an overseer must be well thought of in the community. The natural implication of this is that he is regularly employed in secular work.

[39] Acts 20:33-35.

[40] According to Elton Trueblood, "Our opportunity for a big step lies in opening the ministry of the ordinary Christian in much the same manner that our ancestors opened Bible reading to the ordinary Christian. To do this means, in one sense, the inauguration of a new Reformation while in another it means the logical completion of the earlier Reformation in which the implications of the position taken were neither fully understood nor loyally followed."

[41] The words of Jesus come to mind: "Woe to you experts in the Law, because you have taken away the key of knowledge . . ." (Luke 11:52).

to how well his congregation likes him. Thus he is not free to speak freely without the fear that he may lose some heavy tithers. Herein lies the scourge of the pastor system.

A further peril of the paid pastor system is that it produces men who are void of any skill—something we inherited from the pagan Greeks.[42] For this reason, it takes a man of tremendous courage to step out of the pastorate.

Unfortunately, most of God's people are deeply naive about the overwhelming power of the pastor system. It is a faceless system that does not tire of chewing up and spitting out its young.[43] Again, God never intended the professional pastorate to exist. There is no Scriptural mandate or justification for such a thing. In fact, it is impossible to construct a Biblical defense for it.[44]

Most frequently, ushers are called upon to handle the reception of the money during the church service. Typically, they do so by passing a "collection plate" to the congregation. The practice of passing the collection plate is another post-apostolic invention. It began in 1662. Although alms dishes and alms chests were present before then.[45]

---

[42] The Greeks despised manual labor. They spoke publicly for a fee. Jewish rabbis learned a skill and could not accept money for religious services. In this way, the modern preacher has adopted the Greek custom rather than the Jewish custom which Paul of Tarsus followed even as a Christian.

[43] See Chapter 4 for the profoundly corrupting influences of this system.

[44] See Chapter 4.

[45] James Gilchrist, *Anglican Church Plate* (A Connoisseur Monograph, 1967), pp. 98-101. Early offering plates were called "alms dishes." The silver alms dish did not appear as a normal part of church furnishing until after the Reformation (Michael Clayton, *The Collector's Dictionary of the Silver and Gold of Great Britain and North America*, New York: The Word Publishing Company, p. 11). According to Charles Cox and Alfred Harvey (*English Church Furniture*, 2nd Edition, Methuen, 1908), the use of alms boxes, collecting boxes, and alms dishes are almost entirely a post-Reformation usage. In medieval times, church buildings had alms-chests with a slot in the lid. In the 14th century, the alms dish appeared. In the 17th century, alms basins began to be passed around by deacons or churchwardens. J.G. Davies, ed. *A New Dictionary of Liturgy & Worship* (SCM Press, 1986), pp. 5-6; Charles Oman, *English Church Plate* 597-1830 (London: Oxford University Press, 1957); J. Charles Cox and Alfred Harvey, *English Church Furniture* (EP Publishing Limited, 1973), pp. 240-245; David C. Norrington, "Fund-Raising: The Methods Used in the Early Church Compared with Those Used in English Churches Today," *EQ 70:2* (1998), p. 130. Norrington's entire article is a worthwhile read. He shows that present day "soliciting" methods in church have no analog in the NT (pp. 115-134).

The usher originated from Queen Elizabeth I's (1533-1603) reorganization of the liturgy of the church of England. Ushers had the job of seeing where the people sat, collecting the offering, and keeping records of who took communion. The predecessor of the usher is the church "porter." The porter was a minor order (lesser clergy) tracing back to the third century.[46] Porters had the duty of superintending lock up and opening of church doors, keeping order in the building, and the general direction of the deacons.[47] Porters were replaced by "churchwardens" in England before and during the Reformation period.[48] Out of the churchwarden grew the usher.

Conclusion

In conclusion, tithing, while Biblical, is not Christian. Jesus Christ did not affirm it. The first-century Christians did not observe it. And for 300 years, God's people did not practice it. Tithing did not become a widely accepted practice among Christians until the eighth century!

Giving in the NT was according to one's ability. Christians gave to help other believers as well as to support apostolic workers, enabling them to travel and plant churches.[49] One of the most outstanding testimonies of the early church has to do with how liberal the Christians were to the poor and needy.[50] This is what

---

[46] "Porter, Doorkeeper," *The Catholic Encyclopedia* (www.newadvent.org/cathen/12284b.htm).

[47] Private Email from Professor John McGuckin, 9/23/2002. The word "usher" comes from Anglo-Saxon and refers to a person who guides people into court or church (Private Email from Professor Eugene A. Teselle, 9/22/2002).

[48] *English Church Furniture*, p. 245.

[49] Helping other believers: Acts 6:1-7; 11:27-30; 24:17; Rom. 15:25-28; 1 Cor. 16:1-4; 2 Cor. 8:1-15; 9:1-12; 1 Tim. 5:3-16. Supporting church planters: Acts 15:3; Rom. 15:23-24; 1 Cor. 9:1-14; 16:5-11; 2 Cor. 1:16; Php. 4:14-18; Titus 3:13-14; 3 Jn. 5-8. There is a close connection between the wallet and the heart. One out of every six verses in Matthew, Mark, and Luke have to do with money. Of the 38 parables in the NT, 12 have to do with money.

[50] A telling and moving historical account of third and fourth-century Christian liberality is found in Alan Kreider's *Worship and Evangelism in Pre-Christendom*, Alan/Gron Liturgical Study, 1995, p. 20. See also Tertullian's testimony of Christian charity in Paul Johnson's *A History of Christianity* (New Your: Simon & Schuster, 1976), p. 75 and Kim Tan's, *Lost Heritage: The Heroic Story of Radical Christianity* (Godalming: Highland Books, 1996), pp. 51-56.

provoked outsiders, including the philosopher Galen, to watch the awesome, winsome power of the early church and say: *"Behold how they love one another."*[51]

Tithing is only mentioned four times in the NT. But none of these instances applies to Christians.[52] Again, tithing belongs to the Old Testament era where a taxation system was needed to support the poor and where a special priesthood was set apart to minister to the Lord. With the coming of Jesus Christ, there has been a "change of law"—the old has been "set aside" and rendered obsolete by the new.[53]

We are all priests now—free to function in God's house. The Law, the old priesthood, and the tithe have all been crucified. There is now no temple curtain, no temple tax, and no special priesthood that stands between God and man. You, dear Christian, have been set free from the bondage of tithing and from the obligation to support an unbiblical clergy system.

---

[51] Tertullian, *Apology* 39:7; Robert Wilken, *The Christians as the Romans Saw Them* (New Haven: University Press, 1984), pp.79-82.

[52] Murray handles all four instances in detail, proving that they are not proof texts for Christians tithing. He also shows that according to Jesus, tithing is linked to legalism and self-righteousness rather than a model to imitate (see *Beyond Tithing*, Chapter 3).

[53] Hebrews 7:12-18; 8:13.

The church, embracing the mass of the population of the Empire, from the Caesar to the meanest slave, and living amidst all its institutions, received into her bosom vast deposits of foreign material from the world and from heathenism . . . Although ancient Greece and Rome have fallen forever, the spirit of Graeco-Roman paganism is not extinct. It still lives in the natural heart of man, which at this day as much as ever needs regeneration by the Spirit of God. It lives also in many idolatrous and superstitious usages of the Greek and Roman churches, against which the pure spirit of Christianity has instinctively protested from the beginning, and will protest, till all remains of gross and refined idolatry shall be outwardly as well as inwardly overcome, and baptized and sanctified not only with water, but also with the spirit and fire of the gospel.

-Philip Schaff

CHAPTER 8

BAPTISM AND THE LORD'S SUPPER: DILUTING THE SACRAMENTS

Many institutions and elements of institutions which have sometimes been thought to belong to primitive Christianity belong, in fact, to the Middle Ages.
-Edwin Hatch

Countless books have been written on the two Protestant sacraments: Baptism and the Lord's Supper. However, nothing exists in print that traces the origin of how we practice them today. In this chapter, we will see how far afield we got in our practice of water baptism and the Lord's Supper.

Diluting the Waters of Baptism

Most evangelical Christians believe and practice "believers baptism" as opposed to "infant baptism."[1] Likewise, most Prot-

---

[1] Infant baptism has its root in the superstitious beliefs that pervaded Greco-Roman culture. According to one scholar, "There is first of all superstition, which in the course of the second century associated itself with the Mysteries, the mystic sacred performances [of the heathen], and then the setting up of the state church. The superstitious ideas which came to be associated with baptism could not but lead to infant baptism" (J. Warns, *Baptism: Its History and Significance*, Exeter: Paternoster, 1958, pp. 73-75, 93-95). Cyprian, a powerful advocate of infant baptism, attributed magical powers to it in its ability to wash away sin (M.A. Smith, *From Christ to Constantine*, Downer's Grove: InterVarsity Press, 1973, p. 139). Echoing the same sentiment, Graydon F. Snyder wrote that "infant baptism was practiced when the social matrix and the religious community had become one and the same" (Graydon F. Snyder, *Ante Pacem: Church Life Before Constantine*, Mercer University Press, 1985, p. 125). The earliest plausible reference to infant baptism is found in Irenaeus (130-200). Tertullian (160-225) was also one of the first to speak on it, but he was opposed to it. Infant baptism seems to have begun in the early second century and had an elaborate theology to go along with it. By the fifth century, infant baptism became a general practice replacing adult baptism (Everett Ferguson, *Early Christians Speak:*

estants believe and practice baptism by "immersion" rather than by "sprinkling." The NT as well as early church history stand with both of these positions.[2]

However, it is typical in most modern churches for baptism to be separated from conversion by great lengths of time. Many Christians were saved at one age and baptized at a much later age. In the first century, this was unheard of.

In the early church, converts were baptized immediately upon believing.[3] One scholar says of baptism and conversion, *"They belong together. Those who repented and believed the Word were baptized. That was the invariable pattern, so far as we know."*[4] Another writes, *"At the birth of the church, converts were baptized with little or no delay."*[5]

In the first century, water baptism was the outward confession of a person's faith.[6] But more than that, it was *the* way someone came to the Lord in Century One. For this reason, the confession of baptism is vitally linked to the exercise of saving faith. So much so that the NT writers often use "baptism" in place of the word

---

Faith and Life in the First Three Centuries, Abilene: A.C.U. Press, Third Edition, 1999, pp. 57-61; Marjorie Warkentin, *Ordination: A Biblical-Historical View*, Grand Rapids: Eerdmans, 1982, pp. 31-32). The Anabaptist Menno Simons dated the "fall of the church" when Pope Innocent I signed the edict that made infant baptism mandatory in 416 (*Ordination*, p. 63). From a theological standpoint, infant baptism divorces two things that the Scriptures consistently join together: 1) Faith and repentance, and 2) Water baptism. In A.D. 197, Tertullian condemned infant baptism along with the baptism of the dead. But Augustine provided a full Biblical justification for the practice (Kim Tan, *Lost Heritage: The Heroic Story of Radical Christianity*, Godalming: Highland Books, 1996, pp. 82, 209).

[2] "Baptism" in the Greek (*baptizo*) literally means immersion. John 3:23 does not make much sense if sprinkling was practiced. Immersion was the common practice of the Christian church until the late Middle Ages in the West (*Early Christians Speak*, pp. 43-51).

[3] Acts 2:37-41; 8:12ff., 27-38; 9:18; 10:44-48; 16:14-15, 31-33; 18:18; 19:1-5; 22:16.

[4] Michael Green, *Evangelism in the Early Church* (Houder and Stoughton, 1970), p. 153.

[5] David F. Wright, *The Lion Handbook of the History of Christianity*, Chapter on "Beginnings," Section on "Instruction for Baptism."

[6] Augustine called baptism a "visible word" (*Tractates on the Gospel According to Saint John*, LXXX,3).

"faith" and link it to being "saved."[7] This is because baptism was the early Christian's initial confession of faith in Christ.

In our day, the "Sinner's Prayer" has replaced the role of water baptism as the initial confession of faith. Unbelievers are told, *"Say this prayer after me, accept Jesus as your 'Personal Savior,' and you will be saved."* But nowhere in all the NT do we find any person being led to the Lord by a "Sinner's Prayer." And there is not the faintest whisper in the Bible about a "Personal Savior."

Instead, unbelievers in the first century were led to Jesus Christ by being taken to the waters of baptism. If I may put it this way, water baptism was the "Sinner's Prayer" in Century One! Baptism accompanied the acceptance of the gospel. It marked a complete break with the past and a full entrance into Christ and His church. Baptism was simultaneously an *act* of faith as well as an *expression* of faith.[8]

So when did baptism get separated from receiving Christ? It began in the early second century. Certain influential Christians taught that baptism must be preceded by a period of instruction, prayer, and fasting.[9] This trend grew worse in the third century when young converts had to wait three years before they could be baptized!

If you were a baptismal candidate in the third century, your life was scrutinized with a fine tooth comb.[10] You had to show yourself worthy of baptism by your conduct.[11] Baptism became a rigid and embellished ritual that borrowed much from Jewish and Greek culture—elaborate with blessing the water, full disrobing, the

---

[7] Mark 16:16, Acts 2:38, Acts 22:16, and 1 Peter 3:21 and some examples.

[8] The importance of water baptism in the Christian faith is depicted in early Christian art (Andre Grabar, *Christian Iconography*, Princeton: Princeton University Press, 1968).

[9] *Early Christians Speak*, p. 33.

[10] David F. Wright, *The Lion Handbook of the History of Christianity*, Chapter on "Beginnings," Section on "Instruction for Baptism." Wright points out that by the fourth century, the clergy took over the instructions for converts and the bishop became personally responsible for the teaching and discipline that preceded baptism. This is the precursor for the pre-baptismal class overseen by the pastor in many modern Protestant churches. From the second century onward, baptisms normally took place at Easter. Herein is the origin of Lent (*From Christ to Constantine*, p. 151).

[11] *Early Christians Speak*, p. 35.

uttering of a creed, anointing oil with exorcism, and giving milk and honey to the newly baptized person.[12] It had devolved into an act associated with works rather than with faith.

The legalism that baptism was shrouded in bled forth an even more startling concept: Only baptism forgives sins. If a person commits sin after baptism, he cannot be forgiven. For this reason, the delay of baptism became quite common by the fourth century. Since it was believed that baptism brought the forgiveness of sins, many felt it was best to delay baptism until the maximum benefits could be obtained.[13] Therefore, some people, like Constantine, waited until they were on their death-beds to be baptized![14]

The Sinner's Prayer and a Personal Savior

As I stated earlier, the "Sinner's Prayer" eventually replaced the Biblical role of water baptism. Though it is touted as gospel today, the "Sinner's Prayer" is a very recent invention. D.L. Moody (1837-1899) was the first to employ it.

Moody used this "model" of prayer when training his evangelistic co-workers.[15] But it did not reach popular usage until the

---

[12] Ibid., pp. 35-36; W.R. Halliday, *The Pagan Background of Early Christianity* (New York: Cooper Square Publishers, 1970), p. 313. The giving of milk and honey was borrowed from paganism. The new convert ("catechumens" as they came to be called, from which "catechism" is derived) was typically baptized on a Sunday Passover or Pentecost. The Thursday beforehand the candidate had to be bathed. He spent Friday and Saturday in fasting, and then he was exorcized by the bishop to drive out any demons. By the end of the second century, this was a fairly uniform baptismal ceremony in the West. Gregory Dix points out that the introduction of the creed in Christianity begins in the first half of the second century with the baptismal creed. The baptism creed was made up of a series of three questions dealing respectively with the three Persons of the Trinity. The Council of Nicea of A.D. 325 carried the creed a step further. The creed evolved to be a test of fellowship for those within the church rather than a test of faith for those outside of it (*The Shape of the Liturgy*, New York: The Seabury Press, 1982, p. 485; David C. Norrington, *To Preach or Not to Preach? The Church's Urgent Question*, Carlisle: Paternoster Press, 1996, p.59).

[13] *Early Christians Speak*, p. 60.

[14] *Evangelism in the Early Church*, p. 156.

[15] C.L. Thompson, *Times of Refreshing, Being a History of American Revivals With Their Philosophy and Methods* (Rockford: Golden Censer Co. Publishers, 1878); Paul H. Chitwood, *The Sinner's Prayer: An Historical and Theological Analysis* (Dissertation: The Southern Baptist Theological Seminary, Louisville, KY, 2001).

1950s with Billy Graham's *Peace With God* tract and later with Campus Crusade for Christ's *Four Spiritual Laws.*[16]

The phrase "Personal Savior" is yet another modern innovation that grew out of the ethos of 19th-century American revivalism.[17] It was spawned in the mid-1800s to be exact.[18] But it grew to popular parlance by Charles Fuller (1887-1968). Fuller literally used the phrase thousands of times in his incredibly popular "Old-Fashioned Revival Hour" radio program which aired in the 1940s, 50s, and 60s. His program reached from North America to every spot on the globe. At the time of his death, it was heard by more than 500 radio stations around the world.[19]

Today, the phrase "Personal Savior" is used so pervasively that it seems Biblical. But consider the ludicrousness of using it. Have you ever introduced one of your friends by such a designation? *"This is my 'Personal Friend,' Fonty Flock."*

Aside from the fact that this phrase has few points of contact with real life, there is a greater problem. The phrase "Personal Savior" *limits* Jesus to what we think of as our personal lives. The fact is that Jesus Christ saves us from every dimension of life—whether personal, impersonal, interpersonal, corporate, etc. He is Savior of every nook, cranny, and room of the building.

Further, the phrase "Personal Savior" reinforces a highly individualistic Christianity. But the NT knows nothing of a "Just-me-and-Jesus" Christian faith. Instead, Christianity is intensely corporate. Christianity is a life lived out among a Body of believers who know Him *together* as Lord and Savior.

---

[16] Here is the classic "Sinner's Prayer" that appears in the "Four Spiritual Laws" tract: *"Lord Jesus, I need You. Thank You for dying on the cross for my sins. I open the door of my life and receive You as my Savior and Lord. Thank You for forgiving my sins and giving me eternal life. Take control of the throne of my life. Make me the kind of person You want me to be."* In the first century, water baptism was the visible testimony that publicly demonstrated the heart of this prayer.

[17] See Chapter 1 for a list of contributions from Finney, Moody, Graham, etc.

[18] The phrase is absent from the "Making of America" data base from 1800-1857. It begins appearing in 1858 in the "Ladies Repository," a periodical put out by the Methodist Episcopal Church during the mid-1800s. Interestingly, 1858 is the year that Charles Finney concluded his prayer revivals which are now so famous.

[19] http://www.cantonbaptist.org/halloffame/fuller.htm

The Lord's Supper

Rivers of blood have been shed at the hands of Protestant and Catholic Christians alike over the doctrinal intricacies related to the Lord's Supper.[20] The Lord's Supper, once precious and living, became the center of theological debate for centuries. Tragically, it moved from a dramatic and concrete picture of Christ's body and blood to a study in abstract and metaphysical thought.

We will not concern ourselves with the theological minutiae that surrounds the Lord's Supper. But Protestants (as well as Catholics) do not practice the Supper the way it was observed in the first century. For the early Christians, the Lord's Supper was a festive meal.[21]

Today, tradition has forced us to take the Supper as a tongue-tickling thimble of grape juice and a tiny, tasteless bite-sized cracker. The Supper is taken with an atmosphere of gloom and doom. We are told to remember the horrors of our Lord's death. We are told to reflect on our sins.

In addition, tradition has taught us that taking the Lord's Supper can be a dangerous thing. Thus most modern Christians would not be caught dead taking it without an ordained clergyman present. All of these elements were unknown to the early Christians. For them, the Lord's Supper was a communal meal.[22] The mood was

---

[20] In the words of H. Ellerbe, "I was brought up to believe that the history of Christianity was a history of Christlike spirituality, which shone through the centuries like a light in the darkness. But I've come to realize that Christianity itself has a dark side, and that the history of Christianity is as much a litany of cruelty as it is a legacy of charity."

[21] See *Rethinking the Wineskin*, Chapter 2; Eric Svendsen, *The Table of the Lord* (Atlanta: NTRF, 1996); F.F. Bruce, *First and Second Corinthians*, NCB (London: Oliphant, 1971), p. 110; James F. White, *The Worldliness of Worship* (New York: Oxford University Press, 1967), p. 85; William Barclay, *The Lord's Supper* (Philadelphia: Westminister Press, 1967), pp.100-107; I. Howard Marshall, *Last Supper and Lord's Supper* (Eerdmans, 1980); Vernard Eller, *In Place of Sacraments* (Eerdmans, 1972), pp. 9-15.

[22] "Throughout the New Testament period the Lord's Supper was an actual meal shared in the homes of Christians" (John Drane); "In the early days the Lord's Supper took place in the course of a communal meal. All brought what food they could and it was shared together" (Donald Guthrie); "At Corinth the holy communion was not simply a token meal as with us, but an actual meal. Moreover it seems clear that it was a meal to which each of the participants brought food" (Leon Morris).

one of celebration and joy. And there was no clergyman to officiate it.[23] The Lord's Supper was essentially a Christian banquet.

Truncating the Meal

So when did the full meal cease, leaving only the bread and the cup? Here is the story. In the first and early second century, the early Christians called the Lord's Supper the "love feast."[24] At that time, they took the bread and cup in the context of a festive meal. But around the time of Tertullian (160-225), the bread and the cup began to be separated from the meal. By the late second century, the separation was complete.[25]

Some scholars have argued that the Christians dropped the meal part because they wanted to keep the Eucharist from becoming profaned by the participation of unbelievers.[26] This may be partly true. But it is more likely that the growing influence of pagan religious ritual removed the Supper from the joyful, down-to-earth, non-religious atmosphere of a meal in someone's living room.[27] By

---

[23] *The Lord's Supper*, pp. 102-103. The Lord's Supper was once a "lay" function, but it eventually devolved into the special duty of a priestly class.

[24] It was called the *Agape*. Jude 1:12.

[25] *The Shape of the Liturgy*, p. 23; *Early Christians Speak*, pp. 82-84, 96-97, 127-130. In the first and early second centuries, the Lord's Supper seemed to have been taken in the evening as a meal. Second-century sources show it was taken only on Sundays. In the *Didache*, the Eucharist is still shown to be taken with the *Agape* meal (love feast). See also J.G. Davies, *The Secular Use of Church Buildings* (New York: The Seabury Press, 1968), p. 22.

[26] *The Table of the Lord*, pp. 57-63.

[27] For the pagan influences on the evolving Christian Mass, see Edmon Bishop's essay, *The Genius of the Roman Rite*; Mgr. L. Duchesne, *Christian Worship: Its Origin and Evolution* (New York: Society for Promoting Christian Knowledge, 1912), pp. 86-227; Josef A. Jungmann, S.J., *The Early Liturgy: To the Time of Gregory the Great* (Notre Dame: Notre Dame Press, 1959), p. 123, 130-144, 291-292; M.A. Smith, *From Christ to Constantine* (Downer's Grove: InterVarsity Press, 1973), p. 173; Will Durant, *Caesar to Christ* (New York: Simon & Schuster, 1950), pp. 599-600, 618-619, 671-672.

the fourth century, the love feast was "prohibited" among Christians![28]

With the abandonment of the meal, the terms "breaking of bread" and "Lord's Supper" disappeared.[29] The common term for the now truncated ritual (just the bread and the cup) was "the Eucharist."[30] Irenaeus (130-200) was one of the first to call the bread and cup an "offering."[31] After him, it began to be called the "offering" or "sacrifice."

The altar-table where the bread and cup were placed came to be seen as an altar where the victim was offered.[32] The Supper was no longer a community event. It was rather a priestly ritual that was to be watched at a distance. Throughout the fourth and fifth centuries, there was an increasing sense of awe and dread associated with the table where the sacred Eucharist was celebrated.[33] It became a somber ritual. The joy that had once been a part of it had vanished.[34]

---

[28] It was prohibited by the Council of Carthage in A.D. 397. *The Lord's Supper,* p. 60; Charles Hodge, *1 Corinthians,* p. 219; R.C.H. Lenski, *The Interpretation of 1 & 2 Corinthians,* p. 488.

[29] *The Early Christians,* p. 100.

[30] Ibid., p. 93. Eucharist means "thanksgiving."

[31] Tad W. Guzie, *Jesus and the Eucharist* (New York: Paulist Press, 1974), p. 120.

[32] Ibid.

[33] Writers as early as Clement of Alexandria, Tertullian, and Hippolytus (early third century) began to use language speaking of a presence of Christ generally in the bread and wine. But no attempt was made at that early stage to argue for a physical realism which "changed" the bread and wine into flesh and blood. Later, some eastern writers (Cyril, Sarapion, Athanasius) introduced a prayer to the Holy Spirit to transform the bread and wine into the body and blood. But it was Ambrose of Milan (late fourth century) who began to locate the consecratory power in the reciting of the words of institution. The words "This is my body" (in Latin *hocest corpus meum*) were believed to contain in them the power to transform the bread and the wine (Josef Jungmann, *The Mass of the Roman Rite,* New York: Benziger, 1951, pp. 52, 203-204; Gregory Dix, *The Shape of the Liturgy,* London: Dacre Press, pp. 239, 240-245). Incidentally, Latin started in North Africa in the late 100s and spread slowly towards Rome until it was common by the end of the 300s (Bard Thompson, *Liturgies of the Western Church,* Cleveland: Meridian Books, 1961, p. 27).

[34] This shift is also reflected in Christian art. There are no gloomy visages of Jesus before the fourth century (Private Email from Graydon Snyder, 10/12/2001; See also his book *Ante Pacem*).

The mystique associated with the Eucharist was due to the influence of the pagan mystery religions.[35] These religions were clouded with mystery and superstition. With this influence, the Christians began to ascribe to the bread and the cup sacred overtones. They were viewed as holy objects in and of themselves.[36]

Because the Lord's Supper became a sacred ritual, it required a sacred person to administer it.[37] Enter now the priest offering the sacrifice of the Mass.[38] He was believed to have the power to call God down from heaven and confine Him to a piece of bread.[39]

Around the 10th century, the meaning of the word "body" changed in Christian literature. Previously, Christian writers used the word body to refer to one of three things: 1) The physical body of Jesus, 2) The church, or 3) The bread of the Eucharist.

The early church fathers saw the church as a faith community which identified itself by the breaking of bread. But by the 10th century, there was a shift in thinking and language. The word "body" was no longer used to refer to the church. It was only used to refer to the Lord's physical body or the bread of the Eucharist.[40] The word "body" had been evacuated from its other meaning: The church.

Consequently, the Lord's Supper became far removed from the idea of the church coming together to celebrate the breaking of bread.[41] The vocabulary change reflected this practice. The

---

[35] *Jesus and the Eucharist,* p. 121.

[36] This occurred in the ninth century. Before this, it was the *act* of taking the Eucharist that was regarded as sacred. But in A.D. 830, a man named Radbert wrote the first treatise that approached the Eucharist by focusing directly on the bread and wine. All the Christians writers before Radbert described what Christians were doing when they took the bread and wine. They described the *action* of taking the elements. Radbert was the first to focus exclusively *on* the elements themselves—the bread and the wine that sat on the altar table (*Jesus and the Eucharist,* pp.60-61, 121-123).

[37] James D.G. Dunn, *New Testament Theology in Dialogue* (Westminister Press, 1987), pp. 125-135.

[38] This started around the fourth century.

[39] Richard Hanson, *Christian Priesthood Examined* (Guildford and London: Lutterworth Press, 1979), p. 80.

[40] *Jesus and the Eucharist,* pp. 125-127.

[41] For many slaves and poor folks, the Lord's Supper was their one real meal. Interestingly, it was not until the Synod of Hippo in A.D. 393 that the concept of fasting the Lord's Supper began to emerge (*The Lord's Supper,* p. 100).

Eucharist had nothing to do with the church, but came to be viewed as "sacred" on its own—even as it sat on the table. It became shrouded in a religious mist. Viewed with awe. Taken with glumness by the priest. Completely removed from the communal nature of the *ekklesia.*

All of these factors gave rise to the doctrine of transubstantiation. In the fourth century, the belief that the bread and wine changed into the Lord's actual body and blood was explicit. Transubstantiation, however, was the doctrine that gave a theological explanation of how that change occurred.[42] (This doctrine was worked out from the 11th through the 13th centuries.)

With the doctrine of transubstantiation, there was a feeling of fear that surrounded the elements. The fear was so intense that God's people were reluctant to approach them.[43] When the words of the Eucharist were uttered, it was believed that the bread literally became God. All of this turned the Lord's Supper into a sacred ritual performed by sacred people and taken out of the hands of God's people. So deeply entrenched was the medieval idea that the bread and cup was an "offering" that even some of the Reformers held to it.[44]

While modern Protestant Christians have discarded the Catholic *notion* that the Lord's Supper is a sacrifice, they have continued to embrace the Catholic *practice* of the Supper. Observe any Lord's Supper service (often called "Holy Communion") in any Protestant church and you will observe the following:

---

[42] *The Early Christians*, pp. 111-112. The full-blown doctrine of transubstantiation is credited to Thomas Aquinas. In this regard, Martin Luther believed that the "opinion of Thomas" should have remained an opinion and not become church dogma (*Christian Liturgy*, p. 307).

[43] Edwin Hatch, *The Growth of Church Institutions* (Hodder and Stoughton, 1895), p. 216. Transubstantiation was defined as a doctrine in the Lateran Council in A.D. 1215 as the result of 350 years of controversy over the doctrine in the West (Gregory Dix, *The Shape of the Liturgy*, New York: The Seabury Press, 1982, p. 630; *Christian Priesthood Examined*, p. 79; Philip Schaff, *History of the Christian Church: Volume 7*, Michigan: Eerdmans, 1910, p. 614).

[44] Ilion T. Jones, *A Historical Approach to Evangelical Worship* (New York: Abingdon Press, 1954), p. 143.

- The Lord's Supper is a bite-size cracker (or a small piece of bread) and a shot-glass of grape juice (or wine). It is removed from the meal just as it is in the Catholic church.
- The mood is somber and glum. Just as it is in the Catholic church.
- Congregants are told by the pastor that they must examine themselves with regard to sin before they partake of the elements. A practice that came from John Calvin.[45]
- Like the Catholic priest, many pastors will sport their clerical robes for the occasion. But always, the pastor will administer the Supper and recite the words of institution: "This is my body" before he dispenses it to the congregation.[46] Just as it is in the Catholic church.

With only a few minor tweaks, all of this is medieval Catholicism through-and-through.

Summary

By our tradition, we have evacuated the true meaning and power behind water baptism. Properly conceived and practiced, water baptism is *the* believer's initial confession of faith before men, demons, angels, and God. Baptism is a visible sign that depicts our separation from the world,[47] our death with Christ, the burial of our old man,[48] the death of the old creation,[49] and the washing of the Word of God.[50]

---

[45] *Protestant Worship: Traditions in Transition* (Louisville: Westminister/John Knox Press, 1989), p. 66. I Corinthians 11:27-33 is not an exhortation to examine oneself with respect to personal sin. It is rather an exhortation to examine oneself in the area of taking the Supper in a "worthy manner." The Corinthians were dishonoring the Supper for they were not waiting for their poor brethren to eat with them, and they were getting drunk on the wine.

[46] Matthew 26:25-27; Mark 14:21-23; Luke 22:18-20.

[47] Acts 2:38-40; 1 Cor. 10:1-2.

[48] Rom. 6:3-5; Col. 2:11-12.

[49] 1 Pet. 3:20-21.

[50] Acts 22:16; Eph. 5:26.

Water baptism is the NT form of conversion-initiation. It is God's idea. To replace it with the human invented "Sinner's Prayer" is to deplete baptism of its God-given testimony.

In the same vein, the Lord's Supper, when separated from its proper context of a full meal, turns into a strange, almost pagan rite.[51] The Supper has become an empty ritual officiated by a clergyman, rather than a shared-life experience enjoyed by the church. It has become a morbid religious exercise, rather than a joyous festival—a stale individualistic ceremony, rather than a meaningful corporate event.

As one scholar put it, *"It is not in doubt that the Lord's Supper began as a family meal or a meal of friends in a private house . . . the Lord's Supper moved from being a real meal into being a symbolic meal . . . the Lord's Supper moved from bare simplicity to elaborate splendour . . . the celebration of the Lord's Supper moved from being a lay function to a priestly function. In the NT itself, there is no indication that it was the special privilege or duty of anyone to lead the worshipping fellowship in the Lord's Supper."*[52]

By our tradition we have nullified the NT experience of water baptism and the Lord's Supper. May you, dear Christian, shun the vain traditions of men and return to the ancient paths as the prophet once cried: *"Thus says the Lord, 'Stand by the ways and see and ask for the ancient paths, where the good way is, and walk in it; and you shall find rest for your souls.'"*[53]

Will you walk in the ancient paths, or will you continue to carelessly adhere to your cherished traditions, stuck in the old rut of our forefathers?

---

[51] Eduard Schweizer, *The Church As the Body of Christ* (John Knox Press, 1964), pp. 26, 36-37.
[52] William Barclay.
[53] Jer. 6:16, NASB.

The Protestant clergy have rescued the Bible from the darkness of papal libraries and have scattered it abroad over the whole earth. They have exalted it in the highest terms of human praise. They have studied, commented, and explained, nay even tortured every word, phrase, and expression in the original and translations, for every possible interpretation. The result is that Christianity is smothered in theology and criticism: the truths of revelation are wire—drawn and spun and twisted into the most fantastical shapes human fancy or human logic can devise. A system of technical Divinity has been constructed which rivals the complexity of all the machinery of the Romish church.

   -Steven Colwell

CHAPTER 9

CHRISTIAN EDUCATION: SWELLING THE CRANIUM

What has Athens to do with Jerusalem?
-Tertullian

In the minds of most Christians, formal Christian education qualifies a person to do the Lord's work. Unless a Christian has graduated from Bible college or seminary, he is viewed as being a "para"-minister. A pseudo Christian worker. Someone less than the big boys. How dare such a person preach, teach, baptize, or administer the Lord's Supper if he has never been formally trained to do such things . . . right?

The idea that a Christian worker must attend Bible college or seminary to be legitimate is horrifyingly ingrained. It is so ingrained that when people feel a "call" of God on their life, they are conditioned to begin hunting for a Bible college or seminary to attend.

Such thinking fits poorly with the early Christian mindset. Bible colleges, seminaries, and even Sunday schools were utterly absent from the early church. All are human inventions that came hundreds of years after the apostles left the human stage.

How, then, were Christian workers trained in the first century if they did not go to a religious school? Unlike today's ministerial training, first-century training was hands-on, rather than academic. It was a matter of apprenticeship, rather than of intellectual learning. It was aimed primarily at the spirit, rather than at the frontal lobe.

In the first century, those called to the Lord's work were trained in two ways: 1) They learned the essential lessons of Christian ministry by *living* a shared life with a group of Christians. In other words, they were trained by experiencing church life as non-leaders. 2) They learned the Lord's work under the tutelage of an older, seasoned worker.

Remarking about the first-century church, Puritan John Owen said, *"Every church was then a seminary, in which provision and preparation was made . . . "*[1] Echoing these words, R. Paul Stevens states, *"The best structure for equipping every Christian is already in place. It predates the seminary and the weekend seminar and will outlast both. In the New Testament no other nurturing and equipping is offered than the local church. In the New Testament church, as in the ministry of Jesus, people learned in the furnace of life, in a relational, living, working and ministering context."*[2]

In stark contrast, modern ministerial training can be described by the religious talk of Job's miserable comforters: Rational, objective, and abstract. It is neither practical, experiential, nor spiritual as it should be.

The actual method by which Christian workers were trained in the first century is beyond the scope of this book. However, a small chorus of books have been dedicated to the subject.[3] In this chapter, we will trace the origin of the seminary, the Bible college, and the Sunday school. We will also trace the history of the youth pastor. And we will discuss how each is at odds with the way of Christ—for all are based upon the educational system of the world.[4]

---

[1] John Owen, *Commentary on Hebrews*, Vol. 3, p. 568.

[2] R. Paul Stevens, *Liberating the Laity* (Downers Grove: InterVarsity Press, 1985), p. 46. Note that these words cannot be said of the modern institutional church. They rather apply to all first-century styled churches.

[3] Among them are Gene Edwards' *Overlooked Christianity* (Sargent: Seedsowers, 1997); Robert E. Coleman's, *The Master Plan of Evangelism* (Grand Rapids: Fleming H. Revell, 1993); A.B. Bruce's *The Training of the Twelve* (Keats, 1979). The following books by Watchman Nee are worth noting. They contain messages given to his younger co-workers during Nee's worker trainings: *The Character of God's Workman*, *The Ministry of God's Word*, and *The Release of the Spirit*. 2 Timothy 2:2 refers to the concept of training Christian workers which is exemplified in both the Gospels and Acts.

[4] For an insightful discussion on the educational aspect of the world system, see Watchman Nee's *Love Not the World* (Wheaton: Tyndale House Publishers, 1978).

Four Stages of Theological Education

Throughout church history there have been four stages of theological education. They are: Episcopal, Monastic, Scholastic, and Pastoral.[5] Let us briefly examine each one:

Episcopal. Theology in the patristic age (third to fifth centuries) was called "episcopal" because the leading theologians of the day were bishops.[6] This theology was marked by the training of bishops and priests on how to perform the various rituals and liturgies of the church.[7]

Monastic. The *monastic* stage of theological education was tied to the ascetic and mystical life. It was taught by monks living in monastic communities (and later cathedral schools).[8] Monastic schools were founded in the third century. These schools sent missionaries to uncharted territories after the fourth century.[9]

During this stage, the eastern church fathers became steeped in

---

[5] John A.T. Robinson, *The New Reformation?* (Philadelphia: The Westminster Press, 1965), pp. 60-65. Robinson argues that Patristic theology was written by bishops, medieval theology was written by university professors, Reformed theology was written by pastors, and the theology of the "new Reformation" will be written by and for the whole people of God. A "theology for the whole people of God" focuses on the concerns and experiences of all Christians, not just the concerns and experiences of a specialized group doing a specialized job (clergy). Contemporary scholars like R. Paul Stevens (*The Abolition of the Laity,* Paternoster Press, 1999; *The Other Six Days: Vocation, Work and Ministry in Biblical Perspective*, Eerdmans, 2000) and Robert Banks (*Reinvisioning Theological Education,* Eerdmans, 1999) have written much on this brand of theology. Also, Harold H. Rowdon's article, "Theological Education in Historical Perspective," *Vox Evangelica*, Vol. VII, 1971, pp. 75-87, gives an overview of theological education throughout history.

[6] Augustine was one such person. A group of clergy gathered around him in the fifth century for training (Harold H. Rowdon, "Theological Education in Historical Perspective," *Vox Evangelica,* Vol. VII, 1971, p. 75).

[7] Episcopal schools did not take on an academic character to train clergy until the sixth century. Before then, prospective priests would learn under the direction of their bishops how to perform rituals and conduct liturgies. Edward J. Power, *A Legacy of Learning: A History of Western Education* (State University of New York Press, 1991), pp. 98, 108.

[8] Before the 12th century, the only education in the West was provided by monastic and cathedral schools.

[9] H.I. Marrou, *A History of Education in Antiquity*, p. 329.

Platonic thought. They held to the misguided view that Plato and
Aristotle were school masters to bring men to Christ. However, the
eastern church fathers' heavy reliance on these pagan philosophers
severely diluted the Christian faith. They did not intend to lead
people astray. It simply happened through the acceptance of a
defiled stream.[10]

Since many of the church fathers were pagan philosophers and
orators prior to their conversions, the Christian faith soon began to
take on a philosophical bent. Justin Martyr (100-165), one of the
most influential Christian teachers of the second century, "dressed
in the garb of a philosopher."[11] Justin believed that philosophy was
God's revelation to the Greeks. He claimed that Socrates, Plato,
and others had the same standing for the Gentiles as Moses had for
the Jews.[12]

After A.D. 200, Alexandria became the intellectual capital of the
Christian world as it had been for the Greeks. A special school was
formed there in A.D. 180.[13] This school was the equivalent of a
theological college.[14]

In Alexandria, we have the beginning of the institutional study
of Christian doctrine.[15] Origen (185-254), one of the school's early
teachers, was deeply influenced by pagan philosophy.[16] He was the

---

[10] In his book, *Ascension and Ecclesia* (Eerdmans, 1999), Douglas Farrow exposes
how Greek thinking took hold of theology through Origen and then Augustine and
how it inevitably affected many areas of church life.

[11] Eusebius, *The History of the Church,* IV, 11, 8.

[12] Norman Towar Boggs, *The Christian Saga* (New York: The Macmillan Company,
1931), p. 151; Edwin Hatch, *The Influence of Greek Ideas and Usages Upon the
Christian Church* (Peabody: Hendrickson, 1895), pp. 126-127.

[13] This school grew to its heights under Origen.

[14] Some say it was founded by Pantaenus, the teacher of Clement of Alexandria.
Others say it was founded by Demetrius. B.H. Streeter, *The Primitive Church* (New
York: The Macmillan Company, 1929), p. 57; James Bowen, *A History of Western
Education: Volume 1* (New York: St. Martin's Press, 1972), p. 240; "Theological
Education in Historical Perspective," p. 76.

[15] *A History of Western Education: Volume. 1,* p. 240; Father Michael Collins and
Matthew A. Price, *The Story of Christianity* (DK Publishing, 1999), p. 25.

[16] Origen was a pupil and friend of Plotinus, the father of Neo-platonism (Will
Durant, *Caesar to Christ,* New York: Simon & Schuster, 1950, p. 610). Neo-
platonism is a pagan philosophy founded by Plotinus (205-270). It flourished in 245-
529 and influenced Christian thought directly through Origen, Clement of Alexandria,
Augustine and Pseudo-Dionysius. According to Neo-platonic thought, an individual

first to organize key theological concepts into a systematic theology.[17]

Of this period Will Durant has observed: *"The gap between philosophy and religion was closing, and reason for a thousand years consented to be the handmaiden of theology."*[18] Edwin Hatch echoes these thoughts saying, *"Within a century and a half after Christianity and philosophy first came into closest contact, the ideas and methods of philosophy had flowed in such mass into Christianity, and filled so large a place in it, as to have made it no less a philosophy than a religion."*[19]

Following the days of Origen in the mid-third century, Christian schools disappeared. Theological education reverted back to the "episcopal" form. Bishops were trained by personal contact with other bishops.[20] The sum and substance of clerical learning at this time was the study of Gregory the Great's (540-604) pastoral theology.[21] Gregory taught bishops how to be good pastors.[22] By the mid-eighth century, bishops' schools were founded. In the 10th century, cathedrals began sponsoring their own schools.[23]

---

must ascend through different stages of purification in order to attain to oneness with God. Such an idea is still very prevalent in Catholic thought. See Philip S. Watson, *Neoplatonism and Christianity: 928 Ordinary General Meeting of the Victoria Institute Vol. 87* (Surrey: The Victoria Institute), 1955.

[17] *Pastor's Notes: A Companion Publication to Glimpses,* Volume 5, No. 2, Worcester: Christian History Institute, 1993, p. 7.

[18] *Caesar to Christ,* p. 611.

[19] *The Influence of Greek Ideas and Usages Upon the Christian Church,* p. 125.

[20] *A History of Education in Antiquity,* p. 329.

[21] Philip Schaff, *History of the Christian Church: Volume 4,* Michigan: Eerdmans, 1910, p. 400.

[22] Gregory's work, *The Book of Pastoral Rule,* was written in A.D. 591. It is a discussion on the duties of the bishop's office.

[23] J.D. Douglas, *Encyclopedia of Religious Knowledge, 2nd Edition* (Grand Rapids: Baker Book House, 1991), p. 289. Notre-Dame was one of the earliest cathedral schools. The university of Paris grew out of a cathedral school. James Bowen, *A History of Western Education: Volume 2* (New York: St. Martin's Press, 1972), p. 111. After 1100, the cathedral schools expanded, being broken up into "grammar schools" for boys and a higher school for advanced learning.

Scholastic. The third stage of theological education owes much to the culture of the university.[24] By 1200, a number of cathedral schools evolved into universities. The university of Bologna in Italy was the first university to appear. The university of Paris came in a close second followed by Oxford.[25]

The university of Paris became the philosophical and theological center of the world at that time.[26] (It would later became the seed of the Protestant seminary.)[27] Higher education was the domain of the clergy.[28] And the scholar was viewed as the guardian of ancient wisdom.

The modern university grew out of the bishops' responsibility to provide clerical training.[29] Theology was regarded as the "Queen of Sciences" in the university.[30] From the mid-12th century to the end of the 14th century, 71 universities were established in Europe.[31]

---

[24] The word "university" comes from the medieval Latin *universitas* which was the term used for the medieval craft guilds (*A History of Western Education: Volume 2*, p. 109).

[25] William Boyd, *The History of Western Education*, 8th ed. (New York: Barnes & Noble, 1967), p. 128. For a discussion on the origin of the university system, see Helen Wieruszowski, *The Medieval University* (Princeton: Van Nostrand, 1966).

[26] *A History of Western Education: Volume 1*, p. 110.

[27] The word "seminary" comes from the Latin *seminarium* meaning seedbed (Daniel G. Reid, *Dictionary of Christianity in America*, Downer's Grove: InterVarsity Press, p. 1071).

[28] *The Story of Christianity*, p.112.

[29] "Theological Education in Historical Perspective," p. 79. The Lateran Council of 1215 exhorted every metropolitan bishop to ensure theology was taught in every cathedral church.

[30] "Theological Education in Historical Perspective," p. 79.

[31] *A Legacy of Learning*, p. 149. The history of university degrees is quite interesting. People who passed academic standards were called *masters*. Lawyers were the first to be called *doctors*. *Doctor* means "one who teaches." It comes from *doctrina* which means learning. A *doctor*, then, is a *master* who teaches. Eager students who wanted recognition were called *bachelors* (p. 153). The Cathedral *chancellor* had ultimate control of the university. *Masters* gave lectures to the *bachelors* who at first lived in privately hired rooms, then later in halls lent to them by the *masters* ("Theological Education in Historical Perspective," p. 79). The word *faculty* which means strength, power, and ability, appeared around 1270. It represented the various subject divisions of the medieval guild. The word "faculty" eventually replaced "guild" and came to refer to the group of scholars in each subject. *A History of Western Education: Volume 2*, p. 111; Charles Homer Haskins, *The Rise of Universities* (New York: H. Holt, 1923), p. 17.

Modern theology cut its teeth on the abstractions of Greek philosophy.[32] University academics adopted an Aristotelian model of thinking which aimed at rational knowledge and logic. The dominating drive in scholastic theology was the assimilation and communication of knowledge. (For this reason, the Western mind has always been fond of creedal formulations, doctrinal statements, and other bloodless abstractions.)

One of the most influential professors in the shaping of modern theology was Peter Abelard (1079-1142). Abelard is partly responsible for giving us "modern theology." His teaching set the table and prepared the menu for scholastic philosophers like Thomas Aquinas (1225-1274).[33]

Distinguished by Abelard, the school of Paris emerged as the model for all universities to follow.[34] Abelard applied Aristotelian logic to revealed truth.[35] He also gave the word *theology* the meaning it has today. (Before him, this word was only used to describe pagan beliefs.[36])

Taking his cue from Aristotle, Abelard mastered the pagan philosophical art of "dialectic"—the logical disputation of truth. He applied this art to the Scriptures.

Christian theological education never recovered from Abelard's influence. Athens is still in its bloodstream. Aristotle, Abelard, and Aquinas all believed that reason was the gateway to Divine truth. So from its beginnings, Western university education involved the fusion of pagan and Christian elements.[37]

Martin Luther had it right when he said, *"What else are the universities than places for training youth in Greek glory."*[38]

---

[32] R. Paul Stevens, *The Other Six Days: Vocation, Work, and Ministry in Biblical Perspective* (Grand Rapids: Eerdmans, 1999), pp. 12-13; R. Paul Stevens, *The Abolition of the Laity* (Carlisle: Paternoster Press, 1999), pp. 10-22.

[33] D.W. Robertson, *Abelard and Heloise* (New York: The Dial Press, 1972), p. xiv.

[34] *A History of Western Education: Volume 2*, p. 109.

[35] A noteworthy quote of Abelard's is: "I do not wish to be a philosopher, if that means I contradict St. Paul; I do not wish to be a disciple of Aristotle, if that means I separate myself from Christ."

[36] To the disgust of many in his day, Abelard called one of his books *Christian Theology* (*Abelard and Heloise*, pp. xii-xiii).

[37] George Marsden, *The Soul of the American University: From Protestant Establishment and Established Nonbelief* (New York: Oxford University Press, 1994), p. 34.

[38] Ibid., p. 35.

Although Luther was a university man himself, his critique was aimed at teaching Aristotelian logic at the university level. [39]

Seminarian. Seminary theology grew out of the "scholastic" theology that was taught in the universities. As we have seen, this theology was based on Aristotle's philosophical system.[40] Seminary theology was dedicated to the training of professional ministers. Its goal was to produce seminary-trained religious specialists. It taught the theology—not of the early bishop, monk, or professor—but of the professionally "qualified" minister. This is the theology that prevails in the modern seminary.

One of the greatest theologians of this century, Karl Barth, reacted against the idea that theological education should be relegated to an elite class of professional orators. He wrote, *"Theology is not a private reserve of theologians. It is not a private affair of professors . . . Nor is it a private affair of pastors . . . Theology is a matter for the church . . . The term 'laity' is one of the worst in the vocabulary of religion and ought to be banished from Christian conversation."*[41]

Concerning the seminary, we can say that Peter Abelard laid the egg and Thomas Aquinas hatched it. More than any other figure, Aquinas has had the greatest influence on modern theological training. In 1879, his work was endorsed by a papal bull as an authentic expression of doctrine to be studied by all students of theology. Aquinas' main thesis was that God can be known through reason. He borrowed this idea from Aristotle.

Today, Protestants and Catholics alike draw upon Aquinas' work, using his outline for their theological studies.[42] Aquinas'

---

[39] Ibid., p. 36. For Luther's ideas on education, see *The History of Western Education*, p. 188ff. Ironically, Luther's co-worker, Melanchthon, combined humanism (which has pagan roots) and Protestantism in the education of Northern Europe.

[40] "Theological Education in Historical Perspective," p. 79.

[41] Karl Barth in *Theologische Fragen und Antworten* (1957), pp. 175, 183-184.

[42] *Christian History*, Issue 28, Vol. IX, No. 4, p. 23. Later in his life, Thomas had a spiritual experience with the Lord. It went beyond his intellect to his spirit. The experience was so profound that Thomas declared: "All that I have hitherto written seems to me nothing but straw . . . compared to what has been revealed to me."After this experience of Christ, Thomas gave up all of his voluminous writing. His

crowning work, *Summa Theologica* (The Sum of All Theology) is the model that is used in virtually all theological classes to-day—whether Protestant or Catholic. Consider the order in which Aquinas' theology is laid out:

God
Trinity
Creation
Angels
Man
The Divine Government (Salvation, etc.)
The Last End[43]

Now compare this outline to a typical systematic theology textbook used in Protestant seminaries:

God
Unity and Trinity
Creation
Angelology
The Origin and Character of Man
Soteriology (Salvation, etc.)
Eschatology: The Final State[44]

Without doubt, Aquinas is the father of modern theology.[45] His influence was mediated to the Protestant seminaries through the

---

mammoth *Summa Theologica* was never completed. He laid down his pen on December 6, 1273, saying, "And I now await the end of my life" (*Summa Theologica*, Great Books of the Western World: Volume 19, Thomas Aquinas I, p. vi; *The Story of Christianity*, p. 113).

[43] *Summa Theologica*, p. vii.

[44] Henry C. Theissen, *Lectures in Systematic Theology* (Eerdmans, 1979), p. v. Any standard Protestant systematic theology text follows this same template. All of it was derived from Aquinas.

[45] Aquinas' theological system continues to get reinforced. For instance, most Protestant seminaries in America and Europe follow what is known as the Berlin Model of theological education. This model started in Berlin in 1800. It was an outgrowth of enlightened rationalism and made theology a cerebral exercise. Most modern seminaries use this model today (*Vantage Point: The Newsletter of Denver Seminary*, June 1998, p. 4).

Protestant scholastics.[46] The tragedy is that Aquinas baptized Aristotle, using the pagan philosopher's logic chopping to expound holy writ. Aquinas also quotes from another pagan philosopher profusely throughout his *Summa Theologica*.[47] Modern theology, therefore, is a blending of Christian thought and pagan philosophy.

So we have four stages of theological education: *Episcopal*, the theology of the bishops. *Monastic*, the theology of the monks. *Scholastic*, the theology of the professor. And *seminarian*, the theology of the professional minister.[48]

Each stage of Christian education is and always has been highly intellectual and study-driven.[49] As one scholar put it, *"Whether a school was monastic, episcopal, or presbyterial, it never separated teaching from religious education, from instruction in church dogma and morals. Christianity was an intellectual religion . . . "*[50] As products of the Reformation, we are taught to be rationalistic (and very theoretical) in our approach to the Christian faith.[51]

The First Seminaries

During the medieval age, clerical education was minimal.[52] At the time of the Reformation, many Protestant pastors who converted from Roman Catholicism had no experience in preaching. They lacked both training and education.

As the Reformation progressed, however, provisions were made

---

[46] Francis Turretin (Reformed) and Martin Chemnitz (Lutheran) were the two leading Protestant scholastics.

[47] Aquinas quotes pseudo-Dionysius, a Neo-platonist, over 100 times in his *Summa Theologica*. Aquinas no doubt thought that the Dionysius he quoted was the man that Paul converted to Christ when in Athens (Acts 17:34). It was not, however. Pseudo-Dionysius was a Neo-platonist who lived much later than Dionysius the Areopagite.

[48] A fifth brand of theology, "lay theology" or a "theology for the whole people of God," is being championed by some contemporary scholars. See footnote #5.

[49] The exception is perhaps the "monastic" form. Some monastic schools studied the writings of the Christian mystics along with Aristotle and Plato.

[50] *A History of Education in Antiquity,* p. 343 in the Epilogue; *The Soul of the American University*, p. 38.

[51] Consider the following quote: "Christ did not appoint professors, but followers. If Christianity . . . is not reduplicated in the life of the person expounding it, then he does not expound Christianity, for Christianity is a message about living and can only be expounded by being realized in men's lives" (Soren Kierkegaard).

[52] *The Soul of the American University,* p. 38.

for uneducated pastors to attend schools and universities. Protestant ministers were not trained in oratory. They were instead trained in exegesis and Biblical theology. It was assumed that if they knew theology, they could preach. (This accounted for the long sermons in the 16th century which often lasted two or three hours!)[53]

This type of theological training produced a "new profession"—the theologically trained pastor. Educated pastors now wielded tremendous influence, holding doctor's degrees in theology or lower academic titles which gave them prestige.[54] By the mid-16th century, most Protestant ministers were university-trained in some way.[55]

So from its inception, Protestantism promoted a well-educated clergy which became the backbone to the movement.[56] Throughout Protestant lands, the clergy would be the best educated citizens. And they used their education to wield their authority.[57]

While Protestant ministers were sharpening their theological savvy, about one fourth of the Catholic clergy had no university training. The Catholic church reacted to this at the council of Trent (1545-1563). In order for the church to fight the new Protestant Reformation, it had to better educate its clergy. The solution? The founding of the very first seminaries![58]

The Catholics wanted their priests to match the learning and devotion of the Protestant pastors.[59] Therefore, the Council of Trent required that all cathedral and greater churches *"maintain, to educate religiously, and to train in ecclesiastical discipline, a certain number of youths of their city and diocese."* So we may

---

[53] *The Ministry in Historical Perspectives*, p. 133.
[54] Ibid., p. 144.
[55] Ibid., p. 142.
[56] *The Soul of the American University*, p. 37.
[57] Ibid., p. 37.
[58] *Concise Dictionary of Christianity in America* (Downers Grove: InterVarsity Press, 1995), p. 309; Will Durant, *The Reformation* (New York: Simon & Schuster, 1957), p. 932. Trent made provision for a seminary in each diocese (A.G. Dickens, *Reformation and Society in Sixteenth-Century Europe,* London: Hartcourt, Brace, & World, Inc, 1966, p. 189; *The Story of Christianity*, p. 149).
[59] "Theological Education in Historical Perspective," p. 81.

credit the founding of the seminary to the Catholics in the late 16th century.

The first Protestant seminary is clouded in obscurity. But the best evidence indicates that the Protestants copied the Catholic model and established their first seminary in America. It was established in Andover, Massachusetts in 1808.[60]

Christian education in the United States was just as Aristotelian and highly systematized as when it thrived in Europe.[61] By 1860, there was a total of 60 Protestant seminaries on American soil.[62] This fast-paced growth was largely the result of the influx of converts produced during the Second Great Awakening (1800-1835) and the perceived need to train ministers to care for them.[63]

Before Andover Seminary was founded, the Protestants had Yale (1701) and Harvard (1636) to train their clergy. Ordination was granted upon completing a formal examination upon graduation.[64] But in time, these universities adopted Unitarianism and rejected orthodox Christian beliefs.[65] The Protestants no longer trusted an undergraduate education at Yale and Harvard, so they established their own seminaries to do the job themselves.[66]

---

[60] *Concise Dictionary of Christianity in America*, p. 113. John Calvin established the Geneva Academy in 1559. But this was not technically a seminary. While the Academy was used to train theologians, it was not conceived originally as a theological school. It gave a total education to non-clergy as well. Interestingly, Theodore Beza (Calvin's right hand man) traced the scholastic pedigree of the Geneva Academy to the Greeks who in turn received their "true philosophy" from the Egyptians. It was argued that this was great since Moses was educated in all the wisdom of the Egyptians (Robert W. Henderson, *The Teaching Office in the Reformed Tradition*, Philadelphia: Westminster Press, 1962, pp. 51-61).

[61] John Morgan, *Godly Learning* (New York: Cambridge University Press, 1986), p. 107. American seminary education was also dominated by the Scottish "common sense" philosophy of Thomas Reid. Later, liberal seminaries came to prefer G.F.W. Hegel while conservative seminaries stuck with Reid.

[62] *Concise Dictionary of Christianity in America*, p. 113.

[63] Ibid., p. 113.

[64] Marjorie Warkentin, *Ordination: A Biblical-Historical View* (Grand Rapids: Eerdmans, 1982), p . 75.

[65] Unitarianism denies the Trinity, the Divinity of Jesus, and other orthodox Christian beliefs.

[66] The first Catholic seminary to hit American soil was established in Baltimore in 1791. Daniel G. Reid, *Dictionary of Christianity in America* (InterVarsity Press), p. 1071.

Bible College

The Bible college is essentially a 19th-century North American evangelical invention. A Bible college is a cross between a Bible institute (training center) and a Christian liberal arts school. Its students major in religion and are trained for Christian service. The founders of the first Bible colleges were influenced by London pastors H.G. Guinness (1835-1910) and Charles Spurgeon (1834-1892).

In response to the revivalism of D.L. Moody (1837-1899), the Bible college movement blossomed in the late 19th and early 20th century. The first two Bible colleges were The Missionary Training Institute (Nyack College, New York) in 1882 and Moody Bible Institute (Chicago) in 1886.[67] Their focus was to train ordinary laypeople to become "full time" Christian workers.[68]

What led to the founding of the Bible college? Since the mid-19th century, little attention had been given to traditional Christian values as an integral part of higher education. Liberal theology began to dominate state universities across America. In the face of these elements, the demand for missionaries, para-church leaders, and ministers provoked the creation of the Bible college to equip "the called" with a Bible education.[69] Today, there are over 400 Bible schools and colleges in the United States and Canada.[70] In short, the Bible college is a minor league version of the seminary.

Sunday School

The Sunday School is also a relatively modern invention, being born some 1700 years after Christ. A newspaper publisher named Robert Raikes (1736-1811) from Britain is credited with being the

---

[67] The Moody Bible Institute was formally constituted in 1889 (*Christian History*, Volume IX, No. 1, Issue 25, p. 28).

[68] *Concise Dictionary of Christianity in America*, pp. 42-43; *Harper's Encyclopedia of Religious Education* (San Francisco: Harper & Row Publishers, 1971), p. 61.

[69] *Harper's Encyclopedia of Religious Education*, p. 61.

[70] "Bible College Movement," *The Evangelical Dictionary of Christian Education* (Grand Rapids: Baker Book House, 2001).

founder of the Sunday School.[71] In 1780, Raikes established a school in "Scout Alley" Gloucester for poor children. Raikes did not found the Sunday School for the purpose of religious instruction. Instead, he founded it to teach poor children the basics of education.

Raikes was concerned with the low level of literacy and morality among common children. Many of the children that attended his school were the victims of social and employer abuse. Because the children could not read, it was easy for others to take advantage of them.

The 1780s was a decade of innovation. The steam engine was the main symbol of progress.[72] Sunday School was born in that climate. Although Raikes was an Anglican laymen, the Sunday School took off like wild fire, spreading to Baptist, Congregational, and Methodist churches throughout England.[73]

The Sunday School movement came to a high peak when it hit the United States. The first Sunday School to appear in America began in Virginia in 1785.[74] Then in 1790, a group of Philadelphians formed the Sunday School Society. Its purpose was to provide education to indigent children so as to keep them off the streets on Sunday.[75] In the 18th and 19th centuries, many Sunday Schools operated separately from churches. The reason: Pastors felt that laymen could not teach the Bible![76]

---

[71] *Harper's Encyclopedia of Religious Education*, p. 625. Most historical books credit Raikes with being the father of the Sunday School. But others are said to have been founders along with Raikes: Hannah Moore and Sarah Trimmers being among them (Thomas W. Laqueur, *Religion and Respectability: Sunday Schools and Working Class Culture, 1780-1850*, p. 21). It has also been said that Rev. Thomas Stock of Gloucester gave Raikes the idea of Sunday education (p. 22).

[72] John Ferguson, *Christianity, Society, and Education: Robert Raikes, Past, Present, and Future*, p. 19.

[73] *Harper's Encyclopedia of Religious Education*, p. 625. The Sunday School grew as part of the Evangelical Revival of the 1780s and 1790s (*Religion and Respectability*, p. 61). When Raikes died in 1811, there were 400,000 children attending Sunday Schools in Great Britain. C.B. Eavey, *History of Christian Education* (Chicago: Moody Press, 1964), pp. 225-227.

[74] John Mark Terry, *Evangelism: A Concise History* (Nashville: Broadman & Holman Publishers, 1994), p. 180.

[75] *Harper's Encyclopedia of Religious Education*, p. 625.

[76] *Evangelism: A Concise History*, p. 181.

In the mid-1800s, Sunday Schools spread far and wide throughout America. In 1810, the Sunday School began to shift from being a philanthropic effort to help poor children to an evangelical mechanism.

D.L. Moody is credited with popularizing the Sunday School in America.[77] Under Moody's influence, the Sunday School became the primary recruiting ground for the modern church.[78] Today, the Sunday School is used both to recruit new converts and train young children in the doctrines of the faith.[79] Public education has taken over the original role for which Sunday School was designed.[80]

It should be noted that the 19th century was an era of institution building in America. Corporations, hospitals, asylums, prisons as well as children's institutions like orphanages, reform schools, and free public schools were formed during this time.[81] The Sunday School was just another institution that grew out of the fury of American institution building.[82] Today, it is a permanent fixture in the institutional church.

As a whole, the modern Sunday School is simply not an effective institution. Over the last two decades, Sunday School attendance has been on the decline.[83] Studies have shown that Sunday School

---

[77] *Christian History,* Volume IX, No. 1, Issue 25, p. 28; *The Story of Christianity,* p. 187. Moody's Sunday School ministry cared for over 1,500 children.

[78] *Sunday School,* p. 167. This was the case by 1880. Arthur Flake developed the Sunday School program within the Southern Baptist Convention. He also popularized Sunday School growth principles that were adopted by other denominations. (*Evangelism: A Concise History,* p. 181). See also Elmer Towns, "Sunday School Movement," *New 20th Century Encyclopedia of Religious Knowledge* (Grand Rapids: Baker Book House, 1991), pp. 796-798.

[79] Ibid., p. 170; *Concise Dictionary of Christianity in America,* p. 331.

[80] *Pastor's Notes: A Companion Publication to Glimpses,* Volume 4, No. 1 (Worcester: Christian History Institute, 1991), p. 6.

[81] Anne M. Boylan, *Sunday School: The Formation of an American Institution 1790-1880* (New Haven: Yale University Press, 1988), p. 1

[82] In 1824, there were 48,681 children in Sunday Schools affiliated with the American Sunday School Union in the United States. In 1832, that figure grew to 301,358 (*Sunday School,* p. 11). The American Sunday School Union was founded in 1824, comprising 724 schools including 68 in Philadelphia. In 1970, the Union was renamed the American Missionary Society (*Concise Dictionary of Christianity in America,* p. 18).

[83] Bobby H. Welch, *Evangelism Through the Sunday School: A Journey of Faith* (Lifeway Press, 1997).

really makes little difference in changing the behavior of young people.[84]

If the truth be told, most youngsters find Sunday School dry, boring, and irrelevant. Sunday School is a dinosaur that is overripe for extinction. It is yet another human tradition that we feel we cannot live without. Yet if we would return to church first-century style, we would open ourselves up to a raft of creative ways to teach and encourage our children in a corporate context.[85] And we would discover anew that we have a God of infinite variety, not of insipid sameness.

Describing the way of the early church, one scholar says, *"There is no evidence to suggest that teachers divided groups on the basis of age and sex. The responsibility of the child's early education and, in particular, religious education lay with the parents . . . No special arrangements seem to have been made for children by the early church. The Christian school was a long way off (around A.D. 372)—the Sunday School even more so."*[86]

The Youth Pastor

On the heels of tracing the origin of the Sunday School, let us take a detour and unearth the hazy roots of the "youth pastor."[87] In 1905, G. Stanley Hall popularized the concept of "adolescent" as being distinct from a young adult and an older child.[88]

Then in the 1940s, the term "teenager" was born. And for the first time a distinct youth subculture was created. People ages

---

[84] Gough, J. E. *Church, Delinquent and Society.* Provocative Pamphlets No. 59. Melbourne: Federal Literature Committee of Churches of Christ in Australia, 1959.

[85] I have been practicing church without Sunday School for over 15 years now. The creative juices resident in the church of Jesus Christ when it concerns what to do for our children have been abundant. Because the children are part of a shared-life community that knows no age segregations, the children in these churches are healthier spiritually and mentally.

[86] David C. Norrington, *To Preach or Not to Preach? The Church's Urgent Question* (Carlisle: Paternoster Press, 1996), p. 59.

[87] Warren Benson and Mark H. Senter III, *The Complete Book of Youth Ministry* (Chicago: Moody Press, 1987), p. 66.

[88] Mark Senter III, *The Coming Revolution in Youth Ministry* (Victor Books, 1992), p. 93

thirteen to nineteen were no longer simply "youths." They were now "teenagers."[89]

After World War II (1945 onward), Americans developed great concern for the young people of our nation. This spilled over into the Christian church. Youth rallies in the 1930s laboring under the banner "Youth for Christ" spawned a parachurch organization by the same name around 1945.[90]

With the influx of these new creatures called "teenagers," there grew up the idea that someone needed to be employed to work with them. Thus was born the professional youth minister. The youth pastor began to emerge in large urban churches in the 1930s and 40s.[91] He then moved to the suburbs in the 1960s.

Calvary Baptist Church in Manhattan had one of the very first youth pastors. Moody Monthly Magazine wrote about him in the late 1930s.[92] During the mid-1950s to the end of the 1960s, the youth pastor became an established part of evangelical churches. (The position was a bit slower to develop in the mainline denominations.)[93]

By the early 1950s, thousands of professional youth ministers emerged to meet the spiritual needs of young people. Teenagers had their own music, dress, literature, language, and etiquette.[94]

---

[89] Michael V. Uschar, *The 1940s: Cultural History of the US Through the Decades* (Lucent Books, 1999), p. 88; Mary Helen Dohan, *Our Own Words* (New York: Alfred Knopf, 1974), p. 289.

[90] Mark Senter III, *The Youth For Christ Movement as an Educational Agency and Its Impact Upon Protestant Churches: 1931-1979* (Ann Arbor: UM, 1990), pp. 7-8. On pages 26ff., Senter discusses the social and historical factors that created a raft of youth organizations. Billy Graham became Youth for Christ's (YFC) traveling evangelist. In the 1950s, YFC established Bible clubs across the country (*Concise Dictionary of Christianity in America*, p. 377). In Manhattan, the charismatic Lloyd Bryant appears to be the first to organize regular youth rallies (*Critique of Modern Youth Ministry*, p. 8).

[91] Calvary Baptist Church in Manhattan (1932), Vista Community Church in North San Diego County (1948), and Moody Memorial Church in Chicago (1949) all hired "youth directors." As Young Life and YFC clubs flourished in the country in the 1930s and 40s, smaller churches began employing youth ministers (*The Coming Revolution in Youth Ministry*, p. 142).

[92] Personal Email from Mark Senter, 9/22/99.

[93] *The Coming Revolution in Youth Ministry*, p. 142.

[94] Christopher Schlect, *Critique of Modern Youth Ministry* (Moscow: Canon Press, 1995), p. 6.

The teenager was viewed as a separate entity with separate needs. Hence, the Christian church began to segregate teenagers from everyone else.

The majority of youth ministers worked for the emerging parachurch organizations that filled the Christian landscape.[95] But from the mid-1970s to the end of the 1980s, youth ministry shifted from the parachurch organizations to institutional churches. The professional youth pastor made the volunteer youth worker a second-class citizen.[96]

Even so, the modern youth pastor is the son of the modern pastor. He is part of the professional clergy. He is built on the modern church's misguided choice to honor divisions that were born in secular culture less than a century ago. Namely, the division between teenager and everyone else.

Put another way, the youth pastor did not exist until we created a separate category called "teenager." In so doing, we created a problem that never before existed. That is, the problem of what to do for (and with) the young people. It is not at all unlike the problem we created when a new class of Christian was invented—the "laymen." The question "How do we equip the laity" was never asked before we made them a separate class of Christian.

Today, the youth pastor is just as much a permanent fixture in the organized church as is the pastor. Both have no root in Scripture.

Exposing the Heart of the Problem

Both Plato and Socrates taught that knowledge is virtue. Good depends on the extent of one's knowledge. Hence, the teaching of knowledge is the teaching of virtue.[97]

[95] Young Life (1941), Youth for Christ (1945), Fellowship of Christian Athletes (1954), Youth With A Mission began (1960). *The Coming Revolution in Youth Ministry*, pp. 27-28, 141; Mark Senter, "A Historical Framework for Doing Youth Ministry," *Reaching a Generation for Christ* (Chicago: Moody Press), 1997.
[96] *The Coming Revolution in Youth Ministry*, p. 143.
[97] William Boyd and Edmund King, *The History of Western Education* (Lanham: Barnes & Noble Books, 1995), p. 28.

Herein lies the root and stem of modern Christian education. It is built on the Platonic idea that knowledge and spirituality are the same. Therein lies the great flaw.

Greek philosophers Plato and Aristotle (both students of Socrates) are the fathers of modern Christian education.[98] To use a Biblical metaphor, modern Christian education, whether it be seminarian or Bible college, is serving food from the wrong tree: The tree of the knowledge of good and evil rather than the tree of life.[99]

Modern theological learning is essentially cerebral. It can be called "liquid pedagogy."[100] We pry open people's heads, pour in a cup or two of information, and close them up again. They have the information, so we mistakenly conclude the job is complete.

Modern theological teaching is data-transfer education. It moves from notebook to notebook. In the process, our theology never gets below the neck. If a student accurately parrots the ideas of his professor, he is awarded a degree. And that means a lot in a day when many Christians obsess over (and sometimes deify) theological degrees in their analysis of who is qualified to minister.[101]

Theological knowledge, however, does not prepare a person for ministry.[102] This does not mean that the knowledge of the world, church history, theology, philosophy, and the Scriptures is without value. Such knowledge can be very useful.[103] But it is not central. Theological competence and a high voltage intellect do not qualify a person to serve in God's house.

---

[98] *A Legacy of Learning*, pp. 29-116.

[99] Time and space will not permit me to explain the meaning of the two trees. For a fuller discussion, I recommend Watchman Nee's *The Normal Christian Life* (Wheaton: Tyndale, 1977), Chapter 7 and Gene Edwards' *The Highest Life* (Wheaton: Tyndale, 1989).

[100] Pedagogy is the art and science of teaching.

[101] One of the key problems in Christianity is that it inherited the intellectual standards of the ancient world (*The Soul of the American University*, p. 34).

[102] Keep in mind that Joseph Stalin attended Tiflis Theological Seminary from ages 14 to 19 (Adam B. Ulam, *Stalin the Man and His Era*, New York : Viking Press, 1973, pp. 18-22; Alan Bullock, *Hitler and Stalin: Parallel Lives*, New York: Knopf, 1992, pp. 6,13).

[103] Paul of Tarsus was highly educated, and he was vital to the spread of early Christianity. Peter, on the other hand, was uneducated.

The fallacy is that men and women who have matriculated from seminary or Bible college are instantly viewed as "qualified." Those who have not are viewed as "unqualified." By this standard, many of the Lord's choicest vessels would have failed the test.[104]

In addition, formal theological training is grossly overrated. According to the *Faith Communities Today (FACT)* study released by Hartford Seminary in Connecticut, seminary graduates and clergymen who had advanced degrees scored lower in both dealing with conflict and having a "clear sense of purpose" than non-seminary graduates.[105]

The survey showed that clergy with no ministerial education or formal certificate program scored the highest on tests that revealed how well one deals with conflict and stress. Bible college graduates scored slightly less. Seminary graduates scored the lowest!

The major finding of the study was that *"congregations with leaders who have a seminary education are, as a group, far more likely to report that in their congregations they perceive less clarity of purpose, more and different kinds of conflict, less person-to-person communication, less confidence in the future and more threat from changes in worship."*[106]

All of this indicates that a person who matriculates from the theory-laden seminary or Bible college has been given no hands-on experience in the crucible of church life. In this way, the seminary is intellectually stultifying on some pretty basic levels.

Still worse is the elitism that the seminary system feeds. The approach taken by seminaries is self-referential. It sets its own

---

[104] Jesus and the twelves apostles were all unlearned men: "The Jews were amazed and asked, 'How did this man [Jesus] get such learning without having studied?'" (John 7:15, NIV); "Now when they saw the boldness of Peter and John, and perceived that they were unlearned and ignorant men, they marveled; and they took knowledge of them, that they had been with Jesus" (Acts 4:13). Some noted Christians used of God who never received formal theological training include A.W. Tozer, G. Campbell Morgan, John Bunyan, C.H. Spurgeon, D.L. Moody, and A.W. Pink. In addition, some of the greatest Bible expositors in church history, such as Watchman Nee, Stephen Kaung, and T. Austin-Sparks, were not seminary trained.

[105] This study was based on more than 14,000 congregations from 41 different denominations and "faith groups." It used 26 different surveys. The *FACT* study is considered to be the most comprehensive look at US religion. The findings are published at www.fact.hartsem.edu

[106] *FACT* study, p. 67.

criteria for who gets to play and on what terms. Then it looks down its nose at those who do not think that criteria is particularly useful or important.

But perhaps the most damaging problem of the seminary and Bible college is that it perpetuates the crippling, unscriptural, humanly-devised clergy system. That system—along with every other outmoded human tradition I have addressed in this book—is protected, kept alive, and spread through our ministerial schools.[107] In the seminary and Bible college, professors and pastors alike illegitimately justify the existence of an unbiblical system in which they live, breath, and have their being.

Instead of offering the cure to the ills of the church, our theological schools worsen them by assuming (and even defending) all of the unscriptural practices that produce them. The words of one pastor sum up the problem nicely:

"I came through the whole system with the best education that evangelicalism had to offer—yet I really didn't receive the training that I needed . . . seven years of higher education in top-rated evangelical schools didn't prepare me to 1) do ministry and 2) be a leader. I began to analyze why I could preach a great sermon and people afterwards would shake my hand and say, "Great sermon, Pastor." But these were the very people who were struggling with self-esteem, beating their spouses, struggling as workaholics, succumbing to their addictions. Their lives weren't changing. I had to ask myself why this great knowledge I was presenting didn't move from their heads to their hearts and their lives. And I began to realize that the breakdown in the church was actually based on what we learned in seminary. We were taught that if you just give people information, that's enough!"[108]

---

[107] Ironically, Protestants are noted for their critical reflection on doctrine. But they have not applied that critical reflection to their church practices.

[108] Dr. Clyde McDowell quoted in *Vantage Point: The Newsletter of Denver Seminary*, June 1998.

The Primitive Church had no New Testament, no thought-out theology, no stereotyped traditions. The men who took Christianity to the Gentile world had no special training, only a great experience—in which 'all maxims and philosophies were reduced to the simple task of walking in the light since the light had come.'

-B.H. Streeter

CHAPTER 10

A SECOND GLANCE AT THE SAVIOR: JESUS, THE REVOLUTIONARY

If Christianity is to receive a rejuvenation it must be by other means than any now being used. If the church in the second half of this century is to recover from the injuries she suffered in the first half, there must appear a new type of preacher. The proper, ruler-of-the-synagogue type will never do. Neither will the priestly type of man who carries out his duties, takes his pay and asks no questions, nor the smooth-talking pastoral type who knows how to make the Christian religion acceptable to everyone. All these have been tried and found wanting. Another kind of religious leader must arise among us. He must be of the old prophet type, a man who has seen visions of God and has heard a voice from the Throne. When he comes (and I pray God there will not be one but many) he will stand in flat contradiction to everything our smirking, smooth civilization holds dear. He will contradict, denounce and protest in the name of God and will earn the hatred and opposition of a large segment of Christendom.

-A.W. Tozer

Jesus Christ is not only the Savior, the Messiah, the Prophet, the Priest, and the King. He is also the Revolutionary. Yet few Christians know Him as such. Doubtlessly, some of my readers have struggled with this thought while reading this book: *"Why do you have to be so negative about the modern church,*

Frank!? Jesus is not a critical person. It is so unlike our Lord to talk about what is wrong with the church. Let us focus on the positive and ignore the negative!"

Such high volume sentiments express complete unfamiliarity with Christ as revolutionary teacher—radical prophet—provocative preacher—controversialist—iconoclast—and the implacable opponent of the religious establishment.

Granted, our Lord is not critical or harsh with His own. He is full of mercy and kindness, and He loves His people passionately. However, this is precisely why He is jealous over His Bride. And it is why He will not compromise with the unbreakable traditions to which His people have been held captive. Nor will He ignore our fanatical devotion to them.

Consider our Lord's conduct while on earth.

Jesus was never a rabble-rouser nor a ranting rebel.[1] Yet He constantly defied the traditions of the scribes and Pharisees. He did not do so by accident, but with great deliberation. The Pharisees were those who, for the sake of the "truth" they saw, tried to extinguish the truth they could not see. This explains why there was always a blizzard of controversy between the "tradition of the elders" and the acts of Jesus.

Someone once said that *"a rebel attempts to change the past; a revolutionary attempts to change the future."* Jesus Christ brought drastic change to the world. Change to man's view of God. Change to God's view of man. Change to men's view of women. Our Lord came to bring radical change to the old order of things, replacing it with a new order.[2] He came to bring forth a new covenant—a new kingdom—a new birth—a new race—a new species—a new culture—and a new civilization.

As you read through the Gospels, behold your Lord, the Revolutionary. Watch Him throw the Pharisees into a panic by intentionally flaunting their conventions. Numerous times Jesus healed on the Sabbath day, flatly breaking their cherished tradition. If the Lord wanted to placate His enemies, He could have waited

---

[1] Matt. 12:19-20.
[2] The following passages throw light on Christ's revolutionary nature: Matt. 3:10-12; 10:34-38; Mark 2:21-22; Luke 12:49; John 2:14-17; 4:21-24.

until Sunday or Monday to heal some of these people. Instead, He deliberately healed on the Sabbath, knowing full well it would make His opponents livid.

This pattern runs pretty deep. In one instance, Jesus healed a blind man by mixing clay with spittle and putting it in the man's eyes. Such an act was in direct defiance to the Jewish ordinance that prohibited healing on the Sabbath by mixing mud with spittle![3] Yet your Lord intentionally shattered this tradition publicly and with absolute resolve. Watch Him eat food with unwashed hands under the judgmental gaze of the Pharisees, again intentionally defying their fossilized tradition.[4]

In Jesus, we have a Man who refused to bow to the pressures of religious conformity. A Man who preached a revolution. A Man who would not tolerate hypocrisy. A Man who was not afraid to provoke those who suppressed the liberating gospel He brought to set men free. A Man who did not mind evoking anger in His enemies, causing them to gird their thighs for battle.

What is my point? It is this: Jesus Christ came not only as Messiah, the Anointed One of God to deliver His people from the bondage of the fall.

He came not only as Savior, paying a debt He did not owe to wash away the sins of mankind.

He came not only as Prophet, comforting the afflicted and afflicting the comfortable.

He came not only as Priest, representing man before God and representing God before man.

He came not only as King, triumphant over all authority, principality, and power.

He also came as *Revolutionary*, tearing apart the old wineskin with a view to bringing in the new.

Behold your Lord, the Revolutionary!

---

[3] In the Mishnah it is stated: "To heal a blind man on the Sabbath it is prohibited to inject wine in his eyes. It is also prohibited to make mud with spittle and smear it on his eyes" (Shabbat 108:20).

[4] According to the Mishna, "One should be willing to walk four miles to water in order to wash your hands rather than to eat with unwashed hands" (Sotah, 4b) . . . "He who neglects hand washing is as he who is a murderer" (Challah, J, 58:3).

For most Christians, this is a new look at Jesus Christ. There-fore, to expose what is wrong with the modern church so that Christ's Body can fulfill God's ultimate intention is simply an expression of our Lord's revolutionary nature. The dominating aim of that nature is to put you and me at the center of the beating heart of God. To put you and me in the core of His eternal purpose—a purpose for which everything was created.[5]

What is needed, then, is a revolution within the Christian faith. Renewal movements will not do it. Revivals will not cut it. Both have been plentiful for the past 50 years. (I might add that they are repackaged every five years.) Renewal movements and revivals have *never* been potent enough to break the immense inertia of religious tradition.

Renewing and inventing new forms for church is like changing clothes on a mannequin. Doing so will never give it life no matter how avant-garde the garb is. No, the axe must be laid to the root of the problem and a revolution ignited!

What is needed is a complete upheaval of our current Christian practices. All traditions that find no soil in Scripture must be forever abandoned. We must begin anew . . . from ground zero. Anything less will prove defective.

If you are a disciple of the Revolutionary from Nazareth . . . the Radical Messiah[6] who lays His axe to the root . . . you will even-tually evoke a specific question. It is the same question that was asked our Lord's disciples while He walked this earth. That question is: *"Why do your disciples break the tradition of the elders?"*[7] On the heels of that statement, the next chapter is the most important of all.

---

[5] See *Rethinking the Wineskin* Chapter 7 for a discussion on the eternal purpose.
[6] The word "radical" is derived from the Latin *radax*, which means "root." A radical, therefore, is someone that goes to the root or origin of something. Jesus Christ was both a radical and a revolutionary. See John A.T. Robinson's definition for both terms at the end of this chapter.
[7] Matt. 15:2.

A true radical must be a man of roots. In words that I have used elsewhere, "The revolutionary can be an 'outsider' to the structure he would see collapse: indeed, he must set himself outside of it. But the radical goes to the roots of his own tradition. He must love it: he must weep over Jerusalem, even if he has to pronounce its doom."
   -John A.T. Robinson

CHAPTER 11

REAPPROACHING THE NT:[1]
THE BIBLE IS NOT A JIGSAW PUZZLE

In handling the subject of ministry in the New Testament it is essential to remember the order in which the books of the New Testament were written. If we assume, as the order in which the books of the New Testament are now presented would lead us to assume, that the Gospels were written first, and then Acts and then the letters of Paul, beginning with Romans and ending with the Pastoral Epistles to Timothy to Titus and the Letter to Philemon, we shall never be able to understand the development of the institutions and the thought of the early church.
- Richard Hanson

Why is it that we Christians can follow the same God-forsaken rituals every Sunday without ever noticing that they are at odds with the NT? Part of the reason has to do with the incredible power of tradition. But there is something else. It concerns our NT. The problem is not in what the NT says. The problem is in how we *approach* it.

The approach most commonly used among modern Christians when studying the Bible is called "proof texting." The origin of proof texting goes back to the late 1590s. A group of men called

---

[1] This chapter is based on a message the author delivered at a house church conference at Oglethorpe University in Atlanta, Georgia on July 29, 2000.

Protestant Scholastics took the teachings of the Reformers and systematized them according to the rules of Aristotelian logic.[2] The Protestant Scholastics held that not only is the Scripture the Word of God, but every part of it is the Word of God in and of itself—irrespective of context. This set the stage for the idea that if we lift a verse out of the Bible, it is true in its own right and can be used to prove a doctrine or a practice.

When John Nelson Darby emerged in the mid 1800s, he built a theology based on this approach. Darby raised proof texting to an art form. In fact, it was Darby who gave fundamentalist and evangelical Christians a good deal of their presently accepted teachings.[3] All of them are built on the proof texting method. Proof texting, then, became *the way* that we modern Christians approach the Bible. It is taught in every Protestant Bible school and seminary on earth.

As a result, we Christians rarely, if ever, get to see the NT as a *whole*. Rather, we are served up a dish of fragmented thoughts that are drawn together by means of fallen human logic. The fruit of this approach is that we have strayed far afield from the practice of the NT church. Yet we still believe we are being Biblical. Allow me to illustrate the problem with a fictitious story.

Meet Marvin Snurdly

Marvin Snurdly is a world renowned marital counselor. In his 20-year career as a marriage therapist, Marvin has counseled thousands of troubled marriages. He has an Internet presence. Each day hundreds of couples write letters to Marvin about their marital sob stories. The letters come from all over the globe. And Marvin answers them all.

---

[2] For a discussion on Protestant scholasticism, see Walter Elwell's *Evangelical Dictionary of Theology* (Grand Rapids: Baker Book House, 1984), pp. 984-985. Francis Turretin (Reformed) and Martin Chemnitz (Lutheran) are the two main shakers among the Protestant Scholastics (*Evangelical Dictionary of Theology*, pp. 1116 & 209 respectively).
[3] Dispensationalism and the pre-tribulational rapture are just two of them. The very successful *Left Behind* series is built upon these teachings (see *Time*, July 1, 2002, pp. 41-48). For the fascinating origin of Darby's pretribulational doctrine, see Dave MacPherson's *The Incredible Cover-Up* (Medford: Omega Publications, 1975).

A hundred years pass, and Marvin Snurdly is resting peacefully in his grave. He has a great, great grandson named Fielding Melish. Fielding decides to recover the lost letters of his great, great grandfather, Marvin Snurdly. But Fielding can only find 13 of Marvin's letters. Out of the thousands of letters that Marvin wrote in his lifetime, only 13 have survived! Nine of them were written to *couples* in marital crisis. Four of them were written to *individual* spouses.

These letters were all written within a 20-year time frame: From 1980 to 2000. Fielding Melish plans to compile these letters into a volume. But there is something interesting about the way Marvin wrote his letters that makes Fielding's task somewhat difficult.

First, Marvin had an annoying habit of never dating his letters. No days, months, or years appear on any of the 13 letters. Second, the letters only portray half the conversation. The initial letters written *to* Marvin that provoked his responses no longer exist. Consequently, the only way to understand the backdrop of one of Marvin's letters is by reconstructing the marital situation from Marvin's response.

Each letter was written at a different time, to people in a different culture, dealing with a different problem. For example, in 1985, Marvin wrote a letter to Paul and Sally from Virginia, USA who were experiencing sexual problems early in their marriage. In 1990, Marvin wrote a letter to Jethro and Matilda from Australia who were having problems with their children. In 1995, Marvin wrote a letter to a wife from Mexico who was experiencing a mid-life crisis.

Take note: 20 years—13 letters—all written to different people at different times in different cultures—all experiencing different problems.

It is Fielding Melish's desire to put these 13 letters in chronological order. But without the dates, he cannot do this. So Fielding puts them in the order of descending length. That is, he takes the longest letter that Marvin wrote and puts it first. He puts Marvin's second longest letter after that. He takes the third longest and puts it third. The compilation ends with the shortest letter that Marvin penned. 13 letters are arranged, not chronologically, but by their length.

The volume hits the presses and becomes an overnight best seller. People are buying it by the truck loads.

100 years pass and *The Collected Works of Marvin Snurdly* compiled by Fielding Melish stands the test of time. The work is still very popular. Another 100 years pass, and this volume is being used copiously throughout the Western World. (Marvin has been resting in his grave for 300 years now.)

The book is translated into dozens of languages. Marriage counselors are quoting it left and right. Universities are employing it in their sociology classes. It is so widely used that someone gets a bright idea on how to make the volume easier to quote and handle.

What is that bright idea? It is to divide Marvin's letters into chapters and numbered sentences (we call them verses). So chapters and verses are born in the *Collected Works of Marvin Snurdly.*

But by adding chapter-and-verse to these once living letters, something changes that goes unnoticed. The letters lose their personal touch. Instead, they take on the texture of a manual.

Different sociologists begin writing books about marriage and the family. Their main source? *The Collected Works of Marvin Snurdly.* Pick up any book in the 24th century on the subject of marriage, and you will find the author quoting chapters and verses from Marvin's letters.

It usually looks like this: In making a particular point, an author will quote a verse from Marvin's letter written to Paul and Sally. The author will then lift another verse from the letter written to Jethro and Matilda. He will extract another verse from another letter. Then he will sew these three verses together upon which he will build his particular marital philosophy.

Virtually every sociologist and marital therapist that authors a book on marriage does the same thing. Yet the irony is here. Each of these authors constantly contradicts the others, even though they are all using the same source!

But that is not all. Not only have Marvin's letters been turned into cold prose when they were originally living, breathing epistles to real people in real places. But they have devolved into a weapon in the hands of agenda-driven men. Not a few authors on marriage begin employing isolated proof texts from Marvin's work to hammer away at those who disagree with their marital philosophy.

How can they do this? How is this being done? How are all of these sociologists contradicting each other when they are using the exact same source!? It is because the letters have been lifted out of their historical context. Each letter has been plucked from its chronological sequence and taken out of its real life setting.

Put another way, the letters of Marvin Snurdly have been transformed into a series of isolated, disjointed, fragmented sentences—free for anyone to lift one sentence from one letter, another sentence from another letter, paste them together to create the marital philosophy of their choice.

An amazing story is it not? Well here is the punch line. Whether you realize it or not, I have just described your NT!

The Order of Paul's Letters

Your NT is made up mostly of Paul's letters. Paul of Tarsus wrote two thirds of it. He penned 13 letters in a 20-year time span. Nine letters were written to *churches* in different cultures, at different times, experiencing different problems. Four letters were written to *individual* Christians. The individuals who received those letters were also dealing with different issues at different times.

Take note: 20 years—13 letters—all written to different churches at different times in different cultures—all experiencing different problems.[4]

In the early second century, someone took the letters of Paul and compiled them into a volume. The technical term for this volume is "canon."[5] Scholars refer to this compiled volume as "the Pauline canon." It is essentially your NT with a few letters added

---

[4] See Donald Guthrie's *New Testament Introduction: Revised Edition* (Downers Grove: InterVarsity Press, 1990). For a good discussion on how we gòt our Bible, see *Christian History,* Issue 43, Vol. XIII, No. 3 and "How We Got our Bible," *Christianity Today,* February 5, 1988, pp. 23-38.

[5] F.F. Bruce's *Paul: The Apostle of the Heart Set Free* (Grand Rapids: Eerdmans, 1977), p. 465. Scholars refer to Paul's canon as the "Pauline corpus." To learn about the history of the NT canon, see F.F. Bruce's *The Canon of Scripture* (Downer's Grove: InterVarsity Press, 1988), Chapters 8-23.

afterwards, the four Gospels and Acts placed at the front, and Revelation tacked on the end.

At the time, no one knew when Paul's letters were written. Even if they did, it would not have mattered. For there was no precedence for alphabetical or chronological ordering.[6] The first-century Greco-Roman world ordered its literature according to decreasing length.[7]

Look at how your NT is arranged. What do you find? Paul's longest letter appears first.[8] It is Romans. 1 Corinthians is the second longest letter, hence the reason why it follows Romans. 2 Corinthians is the third longest letter. Your NT follows this pattern until you come to that tiny little book called Philemon.[9]

Here is the present order as it appears in your NT. The books are arranged according to descending length:[10]

Romans
1 Corinthians
2 Corinthians
Galatians
Ephesians[11]
Philippians

---

[6] Jerome Murphy-O'Connor, *Paul the Letter-Writer* (Collegeville: The Liturgical Press, 1995), p. 121.

[7] Ibid., p. 120. This practice is known as stichometry.

[8] For a thorough discussion on the order of the Pauline canon, see *Paul the Letter-Writer*, Chapter 3.

[9] Hebrews does not appear to be Pauline, so it was not part of the Pauline corpus.

[10] In 1864, Thomas D. Bernard delivered a series of talks called "the Bampton lectures." These lectures were published into a book in 1872 entitled *The Progress of Doctrine in the New Testament*. In the book, Bernard argues that the present order of Paul's letters in the NT were Divinely inspired and commended. This book became very popular among Bible teachers of the 19th and 20th centuries. As a result, virtually every theological text, exegetical text, or Biblical commentary written this century follows the present chaotic order, not realizing how much it has blinded us from seeing the entire panoramic view of the NT. "Canonical criticism" is big among seminarians. This is the study of the canon as a unit in order to acquire an overall Biblical theology. What is needed today is a theology built, not on the present canon and its misarrangement, but on the chronological story of the early church.

[11] Ephesians is actually a hair longer than Galatians, but the books were misarranged due to a scribal gloss. This is not surprising since the difference in length is so slight (*Paul the Letter-Writer*, p. 124).

Colossians
1 Thessalonians
2 Thessalonians
1 Timothy
2 Timothy
Titus
Philemon

What, then, is the proper chronological order of these letters? According to the best available scholarship, here is the order in which they were written:[12]

Galatians
1 Thessalonians
2 Thessalonians
1 Corinthians
2 Corinthians
Romans
Colossians
Philemon
Ephesians
Philippians
1 Timothy
Titus
2 Timothy

The Addition of Chapters and Verses

In the year 1227, a professor at the University of Paris named Stephen Langton added chapters to all the books of the NT. Then

---

[12] See Donald Guthrie's *New Testament Introduction: Revised Edition*; F.F. Bruce's *The Letters of Paul: An Expanded Paraphrase* (Grand Rapids: Eerdmans, 1965); F.F. Bruce's *Paul: The Apostle of the Heart Set Free* (Grand Rapids: Eerdmans, 1977).

in 1551, a printer named Robert Stephanus[13] numbered the sentences in all of the books of the NT.[14]

According to Stephanus' son, the verse divisions that his father created do not do service to the sense of the text. Stephanus did not use any consistent method. While riding on horseback from Paris to Lyons, he versified the entire NT within Langton's chapter divisions.[15]

So verses were born in the pages of holy writ in the year 1551.[16] And since that time God's people have approached the NT with scissors and glue, cutting-and-pasting isolated, disjointed sentences from different letters, lifting them out of their real-life setting and lashing them together to build floatable doctrines. Then calling it "the Word of God."

This half-baked approach still lives in our seminaries, Bible colleges, churches, Bible studies, and (tragically) our house churches today.[17] Most Christians are completely out of touch with the social and historical events that lay behind each of the NT letters. Instead, they have turned the NT into a manual that can be wielded to prove any point. Chopping the Bible up into fragments makes this relatively easy to pull off.

---

[13] He is also called Robert Estienne.

[14] Norman Geisler and William Nix, *A General Introduction of the Bible: Revised and Expanded* (Chicago: Moody Press, 1986), pp. 340-341, 451; Bruce Metzger and Michael Coogan, *The Oxford Companion to the Bible* (New York: Oxford University Press, 1993), p. 79.

[15] H. von Soden, *Die Schriften des Newen Testamentes* (Goettingen: Vandenhoek, 1912), I, 484; W. Kenneth Connolly, *The Indestructible Book* (Grand Rapids: Baker Books, 1996), p. 154. One Bible historian made this remark about Stephanus' versification of the NT: "I think it had been better done on his knees in a closet."

[16] The versification of the Hebrew Bible occurred in 1571. Theodore Beza put Stephanus' verses in his version of the Textus Receptus (1565) which gave them the preeminent place that they have today (*Die Religion in der Geschichte und der Gegenwart* (3rd ed., III, 1141 f.).

[17] In seminary, the story of the early church is taught in a "church history" class while the books of the NT are taught in an "NT studies" class. And never do the twain meet. So seminarians are rarely if ever given a panoramic view of the free-flowing story of the early church with the books arranged in their chronological order. If you do not believe me, try this: The next time you meet a seminary student (or graduate) ask him or her to rehearse for you the entire series of events from Paul's writing of Galatians to his writing of Romans. Ask them to include dates, places, names of important characters, and the events mentioned in Acts.

How We Approach the NT

We Christians have been taught to approach the Bible in one of seven ways. See how many you can tick off with a pencil that apply to you:

- You look for verses that inspire you. Upon finding such verses, you either highlight, memorize, meditate upon, or put them on your refrigerator door.

- You look for verses that tell you what God has promised so that you can confess it in faith and thereby obligate the Lord to do what you want. (If you are part of the "name-it-claim-it," "blab-it-grab-it" movement, you are masterful at doing this.)

- You look for verses that tell you what God commands you to do.

- You look for verses that you can quote to scare the devil out of his wits or resist him in the hour of temptation.

- You look for verses that will prove your particular doctrine so that you can slice-and-dice your theological sparring partner into Biblical ribbons. (Because of the proof-texting method, a vast wasteland of Christianity behaves as if the mere citation of some random, de-contextualized verse of Scripture ends all discussion on virtually all subjects.)

- You look for verses in the Bible to control and/or correct others.

- If you are a preacher, you look for verses that "preach" well for next Sunday morning's sermon. (This is an on-going addiction for preachers. It is so ingrained that many of them are incapable of reading their Bibles in any way other than to hunt for sermon material.)

Now look at this list again. Did you find yourself there? Notice how each of these approaches is highly individualistic. All of them put *you*, the individual Christian, at the center. Each approach ignores the fact that most of the NT was written to corporate bodies of people (churches), not to individuals. But that is not all. Each of these approaches is built on isolated proof-texting. They treat the NT like a manual and blind us to its real message. It is no wonder that we can approvingly nod our heads at paid pastors, the Sunday morning order of worship, sermons, church buildings, religious costumes, choirs, worship teams, seminaries, and a passive priesthood—all without wincing.

We have been taught to approach the Bible like a jigsaw puzzle. For most of us, we have never been told the entire story that lies behind the letters that Paul, Peter, James, John, and Jude wrote. We have been taught chapters and verses, not the historical context.[18]

For instance, have you ever been taught the story behind Paul's letter to the Galatians? Before you nod your head, see if you can answer these questions off the top of your head: Who were the Galatians? What were their issues? When and why did Paul write to them? What happened just before Paul penned his Galatian treatise? Where was he when he wrote it? What provoked him to write the letter? And where in Acts do you find the historical context for this letter? All of these background matters are indispensable for understanding what our NT is about. Without them, we simply cannot understand the Bible clearly or properly.[19]

One scholar put it this way, *"The arrangement of the letters of Paul in the New Testament is in general that of their length. When we rearrange them into their chronological order, fitting them as far as possible into their life-setting within the record of the Acts of the Apostles, they begin to yield up more of their treasure; they become self-explanatory, to a greater extent than when this background is ignored."*[20]

---

[18] Some of us have been taught a little about the historical background of the Bible. But it is just enough to inoculate us from searching further and getting the whole story.

[19] F.F. Bruce, ed., *The New International Bible Commentary* (Grand Rapids: Zondervan, 1979), p. 1095.

[20] G.C.D. Howley in "The Letters of Paul," *New International Bible Commentary* (Grand Rapids: Zondervan, 1979), p. 1095.

Another writes, *"If future editions [of the New Testament] want to aid rather than hinder a reader's understanding of the New Testament, it should be realized that the time is ripe to cause both the verse and chapter divisions to disappear from the text and to be put on the margin in as inconspicuous a place as possible. Every effort must be made to print the text in a way which makes it possible for the units which the author himself had in mind to become apparent."*[21]

I call our method of studying the NT the "clipboard approach." If you are familiar with computers, you are aware of the component called the clipboard. If you happen to be in a word processor, you may cut-and-paste a piece of text via the clipboard. The clipboard allows you to cut a sentence from one document and paste it into another.

Pastors, seminarians, and laymen alike have been conditioned by the clipboard approach when studying the Bible. This is how we justify our human-laden, earth-bound, man-made, encrusted and encased structures and pass them off as "Biblical." It is why we routinely miss what the early church was like whenever we open up our NTs. We see verses. We do not see the whole picture.

Let me demonstrate to you how this approach is still alive and well today, and how deeply it governs our minds.

Meet Joe Housechurch

Enter now Mr. Joe Housechurch. Joe Housechurch grew up in the institutional church. For the last 10 years, he has been dissatisfied with it.

Joe picks up a book on "house church," and he has a crisis of conscience. He ends up learning some amazing things. Namely, that there is no modern pastor in the NT. There are no church buildings. There is no paid clergy, and church meetings are open for all to share.

All of these discoveries rock Joe's world. So much so that he leaves the institutional church. Not without facing the fury of the pastor, by the way. You see, Joe made the mistake of sharing these

---

[21] H. von Soden, *Die Schriften des Newen Testamentes*, p. 482.

"great revelations" with other people in his church. As a result, the pastor got wind of it, and Joe found himself in the pastor's crosshairs. From the pulpit, Joe was branded as a "dangerous heretic," and the congregation was instructed to cut off all fellowship with him.

After licking his wounds, Joe picks up his NT, never realizing that the cut-and-paste approach still lives in his brain. The "clipboard mentality" was never dissected from his thinking. But he is blissfully unaware of it—as are most Christians.

Joe begins looking for the ingredients to start a "NT church." So he begins to do what most Christians are conditioned to do when seeking God's will. He cherry-picks verses out of the NT, ignoring the social, historical background of those verses.

Joe comes across Matthew 18:20: *"Where two or three are gathered together in my name, there am I in the midst of them."* Joe keeps reading and comes across Acts 2:46, *"And they met from house to house."* Joe gets a revelation. *"All I have do is open up my house, have two or three people gather here, and voila! I have planted a NT church!"*

So the next Sunday, Joe opens his home and starts a "house church" based on the NT (so he thinks).

Joe gets another revelation: *"I am a church planter like Paul. I started a house church just like he did."* Joe does not realize that he has just lifted two sentences from two documents—completely out of historical context—and sewn them together to do something that has no root in Scripture.

Matthew 18:20 is not a recipe for founding a church. That passage is dealing with an excommunication meeting! Acts 2:46 is simply a report of what the early Christians did. Yes, the early Christians met in homes. And it is highly recommended that we meet in homes today.[22] But, opening up one's home and inviting people to meet there does not make a church. Nor does it make the owner of the home a "church planter!"

The churches that were planted in the first century were planted out of blood and sweat. The men that planted them did not leave the synagogue on Saturday and decide they were going to plant

---

[22] See *Rethinking the Wineskin*, Chapter 3.

house churches on Sunday. Every man in the NT that was involved in planting churches was first an ordinary brother in an *already existing* church. And in time that man—after a lot of tribulation and exposure in a church that knew him so well they could read him like a phone directory—was recognized and *sent* with the approval of that church. This is a consistent pattern throughout the NT.[23]

You can prove anything with verses, dear reader. Seeing the birth of a church that maps to the churches of the first century takes a whole lot more work than opening up your house and having people sit on comfy couches to drink Java, eat cookies, and talk about the Bible.

What do I mean by a first-century styled church? I am talking about a group of people who know how to experience Jesus Christ and express Him in a meeting without any human officiation. I am talking about a group of people who can function together as a Body when they are left on their own after the church planter leaves them.[24]

The man who plants a first-century styled church leaves that church without a pastor, elders, a music leader, a Bible facilitator, or a Bible teacher. If that church is planted well, those believers will know how to touch the living, breathing Headship of Jesus Christ in a meeting. They will know how to let Him invisibly lead their gatherings. They will bring their own songs, they will write their own songs, they will minister out of what Christ has shown them—with no human leader present![25]

To equip a people to do that takes a lot more than opening up your house and saying, *"Come, let us have Bible study."*

Let us go back to our story. Joe Housechurch now has a "NT church." As in all small groups like Joe's, the issue of leadership is raised. What does Joe do? He gets his cherry-picker out and begins looking for verses on leadership. He stops at Acts 14, and

---

[23] See Gene Edwards' *Overlooked Christianity* (Sargent: Seedsowers, 1997).

[24] This does not mean that church planters never return. There are many times when they are needed to help the church. But after planting a church, church planters should be absent more than they are present.

[25] What I am describing here is not arm-chair philosophy. I have worked with churches that fit this bill.

he is arrested by verse 23. It says, *"And they appointed elders in every church."* Joe gets another revelation! *"The word of God declares that every NT church has elders,"* he musses. *"Therefore, our house church needs elders!"*

Joe makes this discovery only two weeks after opening up his home! *"Every NT church had elders,"* says Joe. So he lifts that verse out of its context and Joe appoints elders. (Joe happens to be one of those elders by the way.)

What is the historical context of Acts 14? Two church planters, Paul and Barnabas, are sent out from their home church in Antioch. Before this sending, both men had already experienced church life as *brothers*, not leaders (Barnabas in Jerusalem and Paul in Antioch).

Acts 14:23 is part of a description of what took place after these two church planters were sent out. They are in South Galatia. The two men have just planted four churches. Now they are returning to visit those churches six months to one year *after* those churches were planted. Paul and Barnabas return to each of the Galatian churches and "publicly endorse old men" in each church.[26]

But Joe has made a mistake even more subtle. The verse says that Paul and Barnabas appointed elders in *every* church. Joe takes this to mean that every genuine church has elders. Yet this text says no such thing. The verse is referring to an event in South Galatia during the first century. *"Every church"* means every church *in South Galatia in A.D. 49!*[27] Luke is talking about the four churches that Paul and Barnabas just planted. Do you see the problem that we run into when we blithely lift verses from their historical setting?

The truth is, Joe Housechurch is totally outside Biblical bounds! First, he is not an itinerant church planter. (These are the men who acknowledged elders in the first century.) Second, the church is far too young to have elders. In Jerusalem, it took at least 14 years for elders to emerge. But Joe Housechurch has his verse, so he is "standing on Scripture" (in his imagination).

---

26 See *Rethinking the Wineskin*, Chapter 5 and *Who is Your Covering?*, Chapter 2.
27 Antioch of Syria and Corinth had no elders as far as we can tell.

Later, the issue of giving money comes up. So Joe parks at 1 Corinthians 16:2, *"On the first day of the week when you are together out of your abundance take up a collection."* Based on this verse, Joe institutes a rule that everyone in his house church should give money to the church fund on Sunday morning.

Again, Joe has taken a passage out of context and built a practice upon it. 1 Corinthians 16:2 is dealing with a one time shot. It was written about A.D. 55 to the church in Corinth. At the time, Paul was collecting money from all the Gentile churches that he had planted. Paul had one goal for this: He wanted to bring that collection to the brothers and sisters in Jerusalem who were going through severe poverty. It was a one shot deal. Paul was saying to the Corinthians, *"By the way, when I come and visit, I want that money up front to bring to Jerusalem. So every Sunday when you come together, would you please gradually lay aside a relief fund?"* 1 Corinthians 16:2, therefore, has nothing to do with a perfunctory ritual of taking up an offering every Sunday morning.[28]

Well there is more. Joe's house church begins to discuss the question of the church's mission. Naturally, Joe takes out his cherry-picker and seeks for verses that will yield an answer. He stops at Matthew 28:19, *"Go ye therefore to all nations, teaching them . . . "* He cross references this to Mark 16:15 which says: *"Go out into all the world and preach the gospel."* He continues on to Acts 5:42 which says, *"And they ceased not to preach and teach Jesus Christ."*

Joe musses to himself, *"Our mission is to preach the gospel. That is why we exist. Why shucks, if God did not want us to preach the gospel He would have killed us after we got saved! So the only reason why we breath oxygen—the only reason why we have house churches—is to preach the gospel. This is what the NT says. I just read it."*

Once again, Mr. Joe Housechurch has lifted three verses totally out of context. In Matthew 28:19 and Mark 16:15, Jesus is not speaking to every Christian. He is speaking to twelve men who had

---

[28] I fully support regularly giving to the needs of the church (*not* pastor salaries or church buildings, mind you). But you cannot use this verse to make a law out of a Sunday morning offering.

never preached the gospel until the Lord *sent* them. And He did not *send* them until He first *trained* them for three years.[29] These men were apostles (church planters). Consequently, the so-called "Great Commission" is a word to those who plant churches. It is not given to every believer.

Further, in the original Greek, the "Great Commission" reads: *"Having gone on your way . . . "* Therefore, it is a prophecy (*"having gone"*), not a command (*"Go"*).[30] The Lord did not tell the twelve apostles to "go." He told them that they would be going.

Who is preaching the gospel in Acts 5? These same men. The apostles. Interestingly, no Christian in Jerusalem other than the twelve apostles preached the gospel until eight years passed.[31] They learned Jesus Christ in the context of church life before they spread the good news. Moreover, when the brothers and sisters in Jerusalem did begin to spread the gospel after those eight years passed, they did not do it out of duty. It spontaneously happened when they were dispersed throughout Palestine. Unlike Christians today, the early believers did not share Christ out of guilt, command, or duty. They shared Him because He was pouring out of them, and they could not help it!

Joe's thought processes about the church's mission have been shaped by two things: 19th-century revivalism (see Chapter 1), and the clipboard approach to the Bible.

The Net Effect of the Clipboard Approach

Let us step back and analyze Joe's story. Joe has grossly mishandled the NT. Is his motive pure? Yes. Does he have a heart for God? Yes. Did this keep him from misapplying Scripture? No.

Joe has come to the NT the same way most of us are taught—with scissors and glue. Ready to cut, paste, and create a basis for our favorite doctrines and practices.

The net effect of the clipboard approach is tragic. It has produced a raft of present-day churches that have no Scriptural

---

[29] The exception is when they went on a very short trial mission in Galilee at the end of their training.
[30] Kenneth S. Wuest, *The New Testament: An Expanded Translation.*
[31] See the *Berkeley Version of the New Testament.*

basis upon which to exist. (I speak of the institutional church as we know it today.) But more, it has generated scores of mechanical pro-forma "house churches" that are lifeless, colorless, and sterile. I am reminded of the vision that Ezekiel had of the valley of dry bones.[32] The Lord took Ezekiel to a valley of bones, and the living, breathing Word of God came forth to resurrect those bones. The Scripture says that bone was put upon bone. The bones were clothed with sinew and flesh. And when the breath of God came into them like a rushing wind, those dead bones became a mighty army.

Most modern house church "planters" can be described as men who have come to the valley of dry bones with glue, needle, thread, and NT verses in hand. They have taken the bones and glued them together. They have put thread through the sinew and stitched flesh upon it. Then they have stood back and said: *"Look, a NT church built on the NT. We have elders, we meet in a house, we do not have a hired clergy, we take up a collection every Sunday, and we preach the gospel."*

But there is no rushing mighty wind!

The church of Jesus Christ cannot be started. It cannot be welded together. There is no blueprint or model that we can tease out of the NT by extracting verses and trying to imitate them mechanically. The church of Jesus Christ is a biological, living entity! It must be born.

If we will see first-century results, the church must be born the same way that all first-century churches were born. If you count all the churches mentioned in the NT, there are about 35 of them. Every one of them was either planted or aided by a traveling church planter who preached only Christ. There are no exceptions. The church was raised up as a result of the apostolic presentation of Jesus Christ.

There are more verses to back this principle up than there are for meeting in homes. There are more verses to back that up than there are for open, participatory meetings. There are more verses to back that up than for taking a collection on Sunday morning. And as we have seen, there is much more Scripture to support this

---

[32] See Ezek. 37.

practice than there is for all the unscriptural things we do in the modern church—including hiring a pastor! The principle of extra-local workers planting and helping a church pervades the NT.

Take note: The NT is not a *manual* for church practice. It is a record of *Emmanuel*—Jesus Christ breathing His Divine life through His people in the first century! The book of Acts is not an instruction book for church order. It is a historical record of how the Head of the church gives birth to His Body and how it expresses itself! The Epistles are not handy texts showing us how to be good Christians. They are living, breathing letters written at different times to different churches living in different cultures experiencing different circumstances!

But they all speak with one voice. And that voice streams out of a consistent, free-flowing saga. A saga that must be unfolded if we will ever return to the primitive Christian mindset and the practice of the early church.

A Practical Remedy

What, then, is the antidote to the clipboard approach to the NT? What is the remedy that will bring you into a living expression of the Body of Christ, first-century style? The antidote begins with understanding our NT.

We have been conditioned to come to the NT with a microscope and extract verses to find out what the early Christians did. We need to abandon that whole mentality, step back, and take a fresh look at the Scriptures. We must learn the whole sweeping drama from beginning to end. We need to learn to view the NT pan-oramically, not microscopically.

F.F. Bruce, one of the greatest scholars of our time, once made a riveting statement. He said that when you read the letters of Paul, it is like listening to one end of a phone conversation. There has been enough done in the field of scholarship over the years that we can reconstruct the entire saga of the early church. Thankfully, we now *can* hear the other side of the conversation![33]

To learn the story of the early church is to be forever cured of the cut-and-paste, clipboard approach to the NT. Learning the story will lay bare the spiritual principles that are in God Himself which are consistent throughout all of the NT. We consistently miss these principles because of the way we approach the Bible. Neither does it help matters that our NT is not in chronological order.

When you learn the story, your verses must bow and bend to it. No longer will you be able to take a verse out of context and say, *"Look, we are supposed to do this."* Many of the verses that we Christians routinely pull out of the Bible will simply not yield. You will be boxed in because for the first time you will understand the whole picture.

Final Challenge

Someone once said, *"There is perhaps nothing worse than reaching the top of the ladder and discovering that you're on the wrong wall."*[34] After reading this book, you should be able to identify with that statement. In this connection, I shall close with a challenge that cuts straight to the heart.

You have learned that the church practices which you have silently assumed to be Biblical are without any Scriptural merit. You have discovered the origin of those practices. You know that they did not originate with God, but with men—mostly pagans. And you know that they thwart God's ultimate intention for His church.[35] You also have become aware that you have been

---

[33] I suggest that you read Gene Edwards' *Revolution: The Story of the Early Church* (Seedsowers), and his *First Century Diaries* (Tyndale). I am also working on a book entitled *From Nazareth to Patmos* which will document the entire story of the first-century church under one cover.

[34] Joseph Campbell is the author of this statement. In a similar vein, Artemus Ward has said, "It ain't so much the things that we don't know that get us in trouble. It's the things we know that just ain't so."

[35] Paul calls this ultimate intention "the eternal purpose" in Eph. 3:11. See *Rethinking the Wineskin*, Chapter 7 for an explanation as well as DeVern Fromke's *Ultimate Intention* (Sure Foundation, 1998).

hopelessly dependent upon these intractable traditions. Even entrapped by them.

In this staggering light, I press the terse query: Will you, pray tell, abandon these traditions? Or will you continue practicing what you know to be at odds with the ways of God?

Are you going to off-handedly ignore what you have read in this book concerning your church practices? Or will you be faithful to the absolute ends of light within you and make a clean break with man's tradition, so as to pursue the fullness of Christ and His church?

After receiving the light that you have been given, will you continue to elevate your religious inventions above the inspired revelation of God? Or will you give heed to the light that is within you?

Will you step out of the institutional church which embraces practices that violate the NT or will you *"invalidate the Word of God for the sake of your traditions"*[36]—traditions that continue to put a great millstone around the neck of the church of Jesus Christ?[37]

Will you continue to sacrifice in Pharaoh's city? Or will you go to the border, survey the land, and take the plunge?

History shows that where conscience and tradition collide, most of God's people go with tradition.[38] Right now, the question before the house is . . .

What are *you* going to do?

---

[36] Matt. 15:6.

[37] Matt. 15:1-9.

[38] This sad trend goes as far back as the Old Testament era. See Isa. 28:9-12; Jer. 5:31; 6:16; Hos. 8:4. In this regard, William Barclay has rightly remarked, "Any business which has lost so many customers as the church has would have tried new ways long ago; but the church tends to resent all that is new."

In the last 50 or 100 years New Testament research has unremittingly and successfully addressed itself to the task of elucidating for us what was known as the 'Ecclesia' in primitive Christianity—so very different from what is to-day called the church both in Roman and Protestant camps . . . This insight—which an unprejudiced study of the New Testament and the crying need of the church have helped us to reach—may be expressed as follows: the New Testament 'Ecclesia,' the fellowship of Jesus Christ, is a pure communion of persons and has nothing to do with the character of an institution about it; it is therefore misleading to identify any single one of the historically developed churches, which are all marked by an institutional character, with the true Christian communion.

-Emil Brunner

APPENDIX: SUMMARY OF ORIGINS

The following summary is neither complete nor detailed. Note that all of these practices are post-Biblical, post-apostolic, and mostly influenced by pagan culture.

Chapter 1: The Order of Worship

- *The Sunday Morning Order of Worship* - Evolved from Gregory's Mass in the sixth century to the revisions made by Luther, Calvin, the Puritans, the Free Church tradition, the Methodists, the Frontier-Revivalists, and the Pentecostals.

- *The Centrality of the Pulpit in the Order of Worship.* Martin Luther in 1523.

- *Two Candles Placed on Top of the "Communion Table" and Incense Burning* - Borrowed from the ceremonial court of Roman Emperors in the fourth century. The "Communion Table" was introduced by Ulrich Zwingli in the 16th century.

- *Taking the Lord's Supper Quarterly* - Ulrich Zwingli (1484-1531).

- *The Congregation Standing and Singing When the Clergy Enters* - Borrowed from the ceremonial court of Roman Emperors in the fourth century. Brought into the Protestant liturgy by John Calvin (1509-1564).

- *Coming to Church with a Somber/Reverent Attitude* - Based on the medieval view of piety. Brought into the Protestant service by John Calvin and Martin Bucer (1491-1551).

- *Condemnation and Guilt Over Missing a Sunday Service* - 17th-century New England Puritans.

- *The Long "Pastoral Prayer" Which Precedes the Sermon* - 17th-century Puritans.

- *The Pastoral Prayer Uttered in Elizabethan English (when the language was outdated)* - 18th-century Methodists.

- *The Goal of All Preaching to Win Individual Souls* - 18th-century Frontier-Revivalists.

- *The Altar-Call* - Invented by 17th-century Methodists and popularized by Charles Finney (1792-1872).

- *The Church Bulletin (written liturgy)* - Originated in 1884 with Albert Blake Dick's stencil duplicating machine.

- *The "Solo" Salvation Hymn, Door-to-Door Witnessing, and Evangelistic Advertising/Campaigning* - D.L. Moody (1837-1899).

- *The Decision Card* - Invented by Absalom B. Earle (1812-1895) and popularized by D.L. Moody.

- *Bowing Heads with Eyes Closed and Raising the Hand in Response to a Salvation Message* - Billy Graham in the 20th century.

- *"The Evangelization of the World in One Generation" Slogan* - John Mott around 1888.

- *Solo or Choral Music Played During the Offering* - 20th-century Pentecostals.

Chapter 2: The Sermon

- *The Modern Sermon* - Borrowed from the Greek sophists, who were masters at oratory and rhetoric. John Chrysostom (347-407) and Augustine (354-430) popularized the Greco-Roman *homily* (sermon) and made it a central part of the Christian faith.

- *The One-Hour Sermon, Sermon Crib Notes, and the Four-Part Sermon Outline* - 17th-century Puritans.

Chapter 3: The Church Building

- *The Church Building* - Started by Constantine around A.D. 327. The first church buildings were patterned after the Roman basilicas which were modeled after Greek temples.

- *The Sacred Space* - Christians borrowed this idea from the pagans in the second and third centuries. The burial places of the martyrs were regarded as "sacred." In the fourth century, church buildings were erected on these burial places, thus creating "sacred" buildings.

- *The Pastor's Chair* - Derived from the *cathedra,* which was the bishop's chair or throne. This chair replaced the seat of the judge in the Roman basilica.

- *Tax-Exempt Status for Churches and Christian Clergy* - Emperor Constantine gave churches tax-exempt status in A.D. 323. He made clergy exempt from paying taxes in A.D. 313, a privilege that pagan priests enjoyed.

- *Stained Glass Windows* - First introduced by Gregory of Tours (538-593) and brought to perfection by Suger (1081-1151), abbot of St. Denis.

- *Gothic Cathedrals* - 12th century. These edifices were built according to the pagan philosophy of Plato.

- *The Steeple* - Rooted in ancient Babylon and Egyptian architecture and philosophy, the steeple was a medieval invention that was popularized and modernized by Sir Christopher Wren in London around 1666.

- *The Pulpit* - Used in the Christian church as early as A.D. 250. It came from the Greek *ambo,* which was a pulpit used by both Greeks and Jews for delivering monologues.

- *The Pew* - Evolved from the 13th through the 18th centuries in England.

Chapter 4: The Pastor

- *The Single Bishop (predecessor of the modern pastor)* - Ignatius of Antioch around A.D. 115. Ignatius' model of one-bishop-rule did not prevail in the churches until the third century.

- *The "Covering" Doctrine* - Cyprian of Carthage (200-258), a former pagan orator. Revived under Juan Carlos Ortiz from Argentina and the "Fort Lauderdale Five" from the United States, creating the so-called "Shepherding-Discipleship Movement" in 1970s.

- *Hierarchical Leadership* - Brought into the church by Constantine in the fourth century. This was the leadership style of the Babylonians, Persians, Greeks, and Romans.

- *Clergy and Laity* - "Laity" first appears in the writings of Clement of Rome (d. 100). "Clergy" first appears in Tertullian (160-225). By the third century, Christian leaders were universally called "clergy."

- *Modern Ordination* - Evolved from the second century to the fourth. It was taken from the Roman custom of appointing men to civil office. The idea of the ordained minister as the "holy man of God" can be traced to Augustine (293-373), Gregory of Nazianzus (329-389), and Chrysostom (347-407).

- *The Title "Pastor"* - Catholic priests who became Protestant ministers were not universally called "Pastors" until the 18th century under the influence of Lutheran Pietists.

Chapter 5: Sunday Morning Costumes

- *Christians Wearing Their "Sunday Best" for Church* - Began in the late-18th century with the Industrial Revolution and became widespread in the mid-19th century. The practice is rooted in the emerging middle class effort to become like their wealthy aristocrat contemporaries.

- *The Clergy Costume* - Began in A.D. 330 when Christian clergy began wearing the garb of Roman officials. By the 12th century, the clergy began wearing everyday street clothes that distinguished them from the people.

- *The Evangelical Pastor's Suit* - A descendent of the black scholar's gown worn by Reformation ministers, the black lounge suit of the 20th century became the typical costume of the modern pastor.

- *The Clerical (Backwards) Collar* - Invented by Rev. Dr. Donald McLeod of Glasgow in 1865.

Chapter 6: Ministers of Music

- *The Choir* - Provoked by Constantine's desire to mimic the professional music used in Roman imperial ceremonies. In the fourth century, the Christians borrowed the choir idea from the choirs used in Greek dramas and Greek temples.

- *The Boys Choir* - Began in the fourth century, borrowed from the boys choirs used by the pagans.

- *Funeral Processions and Orations* - Borrowed from Greco-Roman paganism in the third century.

- *The Worship Team* - Calvary Chapel in 1965, patterned after the secular rock concert.

Chapter 7: Tithing and Clergy Salaries

- *Tithing* - Did not become a widespread Christian practice until the eighth century. The tithe was taken from the 10% rent-charge used in the Roman Empire and later justified by the Old Testament.

- *Clergy Salaries* - Instituted by Constantine in the fourth century.

- *The Collection Plate* - The alms dish appeared in the 14th century. Passing a collection plate began in 1662.

- *The Usher* - Began with Queen Elizabeth I (1533-1603). The predecessor of the usher is the church porter which traces back to the third century.

Chapter 8: Baptism and the Lord's Supper

- *Infant Baptism* - Rooted in the superstitious beliefs that pervaded the Greco-Roman culture, it was brought into the Christian faith in the late second century. By the fifth century, it replaced adult baptism.

- *Sprinkling Replacing Immersion* - Began in the late Middle Ages in the Western churches.

- *Baptism Separated from Conversion* - Began in the early second century as a result of the legalistic view that baptism was the only medium for the forgiveness of sins.

- *The "Sinner's Prayer"* - Invented by D.L. Moody (1837-1899) and made popular in the 1950s with Billy Graham's *Peace With God* tract and later with Campus Crusade for Christ's *Four Spiritual Laws*.

- *Use of the Term "Personal Savior"* - Spawned in the mid-1800s by the Frontier-Revivalist influence and popularized by Charles Fuller (1887-1968).

- *The Lord's Supper Condensed From a Full "Agape" Meal to Only the Cup and the Bread* - The late second century as a result of pagan ritual influences.

Chapter 9: Christian Education

- *The Catholic Seminary* - The first seminary began as a result of the Council of Trent (1545-1563). The curriculum was based on the teachings of Thomas Aquinas which was a blending of Aristotle's philosophy, Neo-Platonic philosophy, and Christian doctrine.

- *The Protestant Seminary* - Began in Andover, Massachusetts in 1808. It too was built on the teachings of Thomas Aquinas.

- *The Bible College* - Influenced by the revivalism of D.L. Moody (1837-1899), the first two Bible colleges were The Missionary Training Institute (Nyack College, New York) in 1882 and Moody Bible Institute (Chicago) in 1886.

- *The Sunday School* - Invented by Robert Raikes from Britain in 1780. Raikes did not found the Sunday School for the purpose of religious instruction. He founded it to teach poor children the basics of education.

- *The Youth Pastor* - Invented in urban churches in the late 1930s and 40s as a result of seeking to meet the needs of a new sociological class called "teenagers."

Chapter 11: Reapproaching the NT

- *Paul's Letters Combined Into a Canon and Arranged According to Descending Length* - Early second century.

- *Chapters Added to the NT* - University of Paris professor Stephen Langton in 1227.

- *Verses Added to the NT* - Printer Robert Stephanus in 1551.

To view new historical findings and updates to this book go to:
www.ptmin.org/paganchristianity.htm